GENDER AND THE SOCIAL GOSPEL

Gender and the Social Gospel

Edited by
Wendy J. Deichmann Edwards and
Carolyn De Swarte Gifford

UNIVERSITY OF ILLINOIS PRESS
URBANA AND CHICAGO

© 2003 by the Board of Trustees
of the University of Illinois
All rights reserved
Manufactured in the United States of America
1 2 3 4 5 C P 5 4 3 2 1

∞ This book is printed on acid-free paper.

Library of Congress Cataloging-in-Publication Data

Gender and the social gospel / edited by Wendy J. Deichmann Edwards
and Carolyn De Swarte Gifford.
p.   cm.
Includes bibliographical references and index.
ISBN 0-252-02795-7 (cloth : alk. paper)
ISBN 0-252-07097-6 (pbk. : alk. paper)
1. Social gospel—History—Congresses. 2. Women in
Christianity—United States—History—19th century—Congresses.
3. Women in Christianity—United States—History—20th century—
Congresses. I. Edwards, Wendy J. Deichmann, 1957–   . II. Gifford,
Carolyn De Swarte.
BR517.G46   2003
261.8'343—dc21   2002010954

To all those women—known and unknown—
who have worked to realize the Kingdom of God,
inspired by the social gospel

CONTENTS

ACKNOWLEDGMENTS

The editors have received help and encouragement from numerous persons and institutions in producing this volume. Christopher H. Evans of Colgate Rochester Crozer Divinity School must be first on the list of those we wish to thank for support in the development of this collection of essays. He organized two conferences on the social gospel hosted by the divinity school, the first in spring 1998 and the second in spring 1999. These conferences helped to spark new interest in social gospel research among scholars. They provided the forum for which most of the essays in this volume were first written.

Three of the essays were subsequently presented in a session on gender and the social gospel at the American Society of Church History meeting in January 2000. We thank Margaret Lamberts Bendroth for her insightful comments on those papers; she raised important interpretive questions that have been incorporated into the Introduction. Rosemary Skinner Keller and Janet Larson, readers for the University of Illinois Press, also gave significant criticism and suggestions, which have informed the revision of the Introduction and the essays. We appreciate their thoughtful comments and their continuing interest in the project.

We are also deeply grateful to those who contributed essays to this volume. They have worked hard and cheerfully to meet our many requests as we put the book together, and their questions and suggestions have sharpened our interpretation of the subject.

Carolyn De Swarte Gifford wishes to thank the Evangelical Scholars Program of the Pew Charitable Trusts for naming her a Research Fellow for 1997–98. Much of the work on her essay was done during this time. She would also like to express gratitude to the Department of Gender Studies, Northwestern University, for appointing her a research associate in 1996 and renewing the appointment yearly.

United Theological Seminary of Dayton, Ohio, and Buffalo, New York, where Wendy Deichmann Edwards is a faculty member, has provided publishing support for this volume, for which we are both grateful. We wish to thank Mary Kelly, our research assistant in Buffalo, for her superb help with the index.

Elizabeth Dulany, our editor at the University of Illinois Press, has given invaluable assistance in negotiating the process to publication. Her colleagues Theresa L. Sears, managing editor, and Carol Betts, copy editor, have also helped us along the path to print.

Finally, we would like to thank those family members who have especially supported our work on this project: Bill Gifford and Jim and Lanse Edwards.

FOREWORD

Christopher H. Evans

Since the publication of Arthur Schlesinger Sr.'s essay "A Critical Period in American Religion" in 1932, the American social gospel movement of the late nineteenth and early twentieth centuries has been a topic that has fascinated historians and theologians. In the present book, Wendy Deichmann Edwards and Carolyn De Swarte Gifford not only contribute to the ongoing scholarly conversation concerning the social gospel's impact in American religious history; they redefine the nature of that dialogue by insisting that gender analysis is essential for interpreting the significance of the social gospel. This collection of essays challenges many well-established historical assumptions about the social gospel. It also suggests the necessity of new definitions and interpretations for understanding this significant topic in American religious history.

Although numerous studies have enhanced and expanded our understanding of the movement, the social gospel's legacy is still too frequently seen primarily through the writings of a small cadre of white middle-class Protestant leaders. While some of these leaders, like Josiah Strong and Walter Rauschenbusch, appear as major historical players in this volume, the reader is reminded of the fact that women were more than a passive audience for these men. Whether emerging from the churches of Protestant and Catholic America or African American urban faith communities, women from diverse cultural and ethnic contexts felt a special call to realize the social hope found in Jesus' teachings. Through organizations such as the Woman's Christian Temperance Union, foreign and home missionary societies, denominational boards, and social work organizations, women published, prayed, preached, and publicly advocated for their own visions of social transformation. At times, their visions complemented the work of male social gospel leaders. At other times, however, their visions brought them into conflict with these men.

This path-breaking book highlights the significant role played by women during this "critical period in American religion." However, the scholarship in this volume goes beyond showing how women's contributions have been "lost" or ignored by successive generations of historians. While the book accomplishes this goal, it moves that argument a step further by actually placing women at the *center* of the social gospel movement. Each chapter suggests that the social gospel was not an ideologically narrow phenomenon that rested primarily within the ecclesiastical corridors of white American Protestantism. Quite simply, the book suggests something missing from many previous studies of this time period: a belief that the social gospel was a compelling popular movement that captured the attention of many Americans living at that time.

Readers may wonder how the disparate perspectives in this volume provide a common framework for understanding this period of American religious history. Yet the purpose of all good scholarship is not just to test hypotheses or theories, but to raise thoughtful and penetrating questions that will inform future scholars and general readers. The reader will be compelled not only to rethink older definitions of the social gospel, but to envision how the social gospel was indeed a *movement* that significantly transformed the lives of women *and* men. It is a book that deserves to be read, reread, and acknowledged for the ways it signals a new direction for understanding the importance of the social gospel in America. This book's contribution toward the field of social gospel scholarship and women's history is timely, profound, and long overdue.

GENDER AND THE SOCIAL GOSPEL

INTRODUCTION: RESTORING WOMEN AND RECLAIMING GENDER IN SOCIAL GOSPEL STUDIES

Wendy J. Deichmann Edwards and
Carolyn De Swarte Gifford

J osiah Strong, general secretary of the Evangelical Alliance for the United States and author of the bestselling *Our Country,* published his second book, *The New Era,* in 1893. This was Strong's first written attempt to articulate the aims and methods of what historians have called the social gospel movement. He sent a complimentary copy to Frances Willard, president of the Woman's Christian Temperance Union (WCTU) and champion of a broad range of women's rights issues, seeking an endorsement of his effort by a highly esteemed colleague whom he regarded as an influential leader in social reform. Willard had a habit of scribbling pertinent remarks in the margins of books she read, often agreeing with the author and elaborating on the author's ideas with her own insights. Occasionally, however, she challenged the author's views with pointed comments. Her marginal note in *The New Era* is telling. "The capital error of this book," she wrote, "is that it makes so little of *woman*."[1] Willard's criticism could have been made about most writings by male social gospel figures and, later, by their biographers and historians of the movement. It succinctly captures the lack of importance ascribed to women and the causes they espoused by the men who were her contemporaries, as well as those who chronicled the history of the movement by taking their cues from celebrated male leaders. With very few exceptions, women's work and thought did not figure in their interpretations. Only recently have some historians begun to question the prevailing narrative of the social gospel movement, as they, like Willard, have noted "that it makes so little of *woman*."

Our purpose is to help reverse the longstanding trend of omitting women and gender from mainstream social gospel historiography. In this volume we highlight aspects of women's participation *and* some of the gender issues that deeply affected both women and men in the movement. We begin with an interpretive summary of earlier scholarship to show the significance of much of the work that has informed our own thinking. We hope to demonstrate the need for further revision of definitions, for gender-inclusive narratives and fresh interpretations of the social gospel movement. This discussion sets the stage for the essays in the main body of the text, each of which advances our knowledge and understanding of the role that women and gender have played in the social gospel movement in North America.[2]

The Problem of Definition

Absence of consideration of women and gender issues is evident in the pioneering historical work of C. Howard Hopkins, long considered the "dean" of social gospel studies. In 1940 he authored *The Rise of the Social Gospel in American Protestantism, 1865–1915.*[3] This influential volume predated historians' interest in social history and subsequent scholarly emphases on gender, race, class, and geographical region as categories of analysis. With its focus on pastors and professors from the northeastern and midwestern United States, it devotes nearly exclusive attention to male Euro-American intellectual and organizational accomplishments. Women are rarely mentioned in its pages or listed in its index. Yet Hopkins's book remains the standard description and analysis of the movement simply because no comprehensive interpretation has been written to supersede it. Packed with detailed descriptions of influential leaders and organizations, it is still the usual place to start if one wishes to understand the social gospel.

Part of Hopkins's legacy was his definition of the social gospel, which, with some elaboration, has remained normative. This definition was partly based upon a description produced earlier by Shailer Mathews, a widely acknowledged social gospel leader. For Mathews the social gospel was, simply, "the application of the teaching of Jesus and the total message of the Christian salvation to society, the economic life, and social institutions such as the state [and] the family, as well as to individuals."[4] Significantly, in his published work, Hopkins omitted Mathews's specific reference to the state and family, subjects that might have invited consideration of a host of women's concerns.[5] Adding historical perspective, Hopkins wrote that the movement was "called into being by the impact of modern industrial society and scientific thought upon the Protestantism of the United States during the half century following the Civil War. . . . It reached its climax in the optimistic prewar years of the twentieth century." He also noted its "criticism of conventional Protestantism, a progressive theology and social philosophy, and an active program of propagandism and reform."[6]

Several decades later, Robert T. Handy further developed what had become the conventional understanding. Handy emphasized the movement's roots in an earlier nineteenth-century reform spirit, which sought to Christianize America. Like Hopkins, Handy underscored social gospel leaders' recognition of the need for new methods to meet the changed conditions in which Christians labored to realize the Kingdom of God on earth. Unprecedented levels of urbanization and industrialization during the Gilded Age had given rise to city slums and inhuman working conditions that shocked the sensibilities of middle-class Protestants. The social gospel movement arose as a theological and practical response to the stark realities of poverty and economic injustice.[7] It was a ringing indictment of the complacency of a Protestantism that had become too comfortable, individualistic, and otherworldly.

These authors' portrayal is still widely accepted today. Thus the common view is of a movement that emerged after the Civil War and developed over the next fifty years, reaching its maturity in the first two decades of the twentieth century before declining in popularity. Its thinkers and activists applied the teachings of Jesus to pronounced social problems characteristic of the era. It is broadly agreed that the primary goal of the social gospel was to effect widespread Christian salvation aimed at transforming both personal lives and the social order. While upholding the need for personal conversion to faith in Jesus Christ, the social gospel called for the conversion of society as well. This societal eschatological emphasis—that the fulfillment of God's will involved the creation of a godly and just social order, the Kingdom of God on earth—was a theological hallmark of the movement. Thus social gospelers perceived themselves to be acting on a divine mandate as they marshaled public opinion, the tools of social science, and the power of the democratic political process in efforts to reconstruct society and its institutions, from the local to the global level, according to Christian ethical principles. This feature distinguished the social gospel from other expressions of social Christianity, which advocated and performed benevolent social ministries, but for the primary or exclusive purpose of saving individual souls. In fact, theological conservatives would disparage the social gospel for its entanglement with secular social science and politics and efforts to reconstruct what they viewed as a hopelessly profane world. Despite such criticism, social gospelers staunchly maintained a view of God's dynamic involvement in the world as both arena and subject of salvation. The goal was to actualize, in cooperation with God's spirit and will, human potential and destiny within what was perceived to be the emerging realm of God's Kingdom on earth.

The definitions that have been put forward by the most prominent social gospel historians have not explicitly excluded women or gender issues from the movement. They have been remarkably non-gender-specific, especially given the time period in which the earliest ones were written, and given the almost exclusively male focus in the narratives about the movement they intend to describe. Sometimes lack of gender specificity theoretically implies gender inclu-siveness. However in the case of social gospel movement historiography, per-sistent failure to specify women's presence in its definitions has only reinforced the tradition of overlooking women that characterizes the movement's predomi-nant narratives. Such definitions, now outdated, exact no accountability for, and require no correction to, the flawed perception of the movement as the domain of elite, white, male intellectuals. They permit and thereby foster continuation of the pattern of omitting women and the causes they espoused from the his-torical understanding of the movement. The difficulties of discerning women's participation in the social gospel movement have been compounded, then, by the nearly universal acceptance of these non-gender-specific definitions.

Women's historians have demonstrated over the past several decades that without the intentional and explicit inclusion of women and gender analysis in our retelling of history, our definitions, descriptions, and interpretations are at best incomplete, and at worst, inaccurate. In recent years, scholars have only begun to apply these insights to the definition and the narration of the social gospel movement and the interpretation of its impact on American religion and society. These efforts have tended to be isolated and their findings have yet to be mainstreamed into the larger scholarly circles and narratives of women's, religious, or cultural historiography. It has become increasingly evident that until much more primary research has been completed, it is impossible to have an adequate understanding of the nature and scope of women's participation in this movement, of the impact of gender issues in its unfolding, and therefore of the movement itself. However, the work that has already been done has been richly rewarding, promising similar rewards from further investigation.

The research in these areas has confirmed what Frances Willard and her fe-male colleagues realized long ago but has since been obscured: that the social gospel movement resulted from the efforts of women and men who jointly ex-pected and labored toward the dawning of the Kingdom of God on earth. Both sexes invoked the teachings of Jesus as the supreme ethical principles fit for the establishment of that kingdom. Women as well as men accepted the challenge of attempting to build a just society in the face of horrific urban, industrial, and labor conditions. In a variety of ways they proclaimed a Christ-centered gospel that was both personally and socially transformational. Adamantly they ex-pressed criticism of individualistic Christianity, which they believed neglected, to everyone's peril, the social causes of sin. Both women and men engaged in active programs of education and reform designed to promote these principles and accomplish these goals.

Recent scholarship suggests that the experiences of women and men in the social gospel movement differed widely in some respects. This difference was determined largely by the Victorian gender ideology that was in vogue during the heyday of the social gospel movement. Both sexes were consciously socialized to operate in separate and complementary spheres of interest and activity. As a result, women presumed responsibility for social conditions that affected women, children, and family life. Men dutifully maintained oversight of industrial, political, and theological concerns. Women rarely ventured to tamper with these male prerogatives, except when they perceived and could demonstrate that the well-being of women, children, or the family was at stake. Women were more likely than men to address social purity issues, including promotion of sex education, opposition to the double sexual standard for men and women, raising of the age of consent, and prevention of prostitution. Women were inclined to take the initiative in setting up kindergartens or day care for the children of working mothers. Women were less likely, with some notable exceptions, to publish theological treatises and philosophical books than men, who were trained and validated in these areas. Men were less disposed than women, again with some exceptions, to use social gospel principles to argue for woman suffrage or for women's ordination or right to preach. Nor would they easily challenge the middle-class Victorian ideals of manhood and womanhood that shaped the popular understanding of the family and its role in society.

Studies of women's participation in the social gospel movement have also shown that there was considerable variation in the nature of women's religiously motivated reform efforts and in their opinions about social gospel issues. The presence of such diversity among male social gospel figures has long been an accepted fact. Some men were Christian socialists, while others repudiated all forms of socialism. Many, but not all, social gospel men were advocates of temperance. Therefore it should come as no surprise that women who were participants and leaders in the social gospel movement also differed from each other. Like men, some were Christian socialists and others were not. Some women believed that temperance was the key to God's Kingdom; others insisted on woman suffrage; still others, that both reforms were indispensable. Many expressed deep concern about child labor and working conditions for women, while others focused their energies on world peace. Some women social gospelers—deaconesses, for example—were given the sanction of the churches, while others functioned in secular settings without benefit of ecclesiastical blessing. Like their male counterparts, the women represented a wide variety of denominational affiliations. Some were wealthy, while others lived in poverty.

Historians have also observed that Euro-American and African American proponents of the social gospel possessed somewhat distinct understandings of what social salvation entailed. Many African Americans worked diligently to address racial justice issues, an area often neglected entirely by Euro-American men and women. This emphasis was evident in the work of both male and female African American social gospel figures. Like their Euro-American counterparts, African American social gospel women often functioned within the constraints of culturally sanctioned gender expectations but sometimes challenged them.

Review of Selected Literature

The first call for revision of the scope and meaning of the social gospel movement was sounded more than a quarter century ago by Ronald C. White and C.
Howard Hopkins. Their anthology, *The Social Gospel: Religion and Reform in
Changing America*, published in 1976, was a watershed in social gospel historiography. Hopkins and White acknowledged the deficiencies of Hopkins's earlier work on the history of the social gospel that had become obvious in light
of the work of social historians beginning in the 1960s. Responding to the growing interest in women's history—as well as African American, immigrant, labor, and regional histories—these authors announced an ambitious purpose:
"to restate and re-vision the social gospel . . . to enlarge [its] definition even as
its geographic, religious, and social boundaries are redrawn and expanded."[8] In
a first step toward accomplishing this goal, they included a chapter on Frances
Willard, illustrating how her leadership of the WCTU became the impetus for
broadening the organization's agenda to include a push for woman suffrage.

In the 1980s, numerous scholars took up the challenge of reinterpreting the
social gospel movement along these new lines. Janet Forsythe Fishburn's *The
Fatherhood of God and the Victorian Family*, published in 1981, introduced a
thoroughgoing gender analysis into social gospel studies. Looking at the theological language favored by movement leaders, Fishburn analyzed the popular
masculine social gospel concepts of "fatherhood of God," "brotherhood of
man," and "Kingdom of God," placing them in their Victorian cultural and
social context. Focusing her study upon previously unscrutinized aspects of
otherwise well-known, white, male social gospel figures, she succeeded in establishing the significance of gender as an important category for further interpretation of the movement. She concluded that for several key male social
gospel leaders the gender arrangement dominant throughout most of the nineteenth century persisted well into the twentieth, affecting their view of women
and women's issues.[9]

Other studies, which appeared that same year, connected turn-of-the-century
women's work in social reform directly with the social gospel's efforts to remake
society into the Kingdom of God on earth and showed that gender-related issues played a central role in these efforts. The first volume of *Women in New
Worlds: Historical Perspectives on the Wesleyan Tradition*, edited by Hilah H.
Thomas and Rosemary Skinner Keller, contains several essays that examine
women and organizations whose contributions to the social gospel movement
were far-reaching. Each of these features the development of the deaconess
vocation as one of Protestantism's strongest responses to the crises of the cities. Mary Agnes Dougherty argued that deaconesses were expressing the essence
of the social gospel movement long before "Protestant churchmen assumed full
paternal responsibility for [it]." Dougherty was one of the first to question why
traditional church history dates the beginning of the movement from its accep-

tance by male ministers and professors, rather than from professional social ministries performed by women, especially deaconesses. She described their work in urban visitation, social analysis, and politics as part of the larger effort to Christianize society. Virginia Lieson Brereton scrutinized some of the many institutions founded at the turn of the century to train deaconesses. These schools were established in order to equip women for a wide range of lay ministries emphasizing service, with innovative curricula offering studies in the new fields of sociology and social service as well as more predictable courses in biblical studies, theology, and church history. Such institutions could be understood as alternatives to denominational theological schools and seminaries where women were not welcome to study. Finally, Miriam Crist recovered the story of a previously unrecognized social gospel figure and placed her squarely in the ranks of the radical wing of the movement, usually represented by well-known male leaders. Winifred L. Chappell, a deaconess trained at one of the institutions featured in Brereton's essay, served on the staff of the Methodist Federation for Social Service (MFSS), the denominational arm charged with carrying out the aims of the social gospel. Fulfilling her responsibility to produce the bimonthly journal of the MFSS, *Social Service Bulletin,* Chappell became a skilled investigative reporter who sought to expose the extent and depth of economic injustice in the United States.[10]

The first modern book-length publication about women and the social gospel movement was published in 1982. John Patrick McDowell's *The Social Gospel in the South: The Woman's Home Mission Movement in the Methodist Episcopal Church, South, 1886–1939,* countered the conclusion of earlier historians that the social gospel movement never caught on in the South. He contended that southern women, working through separate women's organizations, were at the forefront of social gospel leadership, and that they relied heavily upon the broader movement's theology and methods in their work. Because earlier southern historians failed to investigate women's activity and organizations, they simply missed evidence of the movement's strength in the region. Basing his findings on close study of the Woman's Home Missionary Society's publications, McDowell discovered that these women tackled some of the most problematic issues of southern life, including discrimination and segregation, lynching, and labor disputes while at the same time addressing national and international questions such as women's rights and global disarmament.[11]

The need to re-vision and redefine the social gospel movement was reiterated by Susan Hill Lindley in her 1990 article "'Neglected Voices' and *Praxis* in the Social Gospel." Lindley argued for encompassing the activities and reflections of heretofore "neglected" figures in defining the movement. To illustrate, she sketched the careers of three overlooked figures whose activities and underlying motivations suggest an integral relationship with the movement: Vida Scudder, a Wellesley professor and settlement leader; Reverdy C. Ransom, a bishop of the African Methodist Episcopal Church; and Nannie Helen

Burroughs, a longtime president of the Woman's Convention of the National Baptist Convention. While holding much in common with well-known white male social gospel figures, these three persons also added "distinctive notes" of their own to the movement: a variety of spiritual underpinnings, a focus upon lay ministry, a consciousness of white racism as a structural sin, and affirmation of both human dignity and egalitarianism.[12]

A growing body of literature has begun to examine the relationship between African American women and the social gospel. The most thorough treatment of this topic, published in 1993, is Evelyn Brooks Higginbotham's *Righteous Discontent: The Women's Movement in the Black Baptist Church, 1880–1920*. Higginbotham unequivocally associated African American women's social activism with the social gospel movement and argued that during the height of the movement the Woman's Convention of the National Baptist Convention increasingly focused its attention on urban conditions and industrialization. Drawing upon minutes and reports of the convention, Higginbotham showed that many of the black church's efforts in social reform were "initiated, funded, and executed" by women, who worked alongside both black ministers and white social reformers. The convention exerted leadership within the black church community, denouncing churches "that refused to include social salvation in the program of saving souls" and countering "the sexism that black churches shared with the dominant white society." Thus the "convention movement," Higginbotham wrote, gave women "the collective strength and determination to continue their struggle for the rights of blacks and the rights of women." The relationships between these struggles and the larger social gospel movement deserve further exploration.[13]

Eleanor Stebner's 1997 study, *The Women of Hull House*, focused upon the relationship between women's spirituality and social gospel reform. She examined the negative encounters with conventional Christianity experienced by women who became leaders of Hull-House. Stebner concluded that the church's inability to recognize and foster women's vocations within ecclesiastical structures tended to alienate many women from its fold. Disillusionment with traditional forms of Christianity prompted them "to reimagine the tradition and focus on spiritual rather than doctrinal aspects." This spiritual focus provided the grounding for individual and communal life at Hull-House as well as for the social reform efforts accomplished by its female leadership. Stebner contended that the religious beliefs that were held by Hull-House women had much in common with the beliefs being proclaimed by well-known social gospel spokespersons. Yet from the perspective of many in the Protestant religious establishment, because of their gender, women like Jane Addams and Ellen Gates Starr were and are considered social reformers outside the movement's Christian parameters. Stebner's analysis of the difficulty women had clarifying their sense of religious vocation within American Victorian culture underscores the important but too little studied relationship between the social gospel movement and women's use of secular institutions to accomplish their religiously or spiritually motivated reform aspirations.[14]

Kathryn Kish Sklar confirmed and expanded this important connection in her plenary address, "Beyond Maternalism: Protestant Women and Social Justice Activism, 1890–1920," delivered at the April 1998 conference on "Women and Twentieth-Century Protestantism." Sklar argued that too often historians have ignored or belittled the religious underpinnings of women's social reform activism. She maintained that the religious views held by women activists of this era significantly shaped their challenges to the status quo, helped to define their political agendas, and encouraged strategic alliances between religious and secular bodies to help accomplish shared goals. Sklar briefly examined the careers of Jane Addams and Florence Kelley, who have often been viewed as secular figures both by historians of the social gospel and historians of women. While not denying their political and secular interests, Sklar contended that "in their work Addams and Kelley relied on religious metaphors and discourse, if not on religious guidance." Both women "transformed" such discourse so that it would function within the secular and broadly ecumenical contexts in which they worked, "but they still lived inside it." She argued that these two "apparently quite secular figures" should be considered part of the social gospel cast.[15]

Current Perspectives

As the brief literature review above indicates, both the search for women actors in the social gospel narrative and efforts to recognize the role of gender in the movement have already yielded important results. However, the task of retelling the history of the social gospel movement with a full cast of players and complete slate of issues has really just begun. The essays in this volume continue the process.[16] They are arranged in five sections. The first—"Setting the Issues"—points to the need for broader definitions and narratives of the movement to include female participation and women's social gospel concerns, as well as gender analysis. The second section—"Perspectives on a Social Gospel Family"—takes a gendered look at a renowned social gospel family, the Rauschenbusches. The third—"Organization and Professionalization of Women's Social Gospel Work"—highlights a variety of women's organizations and the methods and strategies they employed to accomplish both charity and social gospel aims. The fourth—"Women and Social Gospel Theology"—discusses the creative engagement of several prominent women in theological and intellectual discourse relative to the movement. The final section—"Expanding the Conventional Boundaries of the Social Gospel Movement"—illustrates the need to reconsider the parameters of the movement with regard to its modes of expression, time frame, and racial and gender inclusiveness.

The first essay in the volume, "'The Woman's Cause Is Man's'? Frances Willard and the Social Gospel," by Carolyn De Swarte Gifford, focuses on one of the few women generally acknowledged as a social gospel leader. Gifford traces the development of the central theme of Willard's thought: the true equality of women and men, and their partnership in pursuit of the Kingdom of God. Because Willard was a vocal critic of Victorian gender ideology, Gifford contends that her most crucial role within the social gospel movement was her indictment of the broader movement for its failure to embrace the social reform— equality of the sexes—that she and many other women considered fundamental to the new Christian social order they envisioned.

Wendy J. Deichmann Edwards's essay, "Women and Social Betterment in the Social Gospel Work of Josiah Strong," examines the attention given to women's social concerns by a prominent male social gospel leader. Analyzing relevant segments from Josiah Strong's publications, she traces the evolution of his support for greater public roles for women as indispensable coworkers in social gospel work and in society at large. She argues that his justification for this development hinged upon his understanding of non-gender-exclusive "social betterment" work as an essential component in building God's Kingdom on earth.

Implicitly challenging Hopkins's earlier thesis that the social gospel was a specifically U.S. contribution to religious history, Eleanor J. Stebner in "More Than Maternal Feminists and Good Samaritans: Women and the Social Gospel in Canada" vividly describes the Canadian context of the movement.[17] In doing so, this essay introduces readers to Canadian women leaders whose work and thought are not well known to scholars in the United States or to Canadian social and religious historians. As she examines the many different forms that women's social gospel work took in Canada, Stebner takes issue with historians who understand women's motivations for that work too narrowly. She contends that the label "maternal feminism" does not adequately define layers of motives women held and strategies they pursued in order to accomplish social gospel goals.

Janet Forsythe Fishburn, in an essay entitled "Walter Rauschenbusch and 'The Woman Movement': A Gender Analysis," exposes ambivalence and apparent contradictions in Rauschenbusch's thinking about "the woman movement." She argues that there was only a small shift in his understanding of gender during the course of his career. Initially, he viewed gender arrangements as a polarity of complementary interests and roles, which had the effect of limiting women to the sphere of home and family. Eventually, he developed a limited acceptance of public roles for some women. Yet he continued to worry about how shifting definitions of gender would impact the family, which he considered the foundation of society. Fishburn presents Rauschenbusch as a man with an essentially Victorian understanding of gender roles who was increasingly ill at ease with some of the social changes in his world after 1910, especially those that challenged reigning nineteenth-century notions of womanhood and family.

Paul William Harris's essay, "The Social Dimensions of Foreign Missions:

Emma Rauschenbusch Clough and Social Gospel Ideology," challenges the traditional linkage of foreign missionary activity with a relentless Western imperialism. The Baptist missionary Emma Rauschenbusch Clough, sister of Walter Rauschenbusch and wife of fellow missionary John Everett Clough, became the interpreter of Baptist efforts to convert Telegu Untouchables. Her two books described the mission to the Telegu people, in which her husband played a leading role. Her work was unusual for the time in that it employed sociological and ethnographic analyses, emphasizing the indigenous social sources of mass conversion, and thereby attributing genuine agency to Untouchable converts. Rauschenbusch Clough portrayed a progressive missionary stance that respected traditional indigenous social forms in work for change in India's rigid caste system instead of simplistically imposing Western stereotypes of helpless passivity on converts.

In "The Woman's Christian Temperance Union in the Pacific Northwest: A Different Side of the Social Gospel," Dale E. Soden looks closely at the broad reform agenda of a self-consciously separate women's organization. Focusing on the religious impulse behind the social and political strategies of the WCTU, he maintains that the organization was motivated by a biblical view of justice and gender equality. The women of the WCTU labored to civilize the rough, often brutal, frontier ethos in their efforts to make their region safe for women and children and a wholesome environment for family life. In so doing, they collaborated with many other women and women's organizations and made women's concerns an integral part of the social gospel movement in the northwestern United States.

Taking a biographical approach, Elizabeth N. Agnew examines the life and work of a pioneering social work theorist in "Shaping a Civic Profession: Mary Richmond, the Social Gospel, and Social Work." Agnew convincingly argues that Richmond's understanding of charity and social work was grounded in the ideals of the social gospel with its aim of social justice. Serving for almost two decades as director of the Charity Organization Department of the Russell Sage Foundation, Richmond typified the many women and men motivated by social gospel ideals who chose an alternative, secular setting from which to address the plight of the cities' poor during the Progressive Era. Richmond helped shape the newly developing methodology of social work, participating in the professionalization of charity work by seeking to organize and systematize it. Yet she also struggled to maintain the ethos of civic responsibility undergirded by religious ideals that she believed to be central to her field as social work became increasingly male-directed and medicalized during the 1920s.

Robert Trawick's essay, "Dorothy Day and the Social Gospel Movement: Different Theologies, Common Concerns," argues against the tendency to lump together unreflectively under the rubric of the social gospel anyone working for social reform during the late nineteenth and early twentieth centuries. Trawick presents Day as a distinctively Roman Catholic voice, whose ideas and actions have certain commonalities with the Protestant social gospel yet also reveal crucial differences in theology, spirituality, and method. Trawick traces Day's uniqueness and shows how she drew deeply from the well of Roman Catholic tradition in creating the Catholic Worker movement in the early 1930s. He compares this movement's understanding of poverty and its relationship to the poor with Protestant social gospel approaches to similar concerns.

Like Trawick, R. A. R. Edwards questions using the social gospel rubric as a kind of umbrella under which too wide a variety of social reformers could be placed. In her essay "Jane Addams, Walter Rauschenbusch, and Dorothy Day: A Comparative Study of Settlement Theology," Edwards looks closely at Addams's beliefs, rejecting the notion that they were deeply Christian, as were Rauschenbusch's and Day's. Edwards insists that Addams believed not in God but in democracy, in a kind of "secularizing religiosity." She contrasts Addams's theologically vague, humanitarian faith with Rauschenbusch's vigorous Protestant theology that indicted social sinfulness. She compares Addams's thought, which she finds nearly stripped of compelling Christian ideas and imagery, with Day's commitment to a Catholic understanding of the mystical body of Christ and incarnational ministry.

Kendal P. Mobley uses Baptist periodical literature to explore two crucial themes: the relationship of the social gospel to women's foreign mission work and the leadership of Helen Barrett Montgomery in steering a middle course between the extremes of fundamentalism and modernism in the first decades of the twentieth century. His essay, "The Ecumenical Woman's Missionary Movement: Helen Barrett Montgomery and *The Baptist*, 1920–30," interprets the writings of one of the most influential leaders of the women's foreign mission movement. Mobley finds in Montgomery a clear commitment to social as well as individual salvation. Like the WCTU, the many denominational women's foreign missionary societies championed fuller freedom and opportunities for women worldwide. Montgomery was a vocal spokesperson for women's equality based on her belief in Jesus as the "great Emancipator of woman." This essay confirms the thesis recently put forth by women's historians that differing theologies of gender played a dominant role in the fundamentalist-modernist controversy.[18]

Susan Hill Lindley's essay, entitled "Gender and the Social Gospel Novel," focuses on the different ways male and female authors portrayed female characters.[19] Her study reveals the endorsement by many male writers of traditional gender roles; that women in male-authored novels tended to appear in stereotypical Victorian, peripheral roles such as victim, supportive minister's wife, or shallow society matron. In contrast, women authors dissented from ideological constraints by presenting more complex female characters who might choose a career of social action over marriage and who underwent serious religious struggle. Lindley's study of the novel also identifies new arenas of women's activity in the social gospel movement. She suggests that because this literary genre was a more socially acceptable form of expression for women than the writing of formal theology, the theological critique of Gilded Age society and religion found in many novels written by women must be taken seriously for its representation of women's voice in social gospel studies.

In "True to Our God: African American Women as Christian Activists in Rochester, New York," Ingrid Overacker portrays a unique social gospel response rooted in African Americans' confrontation with white racism. Race issues overrode gender issues in the lives of the African Americans in this upstate New York community during the first half of the twentieth century. By implication, Overacker suggests that this stark fact was true for African Americans generally. She profiles strong, faithful women for whom the traditional maternal role with its concern for moral and intellectual education provided a lifeline for their families, imbuing them with courage and determination to endure and rise above the effects of racism. These women, and many others like them, were the backbone of their churches, the institutions that played the most vital role in sustaining and equipping African Americans in their quest for justice during a time when they were denied nearly every other vehicle for social change.

Several of the essays in this volume make a strong case for extending the periodization of the social gospel movement beyond the end of World War I, the time when many earlier historians of the movement saw its abrupt decline.[20] Michael Dwayne Blackwell's essay, "In the Legacy of Dr. Martin Luther King Jr.: The Social Gospel of Faye Wattleton and Marian Wright Edelman," explores the influence of social gospel ideas, goals, and methods beyond the 1920s. Blackwell asserts that a revitalized social gospel vision should still be an animating force at the beginning of the twenty-first century. He traces the careers of three African Americans who have devoted their lives to bringing into being the Kingdom of God on earth. The civil rights movement led by Martin Luther King Jr. responded to the enduring white racism that an earlier generation of white social gospel leaders failed to confront in any thoroughgoing way. Faye Wattleton's efforts in the area of reproductive rights and gender equality broadened the vision held by Frances Willard and Helen Barrett Montgomery decades before, when they pinpointed health issues as social gospel concerns. The needs and rights of children have been the focus of Marian Wright Edelman's advocacy, echoing and extending the work of numerous Progressive Era institutions devoted to child protection. These three figures—and many others that must be reclaimed and made known—represent a vital social gospel legacy that bears hope for a just future.

New Directions for Social Gospel Research

Along with other recent work, the essays in this volume raise some important questions of interpretation.[21] First, what difference does it make when we view the social gospel movement through the lens of gender? Does something utterly new emerge? Or is it basically the same story—just a bit more complicated? The past three decades of scholarship on women, gender, and the social gospel have begun to lay the groundwork for an informed response to these questions. Much that is new *has* emerged, *and* the story has become much more complex. The same characters that were there before do remain, but there is a much larger cast than previously recognized. Women have emerged as definers of the movement instead of being seen merely as passive recipients of its ideas and methods. Although gender-related issues like women's roles in business, industry, politics, and education may seem brand new to the telling of social gospel history, these and many other concerns were always a part of the real story. To reclaim these valid but forgotten elements does add to the challenge for historians. As these lost components are found and restored, the story of the social gospel will continue to become both more intricate and more accurate.

Research findings in this field of study collectively signal the need for a revised, expanded definition of the social gospel movement. This definition must reflect, unambiguously, the gender-inclusiveness that characterized the movement and encompassed the women and men of various races and classes that were its constituents and its leaders. It is essential to embrace the wide range of issues, including gender-related ones, for which its varied advocates crusaded. The definition should be informed not only by theological treatises, sermons, and philosophical monologues, but also by minutes of meetings and other publications produced by women's home missionary, temperance, and other organizations; women's periodicals; journals; novels; poetry; and letters. The research undergirding this new definition must attend, as equitably as possible, to all the movement's participants. It will be the product not only of the literature reviewed and presented in this volume, but future research as well.

Viewing the social gospel movement through the lens of gender provokes new questions and suggests exciting new directions for research. Most basically, what additional bibliographical and archival resources can be mined to help us learn more about the women and the gender issues that were part of the social gospel movement? Which organizations, religious and secular, provide the kinds of written records that would be most informative? Which women should be the subjects of further biographical work? Which educational institutions, broadly defined, should be investigated because of their roles in inspiring and training women for social gospel work? What kinds of informal mentoring did women receive that led them into social gospel work? How did contacts with women from other continents through international organizations such as the WCTU and the Young Women's Christian Association influence women's social gospel perspectives and strategies?

Comparative studies would also be useful. What were some of the differences between the social gospel work performed by women and that undertaken by men? For instance, how, if at all, did settlement houses directed by women differ from those directed by men? Were there gender-related differences in the nature of social gospel spiritualities, and if so, what were they and why? How did the social gospel's responses to gender issues compare with the responses given by the precursors of the fundamentalist movement, on the one hand, and by society at large, on the other? What role did gender play in the face-off between fundamentalists and social gospel–influenced modernists? What effect did denominational affiliation or theological tradition have on the extent to which women and men aligned themselves with or rejected particular social gospel principles? What was the nature of this alignment? How often did women who felt called to Christian ministry channel their gifts and graces into forms of secular social gospel work because they were denied a position within the church on account of gender? Were there regional distinctions in women's response to the social gospel? How did attitudes toward women and gender issues in the movement change over time, and how did these attitudes affect organizational, especially denominational, structures and practices? What effects did the professionalization of social work have upon the social gospel movement, given the growing preponderance of women in that field? How are all these issues complicated by attending to race and class differences, as well as gender?

The answers to these questions and many more that other scholars will propose will require extensive research. The time has not yet arrived for a definitive account of the role of women and gender in the social gospel movement. However, in the meantime, it is inexcusable *not* to incorporate the many things we *have* learned about women, gender, and the social gospel into future definitions, narratives, and interpretations of the movement. It is easy enough to explain away Josiah Strong's myopia about women in his 1893 book *The New Era*, demonstrating apologetically its roots in Victorian gender ideology. However, this "capital error"—the exclusion of women from the social gospel story, which so incensed Frances Willard in the late nineteenth century—should not be allowed to persist into the twenty-first century. Instead of making "so little of woman," we hope that scholarship in *this* new era will do much to advance our understanding of how *both* women and men tried, in the social gospel movement, to build the Kingdom of God on earth.

Notes

1. Frances E. Willard, handwritten marginal note in her personal copy of Josiah Strong, *The New Era: or The Coming Kingdom* (New York: Baker and Taylor, 1893), 132. Willard's personal library, Frances E. Willard Memorial Library, WCTU Archives, Evanston, Ill.

2. It is beyond the scope of this essay to provide a complete survey of all the literature that has contributed to the growing understanding of how women and gender issues shaped the social gospel movement. Our review is meant to be suggestive of the nature of the work that has been done, not exhaustive. Readers will discover a broad array of further sources in the notes for the essays in this volume.

3. C. Howard Hopkins, *The Rise of the Social Gospel in American Protestantism, 1865–1915* (New Haven: Yale University Press, 1940).

4. The full quote of Mathews's definition is found in Shailer Mathews, "Social Gospel," in *A Dictionary of Religion and Ethics,* ed. Shailer Mathews and G. B. Smith (New York: Macmillan, 1921), 416–17; and also in Willem A. Visser 'T Hooft, *The Background of the Social Gospel in America* (1928; reprint, St. Louis, Mo.: Bethany Press, 1962), 16.

5. This unfortunate omission was repeated in Ronald C. White Jr. and C. Howard Hopkins, eds., *The Social Gospel: Religion and Reform in Changing America* (Philadelphia: Temple University Press, 1976), xi; and Ronald C. White Jr., *Liberty and Justice for All: Racial Reform and the Social Gospel* (San Francisco: Harper and Row, 1990), xvii. This omission could serve only to reinforce inattention to family and related political and legal issues in subsequent social gospel scholarship, especially given the dependence of other scholars upon these works.

6. Hopkins, *Rise of the Social Gospel,* 3.

7. Robert T. Handy, *A Christian America: Protestant Hopes and Historical Realities,* 2d ed. (New York: Oxford University Press, 1984), 135. He enumerated theological emphases of the movement in the introduction to *The Social Gospel in America, 1870–1920: Gladden, Ely, and Rauschenbusch,* ed. Robert T. Handy (New York: Oxford University Press, 1966), 10–11.

8. White and Hopkins, *The Social Gospel: Religion and Reform,* xi.

9. Janet Forsythe Fishburn, *The Fatherhood of God and the Victorian Family: The Social Gospel in America* (Philadelphia: Fortress, 1981). A decade later, William D. Lindsey's article "The Social Gospel and Feminism" (*American Journal of Theology and Philosophy* 13, no. 3 [September 1992]: 195–210) issued a caveat against viewing male social gospel leaders' attitudes about gender as monolithic.

10. Mary Agnes Dougherty, "The Social Gospel According to Phoebe" (200–216); Virginia Lieson Brereton, "Preparing Women for the Lord's Work" (178–99); and Miriam J. Crist, "Winifred L. Chappell: Everyone on the Left Knew Her" (362–78), all in *Women in New Worlds: Historical Perspectives on the Wesleyan Tradition,* vol. 1, ed. Hilah F. Thomas and Rosemary Skinner Keller (Nashville: Abingdon Press, 1981). See also Mary Frederickson, "Shaping a New Society: Methodist Women and Industrial Reform in the South, 1880–1940," in the same volume (345–61).

11. John Patrick McDowell, *The Social Gospel in the South: The Woman's Home Mission Movement in the Methodist Episcopal Church, South, 1886–1939* (Baton Rouge: Louisiana State University Press, 1982).

12. Susan Hill Lindley, "Neglected Voices and *Praxis* in the Social Gospel," *Journal of Religious Ethics* 18 (Spring 1990): 75–76, 94–98. Douglas M. Strong also treats Vida Scudder as a social gospel theologian in *They Walked in the Spirit: Personal Faith and Social Action in America* (Louisville, Ky.: Westminster John Knox Press, 1997), 66–75. Lindley has continued to feature previously neglected figures in her work since the early 1990s and has offered revised definitions of the social gospel in her most recent writing. See Susan Hill Lindley, *You Have Stept Out of Your Place: A History of Women and Religion in America* (Louisville, Ky: Westminster John Knox Press, 1996) 135–47; "Deciding Who Counts: Toward a Revision of the Social Gospel," in *The Social Gospel Today,* ed. Christopher H. Evans (Louisville, Ky.: Westminster John Knox Press, 2001); and "The Social Gospel," in *Encyclopedia of Women and Religion in North America,* ed. Rosemary Skinner Keller and Rosemary Radford Ruether (Bloomington: Indiana University Press, forthcoming).

13. Evelyn Brooks Higginbotham, *Righteous Discontent: The Women's Movement in the Black Baptist Church, 1880–1920* (Cambridge, Mass.: Harvard University Press, 1993), 18 (fourth quote), 121 (third quote), 174–80 (first and second quotes). The roles of African American women in social activism are also explored in Delores C. Carpenter, "Black Women in Religious Institutions: A Historical Summary from Slavery to the 1960s," *Journal of Religious Thought* 46 (1989–90): 7–27; and Mary A. Sawyer, "Black Women and Social Change: Women in Leadership Roles," *Journal of Religious Thought* 47 (1990–91): 16–21. Some African American women are found in the indexes to both White's *Liberty and Justice for All* and Ralph E. Luker's *The Social Gospel in Black and White: American Racial Reform, 1885–1912* (Chapel Hill: University of North Carolina Press, 1991).

14. Eleanor J. Stebner, *The Women of Hull House: A Study in Spirituality, Vocation, and Friendship* (Albany: State University of New York, 1997), 4, 7, 23, 103, 186 (quote).

15. Kathryn Kish Sklar, "Beyond Maternalism: Protestant Women and Social Justice Activism, 1890–1920," *Women and Twentieth Century Protestantism* 3 (Winter 1999): 2–7.

16. All but two of the essays in this volume were initially presented at the second annual Social Gospel Conference held at Colgate Rochester Divinity School in the spring of 1999.

17. This essay was written specifically for this volume—it was not presented at the Social Gospel Conference.

18. This thesis is presented in Margaret Lamberts Bendroth, *Fundamentalism and Gender, 1875 to the Present* (New Haven: Yale University Press, 1993); and Betty A. DeBerg, *Ungodly Women: Gender and the First Wave of American Fundamentalism* (Minneapolis: Fortress, 1990).

19. This essay was first published by Lindley as "Women and the Social Gospel Novel," *Church History* 54, no. 1 (March 1985): 56–73, and is reprinted here, with minimal alterations, with permission from the American Society of Church History. This essay remains unique and definitive more than a decade and a half after its first publication.

20. See, for instance, Hopkins, *Rise of the Social Gospel*, 327. Others, such as William D. Lindsey, have recently challenged this view of its demise. See Lindsey, "Taking a New Look at the Social Gospel," introduction to his *Shailer Mathews's Lives of Jesus: The Search for a Theological Foundation for the Social Gospel* (Albany: State University of New York Press, 1997), 1–33.

21. As other women's historians have also done, Margaret Lamberts Bendroth raised some of these questions during a discussion on "Women and the Social Gospel" at the annual meeting of the American Society of Church History in January 2000.

PART 1

Setting the Issues

CHAPTER 1

"The Woman's Cause Is Man's"? Frances Willard and the Social Gospel

Carolyn De Swarte Gifford

Over the past several decades, a new generation of historians has been reassessing the social gospel movement. With women's history emerging as a leading focus of historical research, historians have been eager to reclaim neglected or forgotten women reformers and place them within the social gospel tradition. Of no figure has this been more true than Frances Willard, whom the venerable American religious historian Sidney Ahlstrom described as "the single most impressive reformer to have worked within the context of the evangelical churches."[1] Ronald C. White Jr. and C. Howard Hopkins, in their 1976 revisionist study of the social gospel, devote a chapter to Willard and her leadership of the Woman's Christian Temperance Union (WCTU). Their attention to Willard, whom they wish to rescue from historical oblivion, indicates that they place her under the broad umbrella of the social gospel movement.[2] Subsequently, the historians Mari Jo Buhle, Ruth Bordin, and Richard Leeman have all referred to Willard as a social gospel leader in the formative years of the movement, but none of them has actually offered an extended discussion of her as a social gospel figure; they simply take it for granted that she is one.[3] Ida Tetreault Miller, in her 1978 dissertation, evaluated Willard "according to the categories of the social gospel," comparing her thought favorably to that of Walter Rauschenbusch, widely recognized as *the* theologian of the social gospel.[4] Miller comes to the predictable conclusion that Willard "measures up" to Rauschenbusch's definition.

Willard certainly can be understood as a social gospel figure and a towering one at that. Her thought and actions during her tenure as president of the WCTU—from 1879 to her death in 1898—show obvious evidence of being motivated by the same visions, goals, and strategies as those of many men whom we immediately identify as social gospel figures, men who were often her friends and allies in the great variety of reforms that she championed. She shared a similar social and religious background and values with early leaders of the movement who grew up during midcentury in a rural and small-town environment. Her family came from New England Puritan roots tempered by evangelical Protestantism—in her case, Methodism—and she spent much of her childhood and adolescence on a farm in southeastern Wisconsin.

With Chicago as the base for her reform career, she plunged into an urban environment, fascinated by its energy and opportunity but concerned by the growing problems of the city. She expressed her ideas in the language of liberal theology, envisioning the Kingdom of God on earth when human institutions would be governed by the Golden Rule, with Jesus as the ethical ideal. She believed in the importance of individual salvation but understood that sinful systems—political, economic, and social—were in dire need of redemption. Her concern for the new urban economy with its inequities between rich and poor; her questioning whether capitalism could ever become a just system; her startling declaration, at the close of the 1880s, that poverty caused intemperance in many cases, and not the other way round, as most still insisted; and her embracing of Christian socialism during the last decade of her life—all these opinions and attitudes that Willard held give ample reason to view her as a social gospel figure. She seems to fit easily, appropriately under the social gospel rubric.

We wonder how we could have overlooked her contribution to that movement and posit that it must have been the blinders of sexism that caused generations of historians to ignore her. Now what we need to do is to put her back where she belongs, to accord her her rightful place in the social gospel narrative, as historians like White and Hopkins suggest. We must simply do the compensatory work necessary to achieve some sort of historical justice in regard to her thought and work. Attempting such a rehabilitation was actually my intent until I began thinking seriously about this essay and about Willard's true aims. Now I want to back away from too easily sliding Willard into the social gospel framework. Instead of asking whether she "measures up" to its categories or "fits" the broad definition of a movement that is beginning to develop during her tenure as the president of the WCTU, I want to reverse the question and ask whether the ideas and aims of the social gospel "measure up" to Willard's dreams for a truly just society.

It is time, I believe, to make this kind of critique of a movement that, in many ways, was admirable, courageous, even heroic, in the face of Gilded Age materialism. Yet I want to argue here that the movement failed—as did most other organizations and movements of the time—to theorize and then realize the ideal that I believe was closest to Willard's heart: the equality of women and men. In her own lifetime, she felt that failure keenly and it was a great disappointment to her. Yet she continued to have confidence that, in the coming twentieth century, with "the dawn of woman's day,"[5] this ideal would finally become a reality. Just as Willard consistently and relentlessly viewed late nineteenth-century society through the lens of gender, we need to focus that lens on the social gospel movement. In order to do this, we must first understand her thoroughgoing critique of male/female relationships and her re-visioning of the ideals of womanhood and manhood. The sort of re-visioning that Willard attempted, I contend, is precisely what most leaders and theologians of the social gospel movement were simply unable to imagine.

In this essay, I want to look closely at three documents that will give us an idea of how Willard understood the equality of women and men. The first document, "The New Chivalry," is the speech with which she launched her reform career in 1871. The second, "'The Woman's Cause Is Man's,'" was written in 1892 at the height of her power and prestige as a reformer. The third, "An Open Letter to Rev. Dr. Charles H. Parkhurst, of New York City," was written in 1895, as she was beginning to comprehend just how difficult it was going to be to realize her ideal of the equality of the sexes. By looking at the background and the context of the first two documents as well as their content, I want to show that the ideal of women's equality was both fundamental to Willard's vision of a renewed society and a longstanding basis for her reform activities. A look at the third document will help to suggest why I believe that we need to critique the ideas and goals of the social gospel movement from Willard's perspective—viewing it through the lens of gender.

Willard's commitment to what she termed "the cause of woman" began to develop well before she actually embarked on her reform career. From her teens on, she had begun to focus the lens of gender on her own environment, noting in her journal inequities in male and female education and the few ways women had to earn a living and gain their independence. Willard pondered women's political inequities as well. In February 1860, when she was just twenty, she noted in her journal her agreement with the popular liberal minister Henry Ward Beecher that women should have the right to vote.[6]

In spring 1868 as Willard prepared to travel to Europe for study, she made a commitment to "the cause of woman" after attending a lecture on "The American Woman" given by Theodore Tilton, editor of *The Independent* and a prominent women's rights speaker. In his address Tilton argued strongly for woman suffrage, as Beecher had nearly a decade earlier. Inspired by his words, Willard wrote in her journal: "Somehow, since I heard Tilton lecture my purpose is confirmed—my object in life is clearer than ever before. What I can do in large and little ways, by influence, by pen, by observation, for *woman,* in all Christian ways, that I will do. And may God help me!"[7] With this commitment, Willard's European trip began to take on added significance. She would study women's status and situation wherever she traveled.

Although she had not decided just what actions she would take on behalf of women, she had already determined that her work would stem from her Christian beliefs. Her faith would inform both her interpretation of "the Woman

Question" and her response to the issues raised by the question. In this she differed from prominent women's rights activists like Elizabeth Cady Stanton and Matilda Joslyn Gage, who grounded their women's rights arguments not in Christian ethics but rather in natural rights philosophy.[8] Unlike them, Willard saw Christianity with its egalitarian possibilities, which she found in biblical passages such as the first Creation account in Genesis (particularly 1:27) and Galatians 3:28, as the wellspring from which women could draw inspiration and strength in their struggle for equality.[9] Although she clearly perceived Christianity's patriarchal structures, she believed that they could be reformed, as Stanton and Gage, finally, did not.[10]

Upon Willard's return to the United States in fall 1870, she began to craft her extensive journal notes on the position of women in Europe and the Middle East into a speech, "The New Chivalry,"[11] which she first gave in March 1871. She had recently accepted the presidency of the newly founded Evanston College for Ladies, a coeducational venture of Northwestern University, so her speech was a way to introduce herself to possible financial supporters, showing them the breadth of her learning and her leadership potential. In the course of drumming up backers for the new college, she delivered it many times in the Chicago area and beyond, mostly to large and enthusiastic church audiences, a constituency that would remain her greatest base of support over the next three decades.

In this speech, Willard described in great detail the oppression of women in the "old world," declaring that it was this "argument from real life . . . which has placed me on the affirmative side of the tremendous 'Woman Question'" (129). Discussing at length women's economic, social, and educational disadvantages in Egypt, Italy, France, Germany, and England, she contrasted their status with the relatively freer status of women in the "new world." Like most American Protestants of her time, Willard fervently believed that her country represented the best hope for a truly democratic society based on Christian values. The United States was destined, she felt, to produce a shining example of a new relationship of equality for women and men. Indeed, she had discovered on her travels that women of the "old world" envied American women for the tremendous freedom they already enjoyed.

Willard agreed that American women had begun to experience a loosening of the gendered bonds that circumscribed old-world women so narrowly, but she realized that they were still a long way from the equality of opportunity she imagined. She also knew that a massive power shift would have to take place in order for women to gain full equality with men. Well aware that men presently held virtually all the power in most institutions, Willard understood that persuading them to share power with women was key to accomplishing women's equality. Thus she proceeded to sketch out a new ideal of manhood, a man sympathetic to woman's advancement, willing to relinquish power to some degree and work along with women who sought equal opportunities.

Central to Willard's speech was her characterization of such a man as a

"knight of the new chivalry" who would be an ally in "the cause of woman."
She gently ridiculed the nineteenth-century notion of the medieval age of chivalry, popularized by such poets and novelists as Alfred Lord Tennyson and Sir
Walter Scott, in which heroic knights protected their ladies from danger. By the
last third of the nineteenth century, Willard declared, a reinterpretation of the
chivalric ideal of knighthood was necessary. The image of "swaggering knights
. . . who could not write their names . . . tilt[ing] . . . their lances to defend the
prestige of 'my lady's beauty,' [and extending to] woman the empty husk of
flattery" (129) was obsolete. Now educated men, who had progressed far beyond
those "swaggering" knights, would gallantly extend equal intellectual opportunity to women. "The Knights of the Old Chivalry drank our health in flowing
bumpers; those of the New invite us to sit down beside them at the banquet of
truth" (140).

Willard did not wish to abandon the chivalrous ideal completely. It had cap-
tivated the imaginations of men and women alike during the nineteenth century, and the language and images of this ideal had helped to define male/fe-
male relationships. The notion of men as women's protectors was prevalent
among "respectables" of the middle-class culture from which Willard and her
audience came. The nineteenth-century knight would defend his family—particularly his wife and daughter—mainly through providing economic security
for them. The man's world, where he wielded most of his power, was the public world of business and politics, while woman's was the home. According to a
dominant Victorian notion, within their separate spheres women and men did
enjoy equality of the sexes.[12] But this was not what Willard meant by the term
"equality." The "knight of the new chivalry" would help to bring into reality a
very different meaning of the equality of men and women. One mark of such
knights would be their willingness to "plac[e] upon the brows of those most dear
to them . . . the helmet of Minerva, and lead . . . them into broader paths of
knowledge and achievement, the fair divinities who preside over their homes"
(140).

In Willard's speech, she identified E. O. Haven, president of Northwestern
University and her strong supporter in Northwestern's coeducational venture,
as "one of the foremost Knights of the New Chivalry."[13] She invited her audience—which, she was certain, contained other chivalrous men—to endorse her
immediate project, women's higher education. At the same time, she was indirectly announcing a far larger goal, that of opening the way through women's
education for her entry into men's world—the wider world beyond the home—
and providing her with the tools of knowledge that she needed to make her way
in that world. The ideas in this speech were only the beginning of what would
become an increasingly radical re-visioning of the ideal of woman and woman's
sphere. Less than a decade later, Willard would further sharpen and strengthen
her definition of the new chivalry by characterizing it as a "chivalry of justice,"
by which she meant justice for women.[14]

In 1874, just three years after Willard gave her first public speech, she left the academic world for temperance reform. She had grown up in a temperance family, and the cause had been a part of her life for a number of years. But she and many other women experienced a renewed interest in temperance, in the wake of the Women's Temperance Crusade the preceding winter when women all over the Midwest and beyond had mobilized against saloon dealers and the liquor industry. Local and state women's temperance organizations formed in many regions of the North, and Willard was recruited by a group in Chicago to lead its campaign. To keep up temperance agitation as the spontaneous crusade activity was waning, women crusaders formed a permanent organization, the Woman's Christian Temperance Union, at a convention in fall 1874. Willard, a delegate to the convention representing both the Chicago and Illinois state women's temperance organizations, participated in this founding meeting. There she was elected corresponding secretary of the national WCTU with the enormous task of building the union through organizing local branches and training women in the leadership skills necessary to mount a sustained battle against a very powerful industry.

Willard quickly became a leading spokesperson for the movement through her speechmaking and writing. Elected president of the WCTU in 1879, Willard proceeded, during the following decade, to mold the organization into a strong voice for a broad spectrum of concerns. The WCTU grew rapidly from a small and struggling group drawing its constituency mainly from the Midwest and Northeast into a truly national organization that reached into the South and the Far West. By the late 1880s it was the largest women's organization of its time. In the mid-1880s, with the advent of the World's Woman's Christian Temperance Union (WWCTU), the organization became an international one, with ties to women all over the world. Under Willard's direction, the WCTU embraced a host of causes beyond its original temperance focus, including woman suffrage, prison reform, the support of the rising labor movement with special attention to the condition of working women, peace and arbitration, social purity (opposition to the double sexual standard for men and women, raising of the age of consent, and rescue of prostitutes), and dress and health reform. At the close of the nineteenth century, the WCTU was one of the most powerful vehicles in the United States for addressing women's issues and producing strong, independent women, who entered the public world, determined to change it.

In 1871 in "The New Chivalry," Willard had begun to define a new ideal of manhood. For the next two decades, she would be intent on defining a corresponding new ideal of womanhood. By 1887, she could confidently declare that "[t]he WCTU is doing no work more important than that of reconstructing the ideal of womanhood."[15] The new woman Willard envisioned would be independent and self-reliant, not needing to lean on men for economic support or physical protection. She would also have to become comfortable wielding power, as men had been doing for millennia. For women who had been socialized to be, or at least to seem, powerless, this was often difficult and frightening to contemplate. But in Willard's estimation it was an absolutely necessary step in women's preparation to enter the world beyond the home and bring about reform in it.

In "'The Woman's Cause Is Man's,'"[16] an 1892 article published in the reform journal *The Arena,* she called on women to take power and use it to participate in shaping all areas of American life. "[Woman] is learning the greatness and sacredness of power," she wrote, "that there is nothing noble in desiring not to possess it, but that to evolve the utmost mastership of one's self and the elements around one's self that can be is, to the individual, the highest possible attainment, if only these forces are used in the spirit of the utmost beneficence toward whatever has life . . . for life should have as its ultimate to bless all other lives" (716). Willard saw the WCTU as, above all, *the* place in which to develop this new woman who was independent and self-reliant and would use power for good. In her article, Willard described the organization as "a training school for greater days whose dawn we see already" (722). She believed that its most important work was shaping Christian women who were devoted to improving society and culture, to reform, philanthropy, patriotism, and religion. The WCTU was, for her, an institution for the development of character with Christ as the model. "Only as our work proves that Christ's working hypothesis of a life has been taken as our own shall we survive" (713), she warned. In contrast to some secularized early twentieth-century versions of the new woman, Willard's ideal was a Christian one, a fitting companion for the "knight of the new chivalry."

The good character of the new WCTU woman would manifest itself in concrete actions aimed at reforming American society, thereby bringing into being a new social order. From its beginnings in the mid-1870s, the WCTU sought to teach its membership how to articulate its aims and strategies effectively through speaking and writing, leading meetings, and working through the political processes by petitioning, lobbying, and influencing party caucuses. The organization ran "schools of methods" in which its leaders drilled women in a whole range of tactics to influence government at all levels from city to county, state, and national. Through a host of different activities, the WCTU created a cadre of women leaders who, in turn, produced thousands of women skilled in organizing for change. WCTU "white ribboners"—who took their name from the symbolic white grosgrain ribbons they wore—definitely learned how to use power.

Willard believed that she could see the effects of women's becoming confident in the uses of power. In the twenty years that had passed since the beginning of her reform career, significant gains had been made in the struggle for women's independence and equality of opportunity through the work of the WCTU and the many other women's organizations that proliferated in the last third of the century. Willard celebrated these gains in "'The Woman's Cause Is Man's,'" listing women's impressive academic achievements as colleges and universities in many parts of the world opened their doors to them. "Forty thousand girls are now studying in colleges," she exclaimed. "What a revolution this little sentence holds" (717). Looking at the political arena, she named countries in which women were moving closer to getting the vote, citing particular legislative victories. Turning to the business world, she mentioned women's access to various jobs and professions, giving examples of women's aptitude for positions formerly viewed as male preserves.

Although Willard eagerly welcomed support from men of the new chivalry, she suspected that they were still few and far between. The new ideal of manhood that she had begun to describe in "The New Chivalry" was only very slowly becoming a reality. In the meantime, she knew that women must be prepared to rely on each other in their struggle for independence and equality. For the present, she defended the separatist nature of the WCTU, "conducted and controlled only by women" (722). It was necessary in the interim as the WCTU shaped the new woman and awaited the day in which the new man would emerge, the man who could accept woman as his equal and welcome her as a full partner in the struggle for reform.

Willard's ideal of the partnership of equals was perhaps the most significant aspect of her revision of the notions of womanhood and manhood. She was interested not only in redefining each of the potential partners in the male/female relationship, but also the notion of the relationship itself. She no longer understood women and men as most Victorians understood them, as complementary partners—each supplying what the other lacked, each presiding over a separate sphere. Instead she saw them as sharing all of the most admirable traits of character and working closely together in one sphere. In her article she listed some of the qualities traditionally attributed to men: courage, intellect, hardihood, and those attributed to women: patience, gentleness, tenderness, chasteness. "Conservatives say, 'let man have his virtues and woman hers,'" she wrote. "Progressives answer, 'let each add to those already won the virtues of the other'" (715). Virtues, then, would not be gendered; they would be neither male nor female, but human qualities, with a single morality prevailing in the home, marketplace, church, and government.

Throughout her reform career, Willard was inspired by lines from Alfred Lord Tennyson's romantic allegorical poem *The Princess,* in which one of the characters, Lady Psyche, the founder and head of a college for women, prophesies a new relationship between women and men. Psyche envisions a future in which women and men will labor together to bring about a better world, both sexes equally active in the domestic realm and the realm beyond the home. Willard often quoted one line from Psyche's vision: "Two heads in council, two beside the hearth," employing it as a kind of shorthand phrase to stand for the new male/female relationship she believed would come about in the near future.

Psyche continues to spin out her vision of an equal partnership, for several more lines that read:

> Two in the tangled business of the world,
> Two in the liberal offices of life,
> Two plummets dropt for one to sound the abyss
> Of science, and the secrets of the mind.[17]

Her prophecy—that women would share with men space formerly viewed as men's alone: the academic, business, and governmental realms, and would, in turn, welcome men into the domestic world—had tremendous appeal for Willard, as the poetic expression of her hope for a new male/female relationship.

Tennyson's poem also furnished the title of her article "'The Woman's Cause Is Man's.'" A male character, who is intrigued by the vision of equality and partnership between the sexes, describes a relationship of interdependence between men and women. "The woman's cause is man's," he says. "They rise or sink together, dwarf'd or godlike, bond or free."[18] Like the character in the poem, Willard believed that the fortunes of women and men were inextricably yoked together. She looked forward to the twentieth century when "poor old humanity with its outraged but ever sacred aspirations shall . . . emerge into the broad, bright, shining upward path where man and woman 'shall woo *perfection* side by side'" (719). Clearly, the new order that Willard awaited—her vision of the Kingdom of God—would be founded on the equality and partnership of women and men as they worked toward reforms that would bring about the perfect society.

Although Willard saw gains for women's equality during the 1880s and early 1890s, there were major setbacks as well, some that were especially disappointing to Willard herself. In 1888, for example, her own Methodist Episcopal Church would not grant laywomen ecclesiastical suffrage, refusing to seat Willard and four other leading Women's Foreign and Home Missionary Society and WCTU leaders as delegates. This was a great blow to Willard and her supporters, provoking her threat to take women out of the denomination and form a new one in which women would enjoy equality in church governance. She even announced that this newly formed church would give itself the power to ordain women.[19] The formation of this new denomination never actually occurred, but Willard's threat indicated how disillusioned she was with her denomination's decision.

The 1880s also saw a backlash against secular woman suffrage with the rise of an organized anti-suffrage movement in which women became the major theoreticians and leaders. By the early 1890s there was even an erosion of the support for woman suffrage in the Prohibition Party, support that Willard and her allies had worked so diligently to build. But perhaps the greatest blow Willard received was the failure of delegates to the 1892 St. Louis Industrial Conference to endorse woman suffrage. The main work of the conference was to organize a third party that would challenge the two major parties in the upcoming presidential election. Willard had used all of the political skill and influence she had developed through her WCTU presidency to help bring together in St. Louis leaders from the growing populist movement, labor groups, and other reform delegates. She served on the platform committee in order to ensure that woman suffrage and prohibition planks would be a key part of the platform and worked through the night persuading the committee to agree. But in what Willard felt to be a betrayal of the committee's promise to include those planks, support for woman suffrage and prohibition were omitted from the committee's report to the full meeting, the following day. The report had been changed after Willard left the meeting, believing that it had ended. It was in St. Louis that Willard realized a bitter truth: she had reached the limits of her political power because she could not deliver a bloc of voters in the November presidential election. The men she had counted on for support—men she thought were "knights of the new chivalry"—sacrificed a portion of women's equality for political victory.[20]

Just three years after "'The Woman's Cause Is Man's'" appeared in *The Arena*—and also three years after the St. Louis Industrial Conference, the *Union Signal*, the weekly newspaper of the WCTU, published an "Open Letter" from Willard to Rev. Dr. Charles H. Parkhurst, pastor and municipal reformer, and someone whose work would surely fit within the parameters of the social gospel movement.[21] Since 1879 Parkhurst had been the minister of Madison Avenue Church, a prominent Presbyterian congregation in New York City. His reputation had skyrocketed during the 1890s when, as president of the Society for the Prevention of Crime, he led a successful fight to topple the corrupt Tammany regime, breaking its control over New York City's government.

Willard began her letter in her usual complimentary fashion, praising Parkhurst for his "dauntless defiance of the Tammany ring" by which he had "won the confidence and good will of all men and women interested in the purity of home life." She observed that Parkhurst's efforts toward municipal cleanup were aided by women who worked alongside men to bring in "a new order of things . . . in the prime city of pestiferous politics." In light of Parkhurst's newly won fame and his stature as a reformer, she was interested to read a series of articles entitled "The True Mission" he had written for a leading women's paper. As one "whose life has been devoted to . . . the uplift of women," Willard was gratified to find that Parkhurst seemed to share some of her most cherished views on woman's sphere of activity and the possibilities of her attainment. She noted his belief that every woman had the "right . . . to be and become all that her capacities permitted so long as her activities were helpful to the world." She listed goals on which they agreed, such as women's access to as much education as schools could furnish and their entry into any profession or industry for which they were fitted.

Then Willard came to her point—a very sharp one. She quoted a paragraph from one of Parkhurst's articles in which he described, in quite condescending language, his understanding of woman's sphere. "Whatever certain adventurous women may think about it . . . ," he wrote, "Nature has so wrought its opinions into the tissue of woman's physical constitution and function that any feminine attempt to mutiny against wifehood, motherhood and domestic 'limitations' is a hopeless and rather imbecile attempt to escape the inevitable." Even though all the "female congresses in the world" passed resolutions that "woman's sphere is coincident with the spherity of the globe or even all of the heavens," Nature had decreed that she was limited to the domestic sphere. "The very idiosyncrasy of her physical build," he continued, "and the limitations essentially bound up in it will sponge out her mass-meeting resolutions as fast as she can pass them."

In her letter, Willard strongly challenged Parkhurst's pronouncements on woman's proper sphere. But first she identified herself as one of those "adventurous women" Parkhurst was attacking. She had been very much involved in the third triennial convention of the National Council of Women, held in February 1895, an event to which Parkhurst undoubtedly alluded in his sarcastic remark about female congresses. As the first president of the council and a member of its executive committee, she was an acknowledged leader in the "mutiny" against Nature that he so decried. Although Parkhurst may not actually have had Willard in mind when he wrote his article, he surely delivered a slap on the wrist—even a slap in the face—to women like her who threatened dominant nineteenth-century gender arrangements.

Willard was clearly distressed—and probably infuriated—by Parkhurst's essentialist claim that woman's physical nature defined her and proscribed her field of activity. For decades she, along with many other women's rights leaders, had been developing a counterclaim, one stating that women ought to be self-defining. They should resist any attempts to restrict their hopes and ambitions to a narrowly circumscribed space, no matter what arguments—natural limitations, societal expectations, biblical injunctions—might be cited in order to curb women's possibilities. Willard's entire reform career had been dedicated to envisioning a new ideal of womanhood, one that encouraged woman's self-development. She had labored tirelessly, through her speeches, her writing, and her leadership of the WCTU, to realize that ideal.

The paragraph Willard quoted from Parkhurst's article must have struck her as a total rejection of what she and other women's rights reformers had struggled for over the years. He also seemed to be contradicting himself. If Nature limited woman to wifehood, motherhood, and the domestic sphere, what would be the use of the higher education he apparently supported? Merely to be a fit companion for her educated husband? To give her something to think about as she went about her household duties? Both of these reasons for women's higher education had indeed been seriously advanced in the last half of the century and

Willard and other women's rights leaders had sometimes used them as part of their argument for women's higher education—but only one small part.

What would be the point of a woman's preparing to enter a profession or other kind of work outside her home, if she were destined to remain within the domestic sphere? Would it be only to have something to fall back on if she were widowed, single, or her husband (or father or brother) were unable to support her because of drunkenness or other disability? These were reasons commonly given for a woman's acquiring a profession or skill other than homemaking. Again, Willard and others—particularly, but not exclusively, WCTU leaders— used them because they were valid and crucial for many women's survival in the event that men could not or would not fulfill their traditional role as women's protectors. But they were not, in Willard's view, the fundamental reasons for women's higher education or their economic independence. Nor were practical reasons like these, which might be given to support any other aspect of women's rights that Willard championed, the fundamental ones. Underlying all the practical reasons was Willard's insistence on woman's basic equality with man and its corollary, that there were, finally, not two spheres, one female and one male, but only one in which women and men would labor together for the good of humanity. Parkhurst's essentialist restatement of the Victorian "doctrine of spheres" undermined Willard's lifelong struggle to realize her goal of woman's equality.

Willard had never before published such an open letter; nor would she do so again, in the few years remaining to her. The letter's unprecedented nature indicates, I believe, the frustration she felt over what she must have seen as the failure of men like Parkhurst to comprehend and embrace her radical vision of women's equality. Parkhurst's series of articles was the immediate target of her anger. But she could have written a similar letter to many—probably most— male reformers (and some women reformers as well) who were allies in a host of causes for which she fought, but who were unable to move completely beyond older images of womanhood and woman's sphere by which they were still constrained. Some sincerely desired and intended to espouse liberal views on women's rights, women's equality, and women's capacities, but they found it difficult to adjust to new ideas about gender relationships. Others simply resisted any reform of those relationships.

The last decades of the nineteenth century were a time of painful transition as ideals of womanhood and manhood were being re-formed. Old and new ideals clashed, often within one individual. Willard certainly experienced this inward clash of ideals, as the journal written in her young adulthood attests. And so did Parkhurst, if his contradictory reasoning in his series of articles is any indication. For nearly a quarter-century, Willard had tried to articulate her vision of a new womanhood and a corresponding new manhood that would revolutionize all human institutions—whether social, political, economic, or religious. But, after twenty-four years of work for "the cause of woman," her patience was wearing thin, as her letter to Parkhurst demonstrates. Just when, she must have despaired, was this vision going to be realized?

* * *

Returning to the question with which the essay began: Should we understand the social gospel movement as one that measured up to Frances Willard's hopes for a just society? As one of the early leaders and thinkers in the social gospel movement, Willard shared much of the background, concerns, and goals of the movement. But we must also understand that a key role she played within the movement was a critical one, exposing a failure of imagination and justice on the part of many, if not most, of the men of the movement. Because they viewed society through a different gendered lens than Willard's, they could not comprehend or welcome the new woman that she and her organization sought to bring into being. Furthermore, they could not accept, much less embrace, her new idea of male/female relationships in which the two sexes would be equals and full partners in reform. As we reassess the social gospel movement, like Willard, we need to call it to account for its limited vision of woman's sphere and capabilities. We must ask what might have been accomplished had the ideas and energy of the dedicated women who heard and responded to the call of the social gospel been more fully integrated into its work for the Kingdom of God. The women of the social gospel movement believed that "man's cause is woman's," but, with very few exceptions, the men of the movement did not truly believe, with Willard, that "'The Woman's Cause Is Man's.'"

Notes

1. Sidney E. Ahlstrom, *A Religious History of the American People* (New Haven: Yale University Press, 1972), 870.

2. Ronald C. White Jr. and C. Howard Hopkins, *The Social Gospel: Religion and Reform in Changing America* (Philadelphia: Temple University Press, 1976), ch. 12.

3. Mari Jo Buhle, *Women and American Socialism, 1870–1920* (Urbana: University of Illinois Press, 1981), 64, 68; Ruth Bordin, *Frances Willard: A Biography* (Chapel Hill: University of North Carolina Press, 1986), 174; and Richard Leeman, *Do Everything Reform: The Oratory of Frances E. Willard* (New York: Greenwood, 1992), 92.

4. Ida Tetreault Miller, "Frances Elizabeth Willard: Religious Leader and Social Reformer" (Ph.D. diss., Boston University, 1978), 174–92.

5. "The Dawn of Woman's Day" was the title of Willard's inaugural address as the newly elected president of the Chicago Woman's League, given on October 4, 1888. The speech text with accompanying headnotes can be found in Amy Rose Slagell, "A Good Woman Speaking Well: The Oratory of Frances E. Willard" (Ph.D. diss., University of Wisconsin–Madison, 1992), 466–83. The quotation is from page 466.

6. The Journal of Frances E. Willard, entry for February 21, 1860, in *Writing Out My Heart: Selections from the Journal of Frances E. Willard, 1855–96,* ed. Carolyn De Swarte Gifford (Urbana: University of Illinois Press, 1995), 59–60.

7. Journal, March 21, 1868, in Gifford, *Writing Out My Heart,* 266.

8. See Elizabeth Battelle Clark, "The Politics of God and the Woman's Vote: Religion in the

Suffrage Movement in America, 1848–1895" (Ph.D. diss., Princeton University, 1989), for a thorough discussion of the differences between Stanton's thought and that of Willard.

9. See Frances E. Willard, *How to Win: A Book for Girls* (New York: Funk and Wagnalls, 1866), reprinted in *The Ideal of the "New Woman" according to the Woman's Christian Temperance Union*, ed. Carolyn De Swarte Gifford (New York: Garland, 1987), 49, for Willard's interpretation of these two biblical passages.

10. See Carolyn De Swarte Gifford, "American Women and the Bible: The Nature of Woman as a Hermeneutical Issue," in *Feminist Perspectives on Biblical Scholarship*, ed. Adela Yarbro Collins (Chico, Calif.: Scholars Press, 1985), 25–31, where differences over the basis for women's rights between Stanton and Gage and Willard are discussed further.

11. Frances E. Willard, "The New Chivalry," in Slagell, "A Good Woman Speaking Well," 128–41. Page numbers for quotations from "The New Chivalry" will appear in parentheses after each quote.

12. See Janet Forsythe Fishburn, *The Fatherhood of God and the Victorian Family: The Social Gospel in America* (Philadelphia: Fortress, 1981), 27–28, 170, for a discussion of the American Victorian ideal of the chivalrous man and of the notion of the "perfect equality of the sexes, each in their own sphere," which prevailed in the middle class for most of the nineteenth century.

13. A clipping from the *Chicago Tribune,* March 22, 1871, reporting on Willard's speech, in scrapbook 3, p. 2, deposited in the Woman's Christian Temperance Union Archive, Frances E. Willard Memorial Library, Evanston, Illinois.

14. Frances E. Willard, "1880 Presidential Address," in *Minutes of the National Woman's Christian Temperance Union* (New York: National Temperance Society and Publication House, 1880), 24. Willard began to use the term "chivalry of justice" as early as 1877 and continued to employ this powerful image throughout her reform career.

15. Frances E. Willard, "President's (1887) Annual Address," in *Minutes of the National Woman's Christian Temperance Union* (Chicago: Woman's Temperance Publication Association, 1888), 90.

16. Frances E. Willard, "'The Woman's Cause Is Man's,'" *The Arena* 5, no. 30 (May 1892): 712–25. Page numbers for quotations from "'The Woman's Cause Is Man's'" will appear in parentheses after each quote.

17. Alfred Lord Tennyson, *The Princess: A Medley,* in *Alfred Lord Tennyson: Poetical Works, Including the Plays* (London: Oxford University, 1954), stanza 2, lines 169–73 (163).

18. Ibid., stanza 7, lines 256–57 (199).

19. See Frances E. Willard, "President's (1888) Annual Address," in *Minutes of the National Woman's Christian Temperance Union* (Chicago: Woman's Temperance Publication Association, 1888), 41–47.

20. In Willard's journal entry for March 22, 1896 (Gifford, *Writing Out My Heart,* 402–3), she refers briefly to this incident. See Jack S. Blocker Jr., "The Politics of Reform: Populists, Prohibition, and Woman Suffrage, 1891–1892" (*The Historian* 34, no. 4 [August 1972]: 614–32), for a fuller discussion of the role Willard played in the politicking before and during the Industrial Conference.

21. Frances E. Willard, "An Open Letter to Rev. Dr. Charles H. Parkhurst, of New York City," dated April 20, 1895, in the *Union Signal,* May 16, 1895, 9. All subsequent quotes from this letter are found on page 9.

CHAPTER 2

Women and Social Betterment in the Social Gospel Work of Josiah Strong

Wendy J. Deichmann Edwards

One day in May 1912, in New York City, Alice and Josiah Strong lifted high a banner showing their support for woman suffrage. Knowing that the annual New York parade championing this issue was a widely publicized event, this refined Congregationalist couple stepped in line with the rest of the demonstrators and marched down the street. Alice Strong later explained to her daughters, "I was the only woman to represent Wyoming, the pioneer state. There was a beautiful banner awaiting me but I could not carry it alone, so what more natural than Father's lending a hand and keeping up the other end? So, though the men were supposed to march by themselves, he and I kept step under the same banner (as we had been doing lo these many years), and attracted much attention along the line of march."[1]

This anecdote about a well-known social gospel leader marching *with his wife* in a national suffrage parade poignantly symbolizes the long-overlooked significance of gender issues and the presence of women in the history of the social gospel movement. It is the purpose of this essay to contribute to both these areas of inquiry. I will argue here that in the course of his career as a highly visible social gospel leader, Josiah Strong not only showed deep interest in women's concerns; he also affirmed and promoted greater public roles for women as indispensable coworkers and as key leaders in the social gospel movement. He indirectly justified this support of women's quasi-religious public leadership roles by equalizing the value of ordained and lay ministries, while also emphasizing the quintessential nature of non-gender-exclusive "social betterment" work as intrinsic to building God's Kingdom on earth. The research undergirding this thesis is based primarily upon Josiah Strong's published writings, but it also draws upon secondary sources, both published and unpublished, for biographical details.

The beginning of this essay identifies five factors from Strong's early life and career that influenced his developing views about women and gender. This is followed by an analysis of Strong's publications and professional activities as general secretary of the Evangelical Alliance for the United States from 1886 to 1898. The final section explores the evidence of Strong's growing support for women in industry, politics, and church leadership during his presidency of the American Institute for Social Service, from 1899 to 1916.

"Honor to Womanhood"

Strong's first known comment upon women's place in society appeared in his most famous publication, *Our Country: Its Possible Future and Its Present Crisis* (hereafter referred to as *Our Country*), which appeared in 1885. In the first chapter Strong wrote that the idea of "honor to womanhood, whose fruitage is woman's elevation, finds its root in the teachings of Christ, and has grown up slowly through the ages to blossom in our own." He praised this notion as one of three *"great ideas"* that had been adopted by society within the past century, placing it in the same category of importance as the ideas of "individual liberty" and an "enhanced valuation of human life." He likened it to remarkable advances in material progress, in science, and in Christian missions during the nineteenth century.[2]

Important though the issue of woman's status was to him, Strong's main interest in mentioning her place in society was to make a larger point about the developmental effects of both Christian teaching and historical progress. He believed that these were providential, "evolutionary" causes, which had led increasingly to improved social relations. *Our Country* was a call for Christian men and women in the United States to respond to the teachings of Christ and to cooperate with historical progress by supporting Protestant home missions in order to establish Christ's Kingdom on earth.

Strong did not develop his point about women's elevated status any further in this volume. However, by putting the development of women's place in society in evolutionary context, Strong had articulated a progressive assessment of women's changing roles, an outlook that would become increasingly visible as he responded to gender issues throughout his career. Paradoxically perhaps, the first of several factors that contributed to his affirming view of women was his gendered Victorian upbringing. Strong was raised under the influence of a cultural ideology that glorified motherhood as the divinely given, noblest role for women, equal in importance in a complementary way to any role that men might fulfill in life. The Victorian view of gender restricted women's sphere to the home, and, to some extent, the church. However, women who faithfully fulfilled what were understood to be their God-appointed duties were accorded deep respect, honor, and support. Although sphere and role expectations would continue to evolve, what remained permanently ingrained in Strong's attitude toward women were the notions that God deemed woman worthy of an important vocation in life, and that the viewpoints of faithful women about issues important to women should always be respected.

[...]'s belief in progress, already alluded to, was the second factor that [...] place in society. His concep-[...] ology upheld by his Puritan [...] stmillennial doctrine of his-[...] views about the evolution of [...] gressive, postmillennial, per-[...] Christian faithfulness.[3] Strong [...] operation, new and beneficial [...] the arena of gender relation-

[...] iew of women was his personal [...] ced a crossing of class bound-[...] optimism and tempered the ri-[...] er. His earliest years were spent [...] Illinois, where both his parents [...] ring his adolescence in Hudson, [...] r. The family became financially [...] nted sister, Mary Strong. She was [...] ol for girls, the Hudson Female [...] was required to perform odd jobs [...] o that his mother would not have [...] able to provide a living wage for [...] onomic standard of the Victorian

[...] g to the reality that it was not al-[...] upport his wife and children at the level of societal expectati[...] [...] s not always feasible or expedient for good Christian women to remain strictly confined to a prescribed, domestic sphere. The fact that women could flourish as providers and competent professionals was never lost on Strong. Throughout his life, he was surrounded and supported by strong, able, and influential women. In his youth, his mother, Elizabeth Strong, and his Aunt Mary Strong managed to keep family life intact through their resourcefulness and determination. As he grew older, he would have been similarly impressed by the professional accomplishments of his sister Mary, who served as a home missionary in Alabama. His own two daughters, Elsie and Margery Strong, never married; instead they went to college, became teachers, and assisted their father in social gospel work in New York City.

The fourth factor that would have contributed to Strong's assessment of women's evolving place in society was his biblical view of the necessary relationship between Christian discipleship and social reform. Like many who became associated with the social gospel, Strong was brought up in a religious family that regarded social reform efforts as an essential ingredient of Christian life. Prior to the Civil War, the Strong family had been avid abolitionists for at least three generations. As such, they were predisposed to emphasize the biblical principles of compassion and prophetic justice for all, and to reject literalistic interpretations of selected biblical texts such as those that fueled proslavery arguments and the repression of women. So it was that Josiah Strong's views about women were supported by principles he derived from the Bible. He clearly believed that both men and women were intended to be the recipients of God's salvation. Because of his conviction that salvation had positive personal and social implications, he viewed the improved social status of women in Christian societies as an aspect of social salvation with divine sanction.

Expediency was the fifth influence upon Strong's attitude toward women. He began his career in the post–Civil War years. Published in 1885, *Our Country* was an ambitious effort on Strong's part to *reunify* the Protestant churches in a common cause. Protestant home missions, he believed, were the one thing that could redeem the losses of the war; heal regional patterns of conflict that were generations old; and galvanize Christians around a common, hopeful purpose in the face of widespread anxiety over cultural changes. Although he supported improved treatment of women early in his career, in his consciousness women's issues were dwarfed by his overriding desire for unity within the church and society. Women's issues were becoming the subject of enormous controversy in public and ecclesiastical circles. Those attracting most attention included women's right to vote, to earn a living wage, to preach, and to be ordained by the church. Even if he had been open in principle to such changes, as an evangelical, midwestern male pastor in the 1880s, Strong was by no means inclined to become a radical crusader on any of these questions. He did not, therefore, venture to discuss women or women's interests at length in *Our Country,* a book about the future of the United States, of which half the population was, of course, female. He had, however, laid the groundwork for what would become an increasingly progressive response to women and the issues they raised throughout the remainder of his career.

"Woman Is Assuming Her Rightful Place"

Strong's *Our Country* quickly became a bestseller when it was published in 1885. Its success propelled him the following year into the position of general secretary of the Evangelical Alliance for the United States (hereafter referred to as the Evangelical Alliance). This organization was the chief interdenominational body in the country, consisting of representatives from the largest Protestant denominations. It had been founded in 1847 as an attempt to promote Christian unity and religious freedom. However, its short history had been fraught with conflict, and it was "almost moribund" when Strong moved his office from Ohio to New York City to assume the position of General Secretary.[4]

Strong was hired by the Evangelical Alliance to provide leadership that would unify and embolden the churches' response to perceived national crises related to urbanization and immigration. In broad strokes, the Evangelical Alliance set ambitious goals, including vigorous church-planting efforts in the West and in rapidly growing cities, closing the relational gap between the church and "the multitude," and "bringing the regenerative power of the gospel to bear upon every character and life."[5]

Immediately Strong began putting together a program designed to accomplish these objectives. It was composed of initiatives in both evangelism and social reform. During the twelve years in which he filled his post, Strong developed his message and methods around evangelism and social transformation with such effectiveness that he would later be designated an important early leader of the social gospel movement. In fact, the historian Sydney Ahlstrom described him as "the dynamo, the revivalist, the organizer, and altogether the most irrepressible spirit of the . . . movement."[6]

As a result of his early life experience and convictions, Strong did not exclude women from involvement in social gospel work. However, the nature of the Evangelical Alliance as a conflicted, relatively conservative, male-led religious organization probably limited both the nature and the extent of women's participation in its programs. Notwithstanding its newly adopted emphasis on addressing national social concerns, the organization never abandoned its ambition of promoting greater religious unity. Had they been entertained, innovations with respect to women's place in the home, church, or society would have invited additional controversy into an already tenuous coalition and interfered with the achievement of this fundamental goal.

In the course of providing direction for meeting the organization's objectives, however, Strong steadily increased women's participation in Evangelical Alliance work and fostered women's leadership in social change in at least three important ways. First, he decisively and publicly affirmed women's roles in house-to-house visitation ministries and as deaconesses, practices accepted by some but not all Protestant churches.[7] He called for the immediate implementation of the visitation role for women at the first national conference of the Evangelical Alliance under his direction, held in 1887. At this event, he invoked the principle of the ministry of all Christians as the foundation for the organization's new outreach initiative. He declared that "aggressive Christian work . . . ought to be the *business* of every Christian." He explicitly called for women's participation in religious visitation as an indispensable component of "systematic," "personal Christian work."[8] Moreover, in his follow-up speech at the Evangelical Alliance's 1889 conference, he highlighted the success women were experiencing in this form of ministry and expressed hope that the following generation of both men and women would "find itself at home in such work."[9]

The second way in which Strong fostered women's involvement in Evangelical Alliance social reform work was by implicitly targeting women's social issues and affirming women's authority on those issues, as properly belonging to the work of the church in building the Kingdom of God. This was not part of a visible crusade to advance women's status. Rather, Strong pursued these aims indirectly, by means of spelling out his grounds for including comprehensive, social salvation in the mission of the church.

Strong's *The New Era,* published in 1893, mandated the inclusion of "social betterment" work as a means to the building of the Kingdom of God on earth and therefore a critical responsibility of the church. Social betterment work consisted of religiously motivated efforts to reform or Christianize society in ways that sometimes exceeded the scope of what ecclesiastical institutions were permitted or willing to do. In Strong's view, the notion of social betterment allowed Christians both to affirm and to counter the official separation of church and state. It was a direct corollary of the social gospel's doctrine of the Kingdom of God, which called for the Christianization of all social institutions and structures, including the state, through the "unbounded influence" of the church upon "the conscience of the social organism."[10] Social betterment was often accomplished through local, national, and even international organizations that dealt with particular social issues through volunteer work, "education of public opinion," and lobbying to affect politics and legislation. Some of the more prolific social betterment organizations at the time were women's clubs, social settlements, the Young Women's Christian Association and the Young Men's Christian Association (YMCA and YWCA), the WCTU, and the National Consumers' League.

In *The New Era,* Strong argued that recent scientific, historical, and theological developments had been providentially timed to disclose the importance of the *social* teachings of Jesus in the late nineteenth century. He criticized as obsolete the *individualistic* approach to spirituality exemplified by the traditional church in its exclusive obsession with saving souls and its focus on the role of the clergy in achieving that end. While affirming the essential importance of individual conversions to faith in Christ, he argued that social salvation had been divinely revealed as the key to establishing the Kingdom of God on earth. The mission of the church, according to the teachings of Jesus, was to encompass both spiritual and physical concerns. It consisted of two equally important components: spiritual ministries to individuals and communities, and social betterment.[11]

In order to accomplish this mission of the church, Strong called for the elimination of the traditional, "thoroughly false and mischievous" distinction between the sacred and the secular with regard to the church's ministry. If the church "is to reach the masses," he wrote, "she must do it on the [physical] plane where the masses live." Moreover, it was incumbent upon the church to embrace the new tools of social science, typically considered secular in nature. Strong believed that these tools had been provided by God to enable the church to accomplish its mission of both personal and social salvation.[12]

Removal of sacred and secular distinctions in the mission of the church in essence equalized the importance of the tasks customarily performed by clergy, who were almost exclusively male, and by laypersons, a majority of whom were female. Those tasks traditionally considered to be sacred, such as preaching and administering the sacraments, were to remain the prerogative of the clergy by virtue of their training and ordination. These functions of the church were important, but no more so than the social betterment efforts that were the duty of every Christian. By extension, this way of thinking equalized the value of men and women's work in service to Christ's Kingdom. Strong did not explicitly state this conclusion, but it was clearly implied in his discussion. He had already committed himself to utilizing women in lay ministries of visitation and in deaconess work. In *The New Era,* he considered such work not only essential to the Evangelical Alliance's outreach initiative, he also made it equal in importance to the ministry of the clergy in both saving souls and building the Kingdom of God. These ministries, he stated, exemplified the mission of Christ. They demonstrated "that his personal love and sacrifice can be shown by the personal love and sacrifice of his followers to the most ignorant, hardened, and vicious, and that with saving power."[13]

In the context of prevailing Victorian gender expectations, elimination of the distinction between the sacred and secular held further implications about the nature of women's service for the Kingdom. In Victorian society, women functioned as the respected experts within their own, limited sphere, which consisted of women's, children's and family concerns. If all social problems were to be addressed as part of building God's Kingdom on earth, as Strong proposed, then women were to be recognized as authorities in addressing the social concerns having to do with women's sphere, making it appropriate for men to defer to women on these matters. Strong's removal of sacred and secular categories had the ultimate effect of giving women newfound authority with regard to how women's issues should be addressed in the process of building the Kingdom of God. This way of thinking not only sanctioned women's church work; it also elevated the importance of women's work in social betterment and in the social sciences as authentic and essential forms of Christian ministry. Thus, women were to be regarded as indispensable coworkers with men in establishing the Kingdom of God on earth.

Later generations as well as some of Strong's contemporaries faulted him for not being more overtly prophetic on some of the more controversial women's issues, especially the one that many see as the most symbolically important—women's ordination. On the surface, his commitment to egalitarianism in the 1890s was limited to elevating the status of the deaconess, visitor, and other, somewhat more socially acceptable roles for women. It is certainly plausible that his promotion and sanctioning of less controversial Kingdom-building roles for women would have diverted talents and energies away from the struggle for women's ordination, thereby reinforcing the growing rift between more radical feminists and the church. Moreover, his broad view of the mission of the church may have convinced some women and men that traditional forms of church involvement were superfluous, contributing to the exodus of well-meaning, religiously motivated social reformers from conventional church institutions. Whether within or outside ecclesiastical institutions, Strong's steadfast commitment was to increase the means and effectiveness by which men and women could work together to fulfill the most urgent and important work of building the Kingdom of God on earth.

The third way in which Strong recognized and promoted women's roles in both Evangelical Alliance work and social reform efforts was by publicizing and showcasing their efforts. In *The New Era,* Strong cited women as authorities on social conditions and social reform methods, including Frances Willard, Maud Ballington Booth, Florence Kelley; and several other, less well-known individuals. In addition, he expressed enthusiastic support for the office of the deaconess.[14] Notwithstanding Frances Willard's justifiable complaint that Strong should have made more of woman's role in his analysis of the "coming Kingdom,"[15] in recognizing these women's work, he had taken a step beyond many of his male contemporaries. As the historian Susan Hill Lindley put it, most male social gospel leaders "simply did not take women seriously as equal partners in dialogue and work in the movement to build a Christian society."[16]

Strong included women as speakers at the Evangelical Alliance's 1893 international conference on the theme "Christianity Practically Applied." This was the first time this ecumenical organization had engaged women as speakers at a gathering of this magnitude.[17] Not surprisingly, his featuring of women as speakers both transcended and expressed Victorian gender expectations. It moved beyond old stereotypes by providing a forum in which women gave public addresses to mixed audiences of church leadership, a practice that was sometimes observed but still not normative among ecclesiastical institutions in the 1890s. However, the nature of the topics about which women spoke strictly conformed to prevailing gender norms. Women addressed the social issues in which they were considered experts and authorities, relating them to the overall theme of applied Christianity. These topics included deaconesses, home-culture clubs, maternal associations, social settlements, working girls' societies, kindergartens, and trained nursing.

As he had done in *Our Country* eight years earlier, Strong made an important summary statement in *The New Era* about the improved status of women. This time he spoke not only of woman's improved status, but also of her equality with man. He also began to spell out the beneficial outcome of this development. He wrote, "Woman is assuming her rightful place at the side of man instead of behind him at a respectful distance or at his feet; and woman's changed status means that her social and industrial and marital relations have improved."[18] Compared with his incidental comment about women in *Our Country,* in which women were cast, if positively, as more or less passive recipients of an honored place in society, this statement depicts woman as rightfully proactive, beginning to reap the benefits of her expanding position in the wide world, both in and beyond the home.

"The Principal Promoters of Movements for Social Betterment"

In 1898, Strong resigned from his position with the Evangelical Alliance to found and became president of his own social betterment organization, the League for Social Service. Located in New York City, this would become the home base of his social gospel work for the remaining eighteen years of his life. Throughout this period, Strong exhibited ever-greater interest in women's issues and growing support and admiration for women's leadership in social betterment. Ultimately, although he remained politically cautious about how and when he expressed his views, he appears to have embraced what approximated a vision of social and political equality between women and men.

The League for Social Service, renamed the American Institute for Social Service (hereafter referred to as the AISS) in 1902, was chartered by the State of New York as an educational institution. Strong called it a "clearing house for social betterment." By means of collecting, studying, and then disbursing information about issues and methods of social reform, Strong intended that the AISS would serve as an effective instrument for building God's Kingdom on earth. Its official purpose was "to be of aid to all organizations and persons desirous of becoming better acquainted with municipal and social questions. It will endeavor, while doing its share of independent investigation, to crystallize the results attained by other organizations."[19]

Strong included prominent female social reformers as advisers, and wealthy women as official sponsors of the AISS, listing their names in publications and on letterhead.[20] With increasing frequency, he afforded women opportunities for publishing their views about social reform issues in the publications that he edited. Women were contributors to the periodicals published by the AISS: the journal, *Social Service,* and the monthly Bible study he coedited, *The Gospel of the Kingdom and What to Do.* For example, the entire July 1905 issue of *Social Service* was devoted to social settlements, with seven of the eleven articles written by women. Additionally, the magazine carried endorsements by Alice Freeman Palmer, former president of Wellesley College; Caroline Hazard, president of Wellesley College; and Mary E. Woolley, president of Mount Holyoke College.

He also affirmed and publicized women's involvement in social betterment by including their names, organizations, and publications in an annual encyclopedia entitled *Social Progress: A Year Book and Encyclopedia of Economic, Industrial, Social and Religious Statistics* (hereafter this series will be referred to as

Social Progress). In the 1906 edition, he featured 28 women among the 183 individuals whose names and addresses were listed as "Workers in Social Reform in the United States." Along with famous men such as Lyman Abbott, William D. P. Bliss, General Ballington Booth, Richard T. Ely, Washington Gladden, and Francis G. Peabody, Strong included Jane Addams, Maud Ballington Booth, Evangeline Booth, Florence Kelley, Vida Scudder, the Reverend Anna Howard Shaw, and a host of other, now less well-known women.[21]

Women's national reform organizations, both secular and religious, were listed in *Social Progress* with their leaders' names as "National Societies." In the section on "Social Settlements," Strong showed that a majority of resident workers in settlement houses were women, a total of 262 compared with 211 men. An even more overwhelming majority of nonresident workers were women: 2,930 compared with 977 men. He noted that of those who "give all their time to the work," there were 497 women and 106 men. Additionally, a majority of those served by the settlement house programs were girls and women, 31,000 out of 55,000.[22]

In the extensive bibliographical section of *Social Progress* were many female authors, including Jane Addams, Vida Scudder, Mary Richmond, Helen Campbell, and Frances Kellor. The publications authored by women addressed not only traditionally feminine matters, such as children, the home, and women's education, but also social, economic, and international issues, such as social progress, unemployment, poverty, factory legislation, and the opium trade. In a similar vein, in his 1900 monograph entitled *Expansion under New World-Conditions,* Strong quoted Jane Addams's views about the new morality and broader humanitarianism that were needed to guide international politics in "the new world life," showing that he was not averse to including a woman's perspective and giving her credit for it, in a serious discussion of international politics.[23]

In addition to the abundant instances in which he referred in his publications to women as leaders in social betterment, Strong offered visible, practical support for causes women espoused. His marching with Alice Strong in the New York City woman suffrage parade has already been mentioned. He also joined forces in 1903 with Florence Kelley of the National Consumers' League; Margaret Dye Ellis, superintendent of legislation of the National WCTU; and Sadie American, a founder of the National Council of Jewish Women, in efforts to prevent the abduction of women into white slavery. This group worked together to pass legislation that would guarantee "the appointment of women inspectors" for "innocent and unwary" female passengers entering the Port of New York. In this case, Strong argued that "the appointment of women to offices formerly monopolized by men is an innovation against which there is always much prejudice. Certain stock objections are made, viz., that the women are not needed, that men can do the work as well or better, etc." Such objections, requiring twenty years to overcome, had been made to the appointment of police matrons, he noted, but "now it would be regarded as a long step backward to dismiss" them. Likewise, he pointed out, the idea of women factory inspectors was initially opposed, but now "their service has justified their appointment and the reform is making progress from state to state."[24]

As Strong clarified his own views about the more controversial women's issues of his time, he expressed them in his writings. In three of his publications he discussed women's presence in the workplace. The first of these, entitled *Religious Movements for Social Betterment,* was published in 1900. It offered information about institutional churches, the Salvation Army, the YMCA and YWCA, and "work by various religious denominations for . . . social and industrial elevation." He applauded these religious organizations and the special programs for social betterment that they sponsored, including those designed to meet women's needs, many of which were led by women.[25]

In *Religious Movements for Social Betterment,* Strong voiced the Victorian view that "the church and the home are the two great saving institutions of society," and he expressed the concern shared with many of his contemporaries that the home was disappearing "at both social extremes," at an alarming rate. However, rather than try to relegate women to the home in an effort to restore order and the salvific influence of the home upon society, Strong argued that it was the duty of the church to help better prepare women for the workplace. He called for the Christianization of the workplace in the same way an earlier generation focused upon the Christianization of the ideal home. In a society that was aiming to establish the Kingdom of God, he reasoned, the worker and the workplace, like the home, should be shaped by Christian principles. He gave three examples of movements that were providing better training for women workers: the deaconess movement, the Girls' Friendly Society of the Episcopal Church, and the Young Women's Christian Association.[26] Notwithstanding later criticism that such organizations attempted to impose white, middle-class Victorian values upon uninterested immigrants, what is important to this discussion is that Strong supported their efforts, by and for women in the workplace, rather than a return of women to the confines of the home.

Strong published two articles that addressed women in the workplace more directly. The first of these articles, which appeared in 1902, was entitled "Women and Social Betterment." Here, he argued that "women who have now been freed from the burdens laid on them by the age of homespun, should devote some of the new leisure thus bestowed to the solution of the new problems" experienced by women who were forced to work in appalling conditions.[27]

In this brief article, Strong affirmed "the new impulse toward higher education among women and the multiplication of colleges which cannot make room for the girls who flock to them," and "the rapid growth of women's clubs which aim at a larger culture." He even capitalized upon Victorian stereotypes of women's nature to suggest that women may possess particular potential for managing labor disputes. "It looks as if women's clubs might take a leading part in the great work of industrial improvement and in establishing right relations between employers and employees," he wrote. "As wives," he explained, club members "sympathize with the perplexities of [employers], and as women they sympathize with the hardships of the [employees]. With a hand upon each they may do much to reconcile both."[28]

Most important for the purposes of this essay, Strong praised women's increasing knowledge, commitment, and leadership in arenas of social reform, even describing female reformers as somewhat superior to their male counterparts. "A large class of women," he wrote, "are much better informed as to social conditions than their husbands, they have also more public spirit, or at least more time to devote to the public good. *Thus it has come about that women are becoming the principal promoters of movements for social betterment*" [emphasis added].[29] This is a profoundly important statement coming from a male social gospel leader who believed that social betterment was a key mandate from the teachings of Christ, essential to building the Kingdom of God on earth.

His second article about women in the workplace, entitled "Women in Industry," was part of a new series of Bible study lessons in the AISS periodical *The Gospel of the Kingdom and What to Do*. In this study, published in 1908, Strong not only used the Bible to justify women's presence in the industrial workplace, he also used it to promote a variety of reforms that would improve conditions for women in the industrial work environment. He began by striking at the myth that the industrial sphere was the rightful domain of men. "Women have always been in industry," he wrote. However the difference between the age of homespun and the early twentieth century was that, earlier, women were "helpers of husbands and brothers," and now they were men's competitors. Moreover, the recent entry of women into "organized industry" was the source of "new industrial, social, and legislative problems," he conceded. It had not only "brought women into competition with men," it had also "greatly increased the labor supply, . . . and tended to depress wages." However, instead of challenging the propriety of this development, Strong placed it in the context of progress. He warned that because of their inherent, natural qualities, "in certain occupations, women, as they gain experience, will become increasingly dangerous competitors of men." He saw in nearly every Victorian stereotype about women a quality he could turn into an advantage for their success in the new industrial scene. He wrote:

> Women are [adept] in that subconscious reasoning which we call intuition. This explains the fact that the average woman is a better judge of character than the average man. Strength is direct and blunt, often brutal. Weakness learns tact and a diplomatic indirection. Strength relies upon itself; weakness learns to rely on its wits. Woman as the "weaker vessel" has learned to observe, to divine, and to manage. With machinery the world's work is becoming less and less a matter of muscle and more and more a matter of brain. Under the new

conditions man's superior physical strength counts for nothing in many occupations, while the finer nervous organization of woman, with all that it
implies—alertness of attitude, quickness of perception, and nimbleness of
action—stands her in good stead.[30]

In addition to praising women's "natural" qualifications for success, Strong
capitalized upon the skills they had acquired through generations of housework
and homemaking. "For ages the housewife has had daily training in petty details," he wrote. "Multitudes of men occupied with great affairs would collapse
with nervous prostration, or go mad, or go on strike, if forced for one month
to go through the minute and repetitious details which their wives carry with
patience and success," he ventured. "In the highly organized competitive industry of to-day," he reiterated, "there are many business positions in which the
above-mentioned qualities are precisely the conditions of success."[31]

Strong voiced his support for women in industry in several additional ways.
First, he sought to dispel vague, negative assumptions about women in the
workplace, calling for the systematic study of effects "on the health of women,
both physical and moral, and its influence on the home and family." Second,
he insisted that legislation was needed to address the "evils" that had "appeared
in connection with women in industry." Third, he again admonished "women
of the leisure class to help address some of the legislative problems associated
with women in industry," which could only mean that women's voices and
concerns must be heard in the political as well as the industrial arena.[32]

Making the most of the Bible study format of *The Gospel of the Kingdom,*
Strong invoked the authority of biblical principles to address some of the
difficulties facing working women. He remarked that there were numerous precedents in the Bible for women working outside the home, as shop managers, a
judge and prophetesses, reigning queens, charity workers, deaconesses, and other
vocations. He added matter-of-factly that "practically all occupations are now
open to women in the United States" and observed that between 1890 and 1900,
women's work increased in 86 out of 303 occupations.[33]

He expressed deep concern over several trends, however. First, the largest gains
in women's employment had been "made in confining or unhealthful occupations," such as those of "tobacco-workers" and bookkeepers. He recorded the
high percentage of working women who were widowed and divorced, and who,
therefore, were trying to support themselves on inadequate incomes. He also
pointed out that a much higher percentage of married African American women
than white women were employed outside the home and that more than half
of all wage-earning African American women were farm laborers. These facts
meant that women's wages were abysmally low, often barely, if enough, for survival. In response to these situations, Strong admonished that in biblical times,
even slaves "got a living" and "were well treated among the Jews" because God's
law forbade oppression and enjoined "prompt payment." He also compared

women's wages and hours with men's, underscoring serious discrepancies for similar work. To ensure better wages, he advised women to seek better training and to join unions. He also endorsed the Consumer's League and its principles, declaring that "the Bible enjoins equity upon all."[34]

In the last section of "Women in Industry," Strong suggested three practical ways for the church to respond to the problems he had defined. First, he defended the "increasing independence" of woman because it allowed her "greater freedom in the choice of her companions, and in the use of discretionary time and money." However, he advised, this did not absolve her "from filial love and duty." The church, he advised, should "teach *men and women alike* that the increasing freedom of modern society necessitates increasing self-control," including taking responsibility for society and nurturing the central role of family within civilization [emphasis added].[35]

Strong's second call for action centered upon the needs of single mothers who spent many hours out of the home, working. "It is an imperative demand upon each individual church to look after her poor mothers," he wrote, "and see to it that the children are not neglected." Thus, he encouraged the churches to "organize boys' and girls' clubs, day-nurseries, play-grounds, out-door gymnasia, etc., where children may spend their time under supervision. If every church did that," he concluded, "the problem would be considerably nearer solution."[36]

Strong's third "duty" for the church was to teach with authority that "good morality is good business," a principle that applied to church members and employers alike. "*Every man and woman* has a duty in regard to the low wages of women, which mean inadequate support of many families," he argued. "It is the bargain-hunter who is in part responsible for starvation wages in the clothing industry." Once again he prodded "honest *men and women*" to support the Consumers' League label and others that guaranteed their goods had been "manufactured under sanitary conditions, with decent wages and hours." He insisted that the churches urge the appointment of more women factory inspectors, declaring that employers were obligated to make conditions "as favorable as possible to [the] physical and moral health of women" [emphasis added above].[37]

In his writings about women in the workplace, Strong applied his social gospel principles to an area of concern that was relatively new: the problems related to women in organized industry. In doing so, he both relied upon and went beyond traditional Victorian assumptions about men's and women's natures and their appropriate spheres. His relatively thorough treatment of the issues surrounding women in industry implies de facto recognition that the two spheres, male and female, were no longer mutually exclusive. Industry outside the home was no longer the sole domain of men. Now it was shared territory between the sexes. In the light of his overarching goal of building the Kingdom of God, Strong wanted to Christianize the gender relationships within this new arrangement.

Women's involvement in politics was another controversial question during the years of Strong's AISS presidency. Although woman suffrage was one of the major reforms advocated by prominent female Christian reformers such as Frances Willard and Anna Howard Shaw, no written statement about woman suffrage has been found with Strong's name attached to it. His lack of outspokenness in print may have been due to a residual Victorian tendency to leave women's issues to women, at least until he clarified his own position on them, or it may have been political expediency. Whatever the cause for his relative quietness on this issue, two pieces of evidence signal his eventual public support for woman suffrage.

The first display of support, already mentioned, was conspicuous. It was his marching with Alice Strong in the New York woman suffrage parade in the spring of 1912. The second instance was less overt, perhaps intentionally so, given the controversial and politically charged nature of this issue within religious circles. One of the featured Bible study topics in the January 1914 issue of *The Gospel of the Kingdom* was "Suffrage for Women." Its contents cannot be directly attributed to Strong, because the periodical was coedited by Strong and W. D. P. Bliss, and James Ecob wrote the editorial for that particular month. However, since Strong was the president of the organization, and no disclaimers were given, he bore a measure of responsibility for the study. Each weekly study in this particular series gave arguments both for and against the issue presented, and woman suffrage was no exception. Significantly, the "pro" arguments in this case were clearly favored by the author of the text, and they were given more than twice as much space as opposing statements.[38]

If woman's presence in industry was not universally accepted, and her participation in politics was highly controversial, a place for her in the upper echelons of church leadership, and in the corresponding intellectual field of theology, was hardly conceivable for most men in the first two decades of the twentieth century. Strong failed to write about women's ordination, even though he repeatedly mentioned in affirming ways the pioneering, ordained clergywoman, the Reverend Anna Howard Shaw. His silence on women's ordination is a two-edged sword, in that it would have invited criticism from both sides. Probably the safest and easiest professional move on his part would have been to condemn it, as did most of his male colleagues at the time.

In 1914, Strong did credit a female theologian with prophetic words for the church, quoting her extensively in the last chapter of his final book, *Our World: The New World-Religion*. The theme of this volume, "the church's conversion to Christ," was, according to Strong, "the first and most fundamental need of the world to-day." Decrying the chronic resistance by the church to the social teachings of Jesus, he argued that the church must allow itself to be converted to the full-orbed gospel of Christ, including his social teachings, before its power to convert the world would finally be realized. This conversion of the church to the social teachings of Christ would both call for, and represent "the Great Renunciation."[39]

Strong attributed this culminating concept, "the great renunciation," to a woman, Professor Vida Scudder of Wellesley College. Both Strong and Scudder believed that the church embodied the "possessing class." By this they meant that the church was the steward of both the spiritual riches of the Christian gospel and sufficient material resources to bring personal and social salvation to the world. As Strong put it, "In asking the possessing class to make the great renunciation, . . . we are simply asking for a genuine conversion to Christ and an honest obedience to his obvious teaching. Let us, rich and poor, make our lives fit our profession."[40]

Strong ended his final book with Walter Rauschenbusch's pastoral "prayer for the church." He had planned two more volumes for the series of which *Our World: The New World-Religion* was a part. However, he became critically ill in the autumn of 1915 and died in April 1916. In quoting Scudder and Rauschenbusch, both fourteen years younger than himself, Strong had symbolically passed his torch to the next generation of prominent social gospelers. In so doing, he recognized that these two persons, who happened to be a laywoman and a clergyman, possessed the necessary qualities for spiritual and theological leadership in building the Kingdom of God on earth.

Conclusion

Josiah Strong is most widely perceived as a narrow-minded racist and nationalist because of the blatant social Darwinism and the unapologetic imperialism expressed in his first and most famous book, *Our Country*. Therefore his relatively progressive attitude toward women, though not completely unaffected by latent Victorian stereotypes, may come as a surprise.

The fact that Strong joined thousands of progressive women and men, including his wife, in the 1912 New York suffrage parade should not be perceived as an anomaly on his part. In the course of his career, Strong had become convinced that for the sake of establishing the Kingdom of God on earth, women and men were meant by God to become equal partners in marriage, the workplace, politics, and even the church. Regrettably, he did not live to develop the full implications of this conviction for all gender issues, or to see society or the church-at-large embrace this ideal of equality.

Notes

1. Elsie and Margery Strong, "Josiah Strong: Social Pioneer," Manuscript I (typed manuscript), "As His Children Knew Him," 17–18, Josiah Strong Papers, Burke Library, Union Theological Seminary, New York.

2. Josiah Strong, *Our Country: Its Possible Future and its Present Crisis* (New York: Baker and Taylor, 1885), 18–19.

3. For further discussion of Strong's views on historical progress, see Wendy J. Deichmann Edwards, "Manifest Destiny, the Social Gospel and the Coming Kingdom: Josiah Strong's Program

of Global Reform, 1885–1916," chap. 5 in *Perspectives on the Social Gospel: Papers from the Inaugural Social Gospel Conference at Colgate Rochester Divinity School,* ed. Christopher H. Evans, Texts and Studies in the Social Gospel series (Lewiston, N.Y.: Edwin Mellen Press, 1999), 81–116; and idem, "Forging an Ideology for American Missions: Josiah Strong and Manifest Destiny," in *North American Foreign Missions, 1810–1914: Theology, Theory, and Policy,* ed. Wilbert R. Shenk (Grand Rapids: Eerdmans, forthcoming).

4. Sydney E. Ahlstrom, *A Religious History of the American People* (New Haven: Yale University Press, 1972), 798. For a history of Strong's relationship with the Evangelical Alliance during this period, see Philip D. Jordan, *The Evangelical Alliance for the United States of America, 1847–1900: Ecumenism, Identity and the Religion of the Republic* (New York: Edwin Mellen Press, 1982), esp. 64–65, 86–87.

5. "Call for the Washington Conference, to the Christian Public," *National Perils and Opportunities: The Discussions of the General Christian Conference, Held in Washington, D.C., December 7th, 8th and 9th, 1887. Under the Auspices and Direction of the Evangelical Alliance for the United States* (New York: Baker and Taylor, 1887), v.

6. Ahlstrom, *Religious History,* 798.

7. The use of women as religious visitors had been accepted by some of the Evangelical Alliance's constituencies since the 1830s and 1840s.

8. Josiah Strong, "Methods of Co-operation in Christian Work," in *National Perils and Opportunities,* 350 (second quote), 352 (first and third quotes).

9. Josiah Strong, "Progress of Christian Co-operation Since the Washington Conference" in *National Needs and Remedies. The Discussions of the General Christian Conference held in Boston, Mass. December 4th, 5th and 6th, 1889, Under the Auspices and Direction of the Evangelical Alliance for the United States* (New York: Baker and Taylor, 1890), 14–16 (quote, p. 16).

10. Josiah Strong, *The New Era: or The Coming Kingdom* (New York: Baker and Taylor, 1893), 234–35.

11. Ibid., 112–13, 222–25.

12. Ibid., 130–31, 225 (second quote), 226 (first quote), 240.

13. Ibid., 277.

14. Ibid., 339–40.

15. See the first paragraph of the introduction to this volume.

16. Susan Hill Lindley, *You Have Stept Out of Your Place: A History of Women and Religion in America* (Louisville, Ky.: Westminster John Knox Press, 1996), 137–38.

17. See *Christianity Practically Applied. The Discussions of the International Christian Conference Held in Chicago, October 8–14, 1893,* 2 vols. (New York: Baker and Taylor, 1894).

18. Strong, *The New Era,* 132.

19. "The Object of the League," *Social Engineering* 1, no. 1 (March 1899): 5.

20. His official list of forty supporters included seven women's names. See Josiah Strong, ed., *Social Progress: A Year Book and Encyclopedia of Economic, Industrial, Social and Religious Statistics, 1904* (New York: Baker and Taylor, 1904), 254. By 1917, the letterhead of the AISS included the following as members of the "National Council" of the organization: Jane Addams, Florence Kelley, Mary E. McDowell, Mary M. Simkhovitch, and Mary E. Woolley. Nathaniel M. Pratt to Albert Shaw, October 4, 1917, carbon copy, Albert Shaw Papers, New York Public Library.

21. *Social Progress, 1906,* 320–23.

22. Ibid., 305 (quote), 310–19.

23. Ibid., 265–87; Josiah Strong, *Expansion under the New World-Conditions* (New York: Baker and Taylor, 1900), 269.

24. "Hearing Given to Mrs. Margaret Dye Ellis, Mrs. Florence Kelley, Miss Sadie American and Josiah Strong, May 22nd, 1903, by Hon. George B. Cortelyou, Secretary Department of Commerce and Labor, Washington, D.C.," typed draft [photocopy], 1–3, Josiah Strong Papers.

25. Strong and Strong, "The AISS," 27.

26. Josiah Strong, *Religious Movements for Social Betterment* (New York: Baker and Taylor, 1900), 45 (first quote), 48 (second quote), 94, 97, 113.

27. Josiah Strong, "Women and Social Betterment," *Social Service* 6, no. 1 (July 1902): 16.

28. Ibid.

29. Ibid.

30. Josiah Strong, "Women in Industry," *The Gospel of the Kingdom and What to Do* 1, no. 2 (November 1908): 10.

31. Ibid.

32. Ibid.

33. Ibid., 11.

34. Ibid., 11–15.

35. Ibid., 15–17.

36. Ibid., 17.

37. Ibid.

38. "Lessons for 1914," *The Gospel of the Kingdom and What to Do* 6, no. 1 (January 1914), inside back cover; and "Suffrage for Women," ibid., 26–27.

39. Josiah Strong, *Our World: The New World-Religion* (Garden City: Doubleday, Page, 1915), 468–518. The quotes are from pages 468, 513, respectively.

40. Ibid., 516. On pages 514–16, Strong quoted extensively from Vida Scudder's "The Church's Great Opportunity," *The Churchman* (February 21, 1914).

CHAPTER 3

More Than Maternal Feminists and Good Samaritans: Women and the Social Gospel in Canada

Eleanor J. Stebner

The classic book on the social gospel in Canada is Richard Allen's *The Social Passion.*[1] Allen analyzes the aims of social reconstruction, the rise and fall of the labor churches and prohibition, and the demise of the movement. Utilizing the typology first suggested by C. Howard Hopkins, Allen identifies social gospelers as encompassing conservative, progressive, and radical strands. He argues that because social gospelers emphasized God's immanence and relied on actions rather than beliefs, the movement ironically contributed to the secularization of society rather than its Christian salvation. While later studies have supported, refined, and refuted Allen's argument, most interesting is the almost complete lack of women (and women's efforts) considered within the social gospel framework.[2]

Scholars who have addressed the movement from a gender perspective have considered a number of different interpretations. Randi Warne argues that whether or not women are included as social gospelers depends on "how the social gospel itself is defined." Dealing specifically with Nellie McClung, Warne warns that it may be both "inappropriate and misleading" to assume women under a social gospel banner since the goals of the women's movement were not prioritized, accepted, or even generally acknowledged.[3] Marilyn Legge notes the lack of women in social gospel scholarship and suggests that this absence may be due to women's practical involvement in it rather than their identification with formal leadership roles. At the same time, she argues that women's work in activities related to the social gospel movement can "rightfully be claimed as the basis of a faith-and-justice activism."[4] Alison Prentice and her coauthors in *Canadian Women* claim that women worked within the movement because some social reform effort was a "logical extension of their maternal role."[5]

Omitting women from scholarship on the social gospel, defining their work as peripheral or perfidious to it, or classifying their involvement as based on values of maternal feminism and personal ethics are not particularly helpful approaches to this topic. Such approaches reinforce gender stereotypes and theoretical frameworks that do not account for the diversity of women's involvements or their multiple—and often evolving—reasons for participating.[6] Between the last decade of the nineteenth century and World War II, women engaged in numerous social reform actions for a variety of reasons. Like their male contemporaries, women did not advocate uniform social gospel principles or agendas. Some women were involved in city missions and suffrage because they were primarily maternal feminists; others were involved in prohibition and morality education because they upheld the theological primacy of being good samaritans; still others were involved in similar actions because they defined themselves as social gospelers and upheld the necessity of working for structural social change. Most, however, exhibited a less segregated and more interactive approach to their faith and works.

In this essay I explore the inclusion of women within the Canadian social gospel movement. I assume a broad definition of the social gospel as relating to the social application of what proponents considered Christian aims. I do not put forth an all-encompassing interpretation of Canadian women and the social gospel, but I argue that current interpretations do not generally account for the fullness of women's experiences. I discuss first the context of Canada. I then analyze women's participation in church-related agencies of missionary societies, deaconess orders, and settlement houses. Finally, I examine the numerous activities and commitments of Beatrice Brigden, a middle-class white woman who has been virtually ignored in social gospel studies; Brigden exemplifies how difficult it is to classify women as simply maternal feminists, good samaritans, or even social gospelers.

One of Canada's most famous novelists and suffragists, Nellie McClung (1873–1951)—who was also an active Methodist laywoman advocating the ordination of women—perhaps best captures the developing involvements of women in her time. Rebuking and rebutting the limited roles assigned to women both in church and society, she states that women had acted the part of good samaritans for too long. While women were still bandaging the wounds of those beaten and robbed along the road to Jericho, McClung observes, a "conviction is growing on them that it would be much better to go out and clean up the road!"[7] Going out and cleaning up the road was a huge task, and it is a most practical metaphor for understanding the multifarious work of women within the social gospel in Canada.

The Lord's Dominion

When the Dominion of Canada was formed by the 1867 British North America Act, it consisted of the provinces of Ontario, Quebec, Nova Scotia, and New Brunswick. The vast lands west and north of the Great Lakes were sparsely inhabited by aboriginal peoples, traders, trappers, missionaries, and a few curious explorers and hearty settlers. The province of Manitoba was added in 1870, followed by British Columbia in 1871 and Prince Edward Island in 1873. The prairie provinces of Alberta and Saskatchewan were officially formed in 1905.[8]

It was one thing to overlay official boundaries on the northern half of the North American continent and quite another thing to build a nation. The formation of the North-West Mounted Police in 1874 (renamed the Royal Canadian Mounted Police in 1920) and the completion of the east-west national railway in 1885 were intended to give Canada symbolic identity, unity, and security ("law and order"). But it was the immigrants—huge numbers from northern, central, and eastern Europe—who were the future hope of the nascent nation; they would settle, clear, and farm the interior and provide the agricultural base for eastern-based entrepreneurs; their very presence would hold back the expansionist tendencies of the United States. Larger than the United States in land mass yet much smaller in population, in 1901 Canada enumerated a population of just over five million. A decade later the population had increased to just over seven million, due largely to European immigrant arrivals.[9]

Within this context, the social gospel movement became a powerful force for nation building. The twin goals—to Christianize and to Canadianize—were based on Anglo-British cultural values and Protestant idealism. While not all Protestants in Canada accepted or supported the social and political aims of the social gospel, all, to greater or lesser degrees and in varying ways, supported the vision that the Dominion of Canada was to be the Lord's Dominion.[10] Methodists most fully embraced the social gospel, especially important since after major consolidations in 1874 and 1884 they accounted for the largest number of Protestants in Canada.[11]

Despite an almost overwhelmingly Protestant presence outside of Quebec, an element of challenge—with an underlying presence of panic—pervaded the dominant national consciousness during these decades. It was fueled by non-English-speaking immigrants who poured into Canada and brought with them their Roman Catholic, Orthodox, Mennonite, and Lutheran religious identities. Already settled Protestant Christians organized schools and missions and worked for prohibition, as an attempt to transmit their particular values to these so-called new Canadians. Urban centers grew in size, and although an economic boom occurred in the first decade of the twentieth century, poverty was an everyday experience for many people. While World War I was enthusiastically supported by Christian churches, postwar disillusionment gave rise to increased labor and class disputes. The Winnipeg General Strike in 1919 revealed class, ethnic, and social tensions. Yet the passage of woman suffrage and prohibition legislation extended middle-class values. Women first received the vote in the provinces of Manitoba, Saskatchewan, and Alberta in 1916, with national suffrage granted in 1918.[12] Prohibition, first legalized in 1900 in Prince Edward Island, was passed by most Canadian provinces in 1916 but, by 1930, it was repealed in every province but Prince Edward Island.

Although neither woman suffrage nor prohibition created the Christian nation for which many had hoped, the social gospel impulse was very much alive in the post–World War I era and during the economic depression of the 1920s and 1930s. Many of its aims were politicized in the 1932 creation of the socialist democratic Co-operative Commonwealth Federation (CCF) party, under the leadership of a Methodist social gospeler, J. S. Woodsworth. The political platform of the CCF was contained in the 1933 Regina Manifesto; the goals of nationalizing essential services and businesses, introducing free and available health care services, and advocating the concerns of laborers and farmers articulated social gospel tenets.[13] The 1925 formation of the United Church of Canada—a union among Methodists, Presbyterians, and Congregationalists— is also often interpreted as resulting from the social gospel. Some scholars argue that the passion of the social gospel in the United Church did not dissipate after the 1930s but rather underwent an institutionalization process that lasted through the 1950s.[14]

Maternal Feminists, Good Samaritans, and Social Gospelers

The formalization of women's organizations expanded in the decades following confederation. Gail Cuthbert Brandt writes that such organizations "moved from being local in nature to being provincial and, sometimes, national in scope."[15] A local branch of the Young Women's Christian Association, for example, was first founded in 1870 in New Brunswick; by 1900, branches existed throughout the nation. The first local Woman's Christian Temperance Union was founded in 1874 by Letitia Youmans in Ontario; by 1883, when the WCTU nationalized, branches were present in every province.[16] While the YWCA and the WCTU garnered the support of countless women, other women participated in missionary societies, deaconess orders, and settlement houses. It is through these latter associations that the issue of women as social gospelers—as well as maternal feminists and good samaritans—is addressed.

Wendy Mitchinson writes that missionary societies were the "largest organizations of Canadian women in the nineteenth century."[17] She shows, however, that major differences existed between the methods and goals of such organizations. Some of the differences related to denominational affiliation. Of the four denominations she examined—Methodist, Presbyterian, Baptist, and Church of England (whose total membership in 1891 accounted for about 50 percent of the Canadian population)[18]—Methodists and Baptists clearly supported mission work at home and abroad. Presbyterian women, on the other hand, directed their efforts toward foreign missions and even refused membership in the National Council of Women when it was formed in 1893.[19] While Mitchinson argues that denominational missionary societies gave women official places within their churches and provided opportunities for leadership development, she concludes that missionary societies were vehicles for religious reform but not "vehicles for social reform."[20]

Religious reform, however, assumed understandings of social reform or, at the least, social control. By and large, women's missionary organizations accepted middle-class ideals regarding Canadianization and Protestant evangelicalism. Michael Owen, in a study on women's missions in Alberta, highlights this relationship when he states that women missionaries exhibited an "unstinting attachment to their church and its self-imposed mission to protect Canada from all that it perceived as non-British and non-Christian." In their attempts to assimilate new immigrant peoples (not to mention their desire to convert and civilize the aboriginal peoples), women's missionary efforts "shifted from Christian evangelism to evangelical Christian community service."[21] They themselves then became more tolerant of cultural differences and began to understand the dangers of ethnocentrism. Yet their participation in such activities may best be understood as stemming from maternal feminism and good samaritanism.

Margaret E. McPherson begs for a more nuanced interpretation based on her study of the Presbyterian missionary society and of Amanda Norris MacKay, one of its key leaders. She notes that Presbyterian women were not as active as Methodist women in work that reflects a social gospel theology, and she concurs that women's missionary societies were not radical entities.[22] Yet McPherson's findings regarding Amanda MacKay add an interesting twist to overarching interpretations. MacKay (b. 1858), a schoolteacher in her home province of Nova Scotia until her marriage, began to work with home missions after she and her husband moved to Manitoba. With other women in the Portage la Prairie area, MacKay began a mission to Native people that developed into a residential school. Residential schools were understood as an efficient way to assimilate Native people into dominant Canadian culture. Like her contemporaries, MacKay held such a view, but she also believed that such schools met the practical and physical needs of aboriginal peoples. After moving into the city of Winnipeg, MacKay became active in the local, provincial, and national organizational structure of the missionary society. She was influential in opening a mission that developed into a church institute, and she spent much time fundraising.

MacKay's efforts were focused on the missionary society; she was active in neither the suffrage movement nor the WCTU. She was, in many ways, typical of the kind of devoted, conventional, and capable woman on which denominational missionary societies relied. Yet MacKay had a political side. When the

Co-operative Commonwealth Federation party was gaining popularity in the 1930s, for example, McPherson says that MacKay was "excited by the social reforms advocated by the new political party." In a letter she wrote to her niece, MacKay even predicted that the CCF will "do great things when they get into power." Toward the end of her life, MacKay lamented that if only she had been born later, she "would have been a politician."[23] MacKay's political interests and aspirations were not visible to most of her contemporaries, yet the fact that they existed makes it necessary to acknowledge that the labels of maternal feminist and good samaritan may cloak more differences than they reveal. While women's missionary societies appeared to support the norm, individuals involved in them were not necessarily opposed to more progressive—or even social gospel—aims. Women simply could not do it all.

If women's missionary societies are generally acknowledged as conservative forces, the activities of women within the deaconess movement provide a more mixed example. Growing out of the women's missionary societies, deaconess orders were promoted by Presbyterians and Methodists beginning in the 1890s. Because Canadian Protestants had no experience with deaconesses, they initially contacted Lucy Rider Meyer's deaconess home in Chicago. Methodists officially recognized a deaconess order in 1908, but Methodist women had already established a Deaconess Aid Society in 1893 and, the next year, had founded a deaconess home and training school; in 1895, they had even designated two women as deaconesses. Presbyterians officially established a deaconess order in 1909, but twelve years earlier, Presbyterian women active in the foreign missionary society had established a training school, "[i]n effect," as Nancy Hall argues, organizing a deaconess order that was "independent of church policy."[24]

The issue of deaconesses in Protestant denominations was highly debated by churchmen. They initially accepted these workers only if they were nonsalaried, single, and of high moral quality. Such women were to be viewed neither as the equivalent of Roman Catholic nuns nor as ordained clergy; they were given a tenuous base within their denominations.[25] Yet it was clear in the 1890s and the early decades of the twentieth century that women workers were needed to engage in the practical applications of Christianity. In this sense, John D. Thomas argues, deaconesses became the "foot soldiers of Methodist applied Christianity."[26]

A product of maternal feminism and the ethic of Christian duty, deaconesses attended to the physical and cultural needs of people, most often children and immigrant women. Focusing on education, evangelism, and health concerns, deaconesses became a major way Protestants addressed problems associated with urban poverty, unwanted pregnancies, and the enculturation of immigrants with Canadian and Christian values. Staffing city missions and institutional churches; teaching Sunday school; visiting the ill, lonely, and displaced; and engaging in efforts toward moral and "redemptive" reform, deaconesses were the hands, faces, and hearts of the social gospel in Canada. While many of their efforts were consumed in bandaging up the wounds of travelers on the road to Jericho, deaconesses worked at making the road a safer place to travel.

Stella Annie Burry (b. 1897) may exemplify this combined approach. Born and reared in Newfoundland, Burry taught in a one-room schoolhouse before attending the Methodist deaconess training school in the early 1920s. She then worked for over a decade in two congregational settings in Toronto. She led Bible studies and engaged in the care of individuals. While she was the male minister's assistant, she took it for granted that she "could do a lot of things," including the standard work with children, visitation, and counseling.[27] In addition, however, she formed a club for working women that addressed some of the major problems facing independent urban women. When she returned to Newfoundland in 1938, she founded a community center that not only provided relief aid and shelter for young women but addressed issues of women's employment. While Burry's work may seem insignificant when compared to the large-scale efforts of some male social gospelers, it provided a tangible, practical, personal, and community-based approach to social transformation. It was a grass-roots endeavor that specifically focused on women's welfare.

Like women involved in missionary societies, deaconesses occupied a narrowly—and officially—defined place within the church. When Methodist and Presbyterian deaconess orders amalgamated with the formation of the United Church, for example, the committee overseeing reorganization defined deaconesses as handmaidens. Deaconesses were also called "angels of mercy." In these ways, the church conveyed the idea that deaconesses were to be "restricted to caring, assisting and remaining submissive, unobtrusive and obedient."[28] Given these parameters, it is amazing that any deaconess managed to do anything more than bandage wounds.

Good samaritanism was the expectation of deaconesses and was based on the church's theological understanding of women's nature and secondary role in society; at the same time, this did not prevent Burry and other women from working within such institutionally imposed limits. Social gospel tenets became popular in deaconess circles not merely because of individual leanings, however. The training schools—or angel factories, as they were jokingly called—themselves endorsed social gospel aims. The United Church Training School in Toronto and the Manitoba College Deaconess Training program in Winnipeg taught necessary "feminine" and etiquette skills. Students, however, were also taught economic, historical, ethical, and social analysis, which, for many, helped define their service as the practical application of the social gospel.[29] Many a social gospeler disguised herself as a humble handmaiden or a harmless angel of mercy.

Some exploration of the settlement house movement may contribute to a broader understanding of women within the social gospel. Settlement houses were established later in Canada than in Great Britain or in the United States, mostly because urbanization and industrialization did not occur until the first decades of the twentieth century. The first Canadian house, Evangelia Settlement, was opened in Toronto in 1902 by Sara Libby Carson with the assistance of her friend Mary Lawson Bell. Carson, who had previously established Christadora House in New York City, founded Evangelia Settlement with the partnership of the Canadian YWCA. A citizen of the United States, a Quaker, and an extremely capable administrator, Carson was later hired by the Presbyterian Church to found or reorganize a total of seven settlements across Canada.[30] Settlements not connected with the church were also founded. The Toronto University settlement (which began as a male-only organization), for example, aimed for a nonreligious ethos.[31]

The programs organized by settlement houses focused on providing social and educational outlets: nursery services for working mothers, clubs for children, English classes for men and women, and so on. Programs were generally practical, not theoretical or philosophical. Yet early social settlements in Canada, which involved a high percentage of women as residents and head residents, had a "strong religious flavour." Allan Irving, Harriet Parsons, and Donald Bellamy in their book *Neighbours* observe that "[v]arious strands of the social gospel movement, particularly as it gathered steam within the Presbyterian and Methodist churches, had a profound influence on the Canadian settlement movement."[32] Brian Fraser pushes the religious connection further by identifying St. Christopher House (founded in 1912 by Carson) in Toronto as "serving two very different groups," namely, the "poor and the immigrants" in the neighborhood, and the "promotion of the social gospel" within the church.[33]

The Presbyterians were clear regarding their social gospel perspective on settlement houses. In 1910, the members of the committee recommending the organization of settlements throughout Canada stated, "[we] are going into this work not merely inspired by a thin, sentimental humanism, but because we are Christian people who seek the advancement of Christ's Kingdom and the saving of men's lives."[34] They intended to found church settlements, not social settlements. Perhaps this is why, despite the social gospel underpinnings of early settlement houses in Canada and their provision of much social service, these settlements never became "spearheads for reform."[35]

Although settlement houses did not develop into centers for radical reform efforts, social gospel underpinnings are easily identified in the formation and goals of settlement leaders. Ethel Dodds Parker (b. 1890), for example, an influential settlement leader, reflected that she had "grown up within the fold of the emerging Social Gospel." Parker was born to farmers in Manitoba, and her childhood home was often the stopping point for male social gospel leaders, such as Charles W. Gordon, a social gospel novelist who wrote under the pen name Ralph Connor. Parker's father, a lay minister who worked among Cree Indians on a nearby reserve, came to the conclusion that evangelical conversions ought to be sought only after a "long period of friendship and teaching." Parker observes that this was her "first experience of the tug between evangelical and social Christianity."[36]

Parker eventually studied at the Toronto Conservatory School of Expression and in 1914 pursued social work at the University of Toronto, at which time she lived at St. Christopher House. She gained more experience at settlement houses in Vancouver and Montreal and was appointed head resident at the Toronto University Settlement (1916–17) and later at St. Christopher House (1917–21). While institutional financial problems consumed much of her energy, Parker identified another source of conflict within the settlement house, namely, the "more general tension between traditional evangelicals and the Social Gospel." She recognized that a few vocal clergymen continually protested the "lack of religious teaching" at settlement houses. Yet she was convinced that her work and the work of her staff was at least "implicitly religious." "Indeed," she continued, "it was often quite explicit."[37]

When Graham Taylor, head resident of the Chicago Commons visited St. Christopher, Parker queried him about what social settlements were to do about teaching religion. She cherished his response: "All religion is vertical and horizontal: the fatherhood of God and the brotherhood of man. Live and teach that and you will offend no Settlement member." Later in life, Parker compared the activities of St. Christopher House with that of Hull-House and other more politically active U.S. settlements. She asked herself if she—and other Canadian social settlement workers—were remiss in not utilizing settlements for more explicit reform. In her own evaluation, St. Christopher was never "bombastically activist," yet it was involved in community organization and the formation of neighborhood coalitions.[38] Torn between doing what came to be called social work and working for change based on social gospel principles, Parker chose the primary path of the good samaritan, while still attempting to establish networks that would address how to clean some of the road traversed by the settlement neighbors.

In examining the activities of women in denominational missionary societies, deaconess orders, and settlement houses, it becomes obvious that the labels "maternal feminist," "good samaritan," and even "social gospeler" are not particularly useful in identifying the motives or the actual work of women. It is not easy to distinguish between them. Middle-class women active in church-related associations walked a narrow line, claiming public authority based on acceptable gender understandings and institutional restrictions while juggling the practical needs of people with their own aspirations of reform, which would go beyond individual care giving. While such organizations provided women with outlets for their skills and energies, they did not offer opportunities for them to engage wholeheartedly in what may be called pure social gospel aims; their multiplex obligations required subtle gerrymandering of gender norms, institutional expectations, and the provision of direct and immediate aid. This may be why women have not been identified as forceful social gospel proponents. Yet such women effected an integrated application of—and community approach to—social gospel aims that has perhaps had a more enduring legacy than that of their brothers.

One Woman's Campaign

The interconnecting, overlapping, and sometimes contradictory associations of women comprise a most interesting aspect of the study of women in this time period. The example of Beatrice Brigden's life and work illustrates the need to expand theoretical interpretations of the social gospel so that women might more fully be included. Valerie Regehr suggests that the social gospel had a male face and a female face, similar but different incarnations of the same movement.[39] Such an interpretation, however, does not account for the differences among women. Nor does it account for how individual women developed and changed. Beatrice Brigden is such a woman. Brigden attained various religious, social, and political positions throughout her long life. Yet, as Allison Campbell points out, she maintained two constants: "her involvement with women's organizations and her search for a society represented by the social gospel ideal— a society of justice, equality and freedom from economic oppression."[40] Brigden provides an example of how one woman, influenced by maternal feminism and motivated by good samaritanism, lived as a social gospeler.

Born in 1888 in Belleville, Ontario, Brigden moved west with her family in 1889 to the area of Deloraine, Manitoba, where they homesteaded. Both of her parents were interested in politics and Christianity and they participated in the prohibition, suffrage, and farmer's cooperative movements. Her mother was a descendant of American Loyalists and was an active Methodist, although she had been a Quaker before moving west. Brigden and her siblings were well read and spent much time discussing politics. While still a child, Brigden met J. S. Woodsworth, who, by coincidence, was then the Methodist circuit minister in their area. Brigden fondly remembers that Woodsworth and her mother engaged in long talks on the state of the world and on the necessity of pacifism: "He was like a bright thread that wove itself in and out and around our lives." Brigden later reflected that she had difficulty remembering a "time when [she] was not of a social gospel orientation."[41]

Brigden's outlook was influenced by her education and other life experiences. She deepened her skills, abilities, and ambitions as a student at Brandon College and then at the Toronto Conservatory of Music, from which she graduated with a degree in speech. It was her exposure to the realities of life in Toronto, however, that began to transform her idealism into practicalities. Joan Sangster writes that Brigden was "shocked by Toronto's slums and widespread poverty. . . . [S]he even took temporary work in a factory" so she could share the experiences of women workers.[42] Upon returning to Manitoba, however, Brigden encountered the dilemma that many young women of her class, race, and education faced: what was she to do with her life?

Deciding against marriage, Brigden needed a job. A male Methodist social purity lecturer suggested that she pursue similar work with girls and women. After some correspondence with Albert Moore, superintendent of Methodist Social Services and Evangelism, Brigden joined the cause. She went to La Crosse, Wisconsin, to train for her upcoming work and took a side trip to Chicago to visit Hull-House and meet Jane Addams. Indeed, Brigden upheld Addams as her role model and described herself as "one of a host of women who follows [Addams] because she understands *best*."[43] From 1914 to 1920, Brigden worked as a Methodist social purity lecturer, traveling and speaking from coast to coast.

Her work was understood within the Methodist Church as evangelistic. Her tasks involved education in the areas of sexual morals for girls and women, fighting venereal disease, and stopping the so-called white slave traffic. Like members of the WCTU and women's missionary societies, Brigden focused on female "maternal qualities of family love and devotion to duty."[44] Her work also involved discussing general social problems. Sometimes her weekly stops were well attended and supported by local Methodists ministers but, at other times, they were ignored.[45] In crisscrossing the country, Brigden connected with local people as well as with other reformers, and these contacts proved to be invaluable in later years. Eventually, Brigden moved from emphasizing the personal choices of individuals to recognizing the social conditions behind them.

Brigden came to consider herself a socialist, although it took her some time to combine her religious and political beliefs. She became annoyed with what she perceived to be a growing backlash on the part of the Methodist Conference against the organization of labor. This point came to a head for her in the 1919 Winnipeg strike and the subsequent departure from the Methodist ministry of J. S. Woodsworth, William Ivens, and A. E. Smith. Richard Allen, in his book *The Social Passion,* discusses the nuances of their departure with academic objectivity, but Brigden interpreted it more directly. In her mind, they were "out of the church entirely due to their social protest on behalf of the poor, the oppressed, their cry for justice and humanity for all." She associates herself with them, saying that their social justice stances were the same as those that she herself had been "advocating in [her] work with the Social Service Department."[46]

Brigden resigned from her position in 1920. She was exhausted, she needed to care for her aging mother, and she was disillusioned with the Methodist Church. She became active in the People's Labour Church in Brandon, Manitoba, organized by A. E. Smith, and began "to give more explicit political expression to [her] social and religious beliefs."[47] She came to understand politics and religion as working together to address the needs of all people. She continued a special focus on women, arguing that women needed to be full participants in the political process and emphasizing their need for education and work opportunities. Speaking, organizing, and educating were her forte. She started a series of People's Forums and organized annual Labor Women's Social and Economic Conferences. In 1930 she ran for political office as a farm-labor candidate.

Brigden moved to Winnipeg after her election defeat, continued her political advocacy work, and wrote a weekly newspaper column for children. She attended the Regina Convention of the Co-operative Commonwealth Federation in 1933 and contributed to the writing of its manifesto; in 1936, she became the Manitoba CCF secretary for a three-year term. Joan Sangster argues that Brigden's feminism developed during these years, changing from an emphasis on maternalism to one based on principles of gender equality.[48] Indeed, after World War I, Brigden's socialism and feminism became fused. Although her involvements changed in later life, when she became active in cultural work, international affairs, and joined the Society of Friends, she was active until her death in 1977.

Brigden is omitted from most of the histories of the CCF, but she was certainly as much a social gospeler as were her male contemporaries.[49] Yet because of her gender—and perhaps because of her primary obligation to the welfare of women, her continued association with women's groups, and her unyielding advocacy for women's rights—scholars have not known how to interpret Brigden's lifelong campaign for social reform. Some might conclude that she was a conservative in her early social-purity-lecturer days who became a progressive and then a radical. Others might see her as a maternal feminist who upheld the necessity of being a good samaritan yet who always claimed at least some kind of social gospel orientation. Neither interpretation recognizes that Brigden was all of these. Of equal importance—and unlike some of her social gospel brothers—she appears never to have lost the faith behind her works.[50]

Women and the Social Gospel

Middle- and upper-middle-class white women in Canada participated in a variety of social-betterment activities from the 1890s through the 1930s. Many of them did so because they believed that, by virtue of their gender, they could make their nation into a more nurturing and loving society. Organizing their efforts through denominational missionary societies, deaconess orders, and settlement houses, women were agents of dominant cultural transmission and also compassionate and caring individuals. The need to do good toward stranger, widow, child, and others who were suffering and oppressed was a motivating biblical imperative that formed women's understandings of maternal feminism and good samaritanism. It also situated many of them within the social gospel movement. Indeed, while bandaging the wounded along the road, many women—drawing on their own skills and accepting limitations imposed on them by religious and social structures—attempted to clean up the road itself.

Notes

1. Richard Allen, *The Social Passion: Religion and Social Reform in Canada, 1914–28* (Toronto: University of Toronto Press, 1971), 17. Another seminal study is C. Howard Hopkins, *The Rise of the Social Gospel in American Protestantism, 1865–1915* (New Haven: Yale University Press, 1940).

2. See Ramsay Cook, *The Regenerators: Social Criticism in Late Victorian English Canada* (Toronto: University of Toronto Press, 1985); David B. Marshall, *Secularizing the Faith: Canadian Protestant Clergy and the Crisis of Belief, 1850–1940* (Toronto: University of Toronto Press, 1992); Nancy Christie and Michael Gauvreau, *A Full-Orbed Christianity: The Protestant Churches and Social Welfare in Canada, 1900–1940* (Montreal: McGill-Queen's University Press, 1996); and Paul T. Phillips, *A Kingdom on Earth: Anglo-American Social Christianity, 1880–1940* (University Park: Pennsylvania State University Press, 1996).

3. Randi R. Warne, *Literature as Pulpit: The Christian Social Activism of Nellie L. McClung* (Waterloo, Ont.: Canadian Corporation for Studies in Religion, Wilfred Laurier University Press, 1993), 5, 149. See also Joan Sangster, *Dreams of Equality: Women on the Canadian Left, 1920–1950* (Toronto: McClelland and Steward, 1989), 21–22.

4. Marilyn J. Legge, *The Grace of Difference: A Canadian Feminist Theological Ethic,* AAR Academy Series Number 80 (Atlanta: Scholars Press, 1992), 50.

5. Alison Prentice et al., *Canadian Women: A History* (Toronto: Harcourt Brace, 1988), 151. Also see Carol Lee Bacchi, *Liberation Deferred? Ideas of the English-Canadian Suffragists, 1877–1918* (Toronto: University of Toronto Press, 1983).

6. Ruth Compton Brouwer suggests that historians themselves are responsible for perpetuating stereotypical views of women, mostly because many historians have "appeared uninterested in or uneasy with the topic of religion" or have even been hostile to it. Brouwer, "Transcending the 'Unacknowledged Quarantine': Putting Religion into English-Canadian Women's History," *Journal of Canadian Studies/Revue d'etudes canadiennes* 27, no. 3 (Fall 1992): 47.

7. Nellie McClung, *In Times Like These* (New York: D. Appleton, 1915), 126. See also her entire chapter "Women and the Church," 102–27. For select studies on McClung, see Mary E. Hallett, "Nellie McClung and the Fight for the Ordination of Women in the United Church of Canada," *Atlantis* 4, no. 2, part 1 (Spring 1979): 2–19, and Randi R. Warne, "Nellie McClung's Social Gospel," in *Changing Roles of Women within the Christian Church in Canada,* ed. Elizabeth Gillian Muir and Marilyn Fardig Whitely (Toronto: University of Toronto Press, 1995), 338–54.

8. Federal jurisdiction was extended north of the provinces to create the territories of the Yukon, the North West, and most recently, Nunavut. Newfoundland joined Canada in 1949.

9. Robert T. Handy, *A History of the Churches in the United States and Canada* (Oxford: Oxford University Press, 1976), 344–45; census figures, 1871–1911, in *The Canadian Protestant Experience, 1760–1990,* ed. George A. Rawlyk (Burlington, Ont.: Welch Publishing Company, 1990), 102–4.

10. See Brian Clarke, "English-Speaking Canada from 1854," in *A Concise History of Christianity in Canada,* ed. Terrence Murphy (Toronto: Oxford University Press, 1996), 261–359; Dennis L. Butcher et al., eds., *Prairie Spirit: Perspectives on the Heritage of the United Church of Canada in the West* (Winnipeg: University of Manitoba Press, 1985); Phyllis D. Airhart, "Ordering a New Nation and Reordering Protestantism, 1867–1914," in *The Canadian Protestant Experience, 1760–1990,* ed. George A. Rawlyk (Burlington, Ont.: Welch Publishing Company, 1990), 98–138; and John Webster Grant, *The Church in the Canadian Era* (Burlington, Ont.: Welch Publishing Company, 1988). See also Richard Allen, ed., *The Social Gospel in Canada,* Papers of the Interdisciplinary Conference on the Social Gospel in Canada, March 21–24, 1973, at the University of Regina, Mercury Series, History Division Paper No. 9 (Ottawa: National Museums of Canada, 1975); see especially Allen's essay, "The Background of the Social Gospel in Canada," 2–35.

11. See the discussion in Phyllis D. Airhart, *Serving the Present Age: Revivalism, Progressivism, and the Methodist Tradition in Canada* (Montreal: McGill-Queen's University Press, 1992), and Neil

Semple, *The Lord's Dominion: The History of Canadian Methodism* (Montreal: McGill-Queen's University Press, 1996).

12. See Jane Errington, "Pioneers and Suffragists," in *Changing Patterns: Women in Canada,* ed. Sandra Burt, Lorraine Code, and Lindsay Dorney (Toronto: McClelland and Stewart, 1988), 69–73, and Jeanne L'Esperance, *The Widening Sphere: Women in Canada, 1870–1940* (Ottawa: Public Archives, National Library of Canada, 1982).

13. See N. K. Clifford, "Religion in the Thirties: Some Aspects of the Canadian Experience," in *The Dirty Thirties in Prairie Canada,* ed. R. D. Francis and H. Ganzevoort, (Vancouver: Tantalus Research Limited, 1980), 125–40, and Howard Wells and Roger Hutchinson, eds., *A Long and Faithful March: "Towards the Christian Revolution," 1930s/1980s* (Toronto: United Church Publishing House, 1989). The CCF was the forerunner of the current New Democratic Party.

14. See Ted Reeve, *Claiming the Social Passion: The Role of The United Church in Creating a Culture of Social Well-being in Canadian Society* (Toronto: Centre for Research in Religion, Emmanuel College, and Moderator's Consultation on Faith and the Economy, United Church of Canada, 1999), and Ian McKay Manson, "'Fighting the Good Fight': Salvation, Social Reform, and Service in the United Church of Canada's Board of Evangelism and Social Service, 1925–1945" (Th.D. diss., Victoria University of the University of Toronto, 1999).

15. Gail Cuthbert Brandt, "Organizations in Canada: The English Protestant Tradition," in *Women's Paid and Unpaid Work: Historical and Contemporary Perspectives,* ed. Paula Bourne (Toronto: New Hogtown Press, 1985), 80. Between 1870 and 1920, the number of women joining Roman Catholic orders greatly increased. See Marta Danylewycz, *Taking the Veil: An Alternative to Marriage, Motherhood, and Spinsterhood in Quebec, 1840–1920* (Toronto: McClelland and Stewart, 1987).

16. See Diana Pedersen, "Providing a Woman's Conscience: The YWCA, Female Evangelicalism, and the Girl in the City, 1870–1930," in *Canadian Women: A Reader,* ed. Wendy Mitchinson et al. (Toronto: Harcourt Brace, 1996), 194–210, and Nancy M. Sheehan, "The WCTU on the Prairies, 1886–1930: An Alberta-Saskatchewan Comparison," *Prairie Forum* 6, no. 1 (1981): 17–33. See also Mariana Valverde, *The Age of Light, Soap, and Water: Moral Reform in English Canada, 1885–1925* (Toronto: McClelland and Stewart, 1991).

17. Wendy Mitchinson, "Canadian Women and Church Missionary Societies," *Atlantis* 2, no. 2, part 2 (Spring 1977): 58.

18. Ibid., 73n.1.

19. Ibid., 72.

20. The National Council of Women was formed under the leadership of Lady Ishbel Aberdeen, who, after participating in the 1893 International Council of Women held at the World's Columbian Exposition in Chicago, realized how "far behind [Canadian women] were in organizing and coordinating their efforts." Brandt, "Organizations in Canada," 84. Several excellent studies are available on Canadian women and foreign missions. See, for example, Ruth Compton Brouwer, *New Women for God: Canadian Presbyterian Women and India Missions, 1876–1914* (Toronto: University of Toronto Press, 1990), and Rosemary R. Gagan, *A Sensitive Independence: Canadian Methodist Women Missionaries in Canada and the Orient, 1881–1925* (Montreal: McGill-Queen's University Press, 1992).

21. Michael Owen, "'Lighting the Pathways for New Canadians': Methodist and United Church WMS Missions in Eastern Alberta, 1904–1940," in *Standing on New Ground: Women in Alberta,* Alberta Nature and Culture Series, ed. Catherine A. Cavanaugh and Randi R. Warne (Edmonton: University of Alberta Press, 1993), 2 (first quote), 15 (second quote).

22. See Margaret E. McPherson, "Head, Heart and Purse: The Presbyterian Women's Missionary Society in Canada, 1876–1925," in Butcher et al., *Prairie Spirit,* 147–70, and her article "'From Caretakers to Participants': Amanda Norris MacKay and the Presbyterian Women's Missionary Society, 1876–1925," *Touchstone* (September 1991): 32–44.

23. McPherson, "Head, Heart and Purse," 167.

24. Nancy Hall, "The Professionalisation of Women Workers in the Methodist, Presbyterian, and United Churches of Canada," in *First Days, Fighting Days: Women in Manitoba History,* ed. Mary Kinnear (Regina: University of Regina, Canadian Plains Research Center, 1987), 125.

25. See Mary Anne MacFarlane, "A Tale of Handmaidens: Deaconesses in the United Church of Canada, 1925 to 1964" (M.A. thesis, University of Toronto, 1987).

26. John D. Thomas, "Servants of the Church: Canadian Methodist Deaconess Work, 1890–1926," *Canadian Historical Review* 65, no. 3 (1984): 371.

27. Nancy Elizabeth Hardy, *Called to Serve: A Story of Diaconal Ministry in the United Church of Canada* (Toronto: Division of Ministry Personnel and Education, United Church of Canada, 1985), 17. See also Morley F. Hodder, "Stella Annie Burry: Dedicated Deaconess and Pioneer Community Worker," *Touchstone* (October 1985): 24–33.

28. MacFarlane, "A Tale of Handmaidens," 23.

29. Sherri McConnell examines the curriculum and role of the training schools in deaconess formation in a manuscript entitled "Call, Vocation, and the Deaconess Tradition," Faculty of Theology, University of Winnipeg, 1999. McConnell is currently working on a master's thesis on the same topic at the University of Winnipeg.

30. Allan Irving, Harriet Parsons, and Donald Bellamy, *Neighbours: Three Social Settlements in Downtown Toronto* (Toronto: Canadian Scholars' Press, 1995), 23–31, 65–83.

31. Sarah Z. Burke, in *Seeking the Highest Good: Social Service and Gender at the University of Toronto, 1888–1937* (Toronto: University of Toronto, 1996), provides a full study of University Settlement, one of Canada's most well known settlement houses.

32. Irving et al., *Neighbours,* 209.

33. Brian Fraser, "Theology and the Social Gospel among Canadian Presbyterians: A Case Study," *Studies in Religion* 8, no. 1 (Winter 1979): 39.

34. Quoted by Ethel (Dodds) Parker, "The Origins and Early History of the Presbyerian Settlement Houses," in Allen, *The Social Gospel in Canada,* 95.

35. Irving et al., *Neighbours,* 73, 211.

36. Parker, "Origins and Early History," 86, 89. Connor's best-known book is *The Foreigner* (Toronto: Westminster, 1909).

37. Parker, "Origins and Early History," 109, 110, 113.

38. Ibid., 113 (first quote), 119 (second quote).

39. Valerie Regehr, "Beatrice Brigden: Her Social Gospel Theology in Its Historical Context" (M.A. thesis, Associated Mennonite Biblical Seminary, Elkhart, Indiana, 1989), 116.

40. Allison Campbell, "Beatrice Brigden: The Formative Years of a Socialist Feminist, 1888–1932" (M.A. thesis, University of Winnipeg, 1991), 15.

41. Beatrice Brigden, "One Woman's Campaign for Social Purity and Social Reform," in Allen, *The Social Gospel in Canada,* 39.

42. Joan Sangster, "The Making of a Socialist-Feminist: The Early Career of Beatrice Brigden, 1888–1941," *Atlantis* 13, no. 1 (Fall 1987): 15.

43. Brigden to Albert Moore, January 28, 1914, quoted by Sangster, "The Making of a Socialist-Feminist," 17.

44. Campbell, "Beatrice Brigden," 67.

45. Brigden, "One Woman's Campaign," 46–51, contains excerpts of her correspondence regarding her many speaking engagements.

46. Brigden, "One Woman's Campaign," 55. See also, Allen, *The Social Passion,* 114–19.

47. Brigden, "One Woman's Campaign," 56. See also, Vera Fast, "The Labor Church in Winnipeg," in Butcher et al., *Prairie Spirit,* 233–49.

48. Sangster, "The Making of a Socialist-Feminist," 22.

49. See, for example, David Lewis, *The Good Fight: Political Memoirs, 1909–1958* (Toronto: Macmillan, 1981), and Albert E. Smith, *All My Life* (Toronto: Progress Books, 1949). Both of these men barely acknowledge Brigden, although she was one of their colleagues.

50. Mary Kinnear, "Religion and the Shaping of 'Public Woman': A Post-Suffrage Case Study," in *Religion and Public Life in Canada: Historical and Comparative Perspectives,* ed. Marguerite Van Die (Toronto: University of Toronto Press, 2001), 196–215.

PART 2

Perspectives on a Social Gospel Family: The Rauschenbusches

CHAPTER 4

Walter Rauschenbusch and "The Woman Movement": A Gender Analysis

Janet Forsythe Fishburn

Walter Rauschenbusch (1861–1918), known to historians as a progressive social theorist and liberal theologian, was a Baptist minister, seminary professor, and well-known leader of the social gospel movement. His reputation as a social prophet was established by the publication of *Christianity and the Social Crisis* in 1907 and expanded through extensive public speaking and writing for church groups, college students, and civic organizations like the Young Men's Christian Association (YMCA). His primary contribution to theology, *A Theology for the Social Gospel*, published in 1917, expressed his conviction that the most vital theology is actively engaged with the culture of its time.

Rauschenbusch's social thought was grounded in assumptions about the evolution of social institutions like the family and the state. As a professor of church history, he was deeply concerned about the role of Christianity in social progress or regress. Like many theologians and politicians at the time he believed that the American democracy undergirded by Christian morality represented a new era of social progress. He also embraced the popular view that if moral values were not instilled in children through family life, democracy would crumble into social chaos. He regarded the family as the building block of democracy.

His views about women and family life were more static than progressive. For biblical and biological reasons, he believed that women were created to be the mothers of the race. Although he regarded "the woman movement" as a social revolution worthy of serious attention, this was a relatively minor theme in his speaking and writing, which were mostly addressed to men. Throughout his career, to the extent that he was concerned about the changing role of women, it was primarily because of the impact this would have on men and social progress.

Gender issues were important to Rauschenbusch because of the way he linked stability in family life to social and economic change. Like most Victorians, he subscribed to a two-sphere theory of gender roles. Like many other social gospel leaders, he thought in terms of the equal but different social roles of men and women. Theoretically, the two spheres set boundaries that divided the social-political world between the public work world of men and the private domestic world of women. Since these boundaries could be adjusted with social change, social theorists like Rauschenbusch weighed whether particular adjustments represented progress, a threat to the present social equilibrium, or, even worse, social regression.

The Progressive Era in American history, roughly 1890 to 1920, coincided with the active years of Rauschenbusch's ministry. Most theories of social evolution at this time were derived from the work of the self-taught English social philosopher Herbert Spencer, who adapted Charles Darwin's theories of natural selection to social theory. Theorists of social progress were concerned with how social equilibrium occurred as well as with the social function of disequilibrium. There were many variations on the theme of social equilibrium. Those adopted by Rauschenbusch differed in some details from those of other social gospel thinkers and were probably influenced by his study of German anthropologists, economic historians, and social theorists. As the son of German-American immigrants, he had earned the equivalent of American high school and college degrees in Germany and returned to study economics there in 1907–8. Throughout his career he was concerned about the ratio of men to women in the American population. He assumed that social equilibrium required a fairly equal proportion of men to women to sustain marriage and family life, and that marriage partners be well matched in terms of education and abilities.

Despite the fact that much of what Rauschenbusch wrote seems clear and direct, it is not always obvious why he has taken a particular position. The narrative that follows is arranged topically in an effort to clarify some of the less obvious presuppositions in his thinking, writing, and speaking about gender, women, and family.

The Role of Gender in the Social Theory of Rauschenbusch

Social historians agree that the rigid delineation of gender that was characteristic of the Victorian period in the United States solidified around 1860, the year Rauschenbusch was born. The decades in which the social roles of women changed most dramatically coincide with those of his career as a pastor, professor, and writer. "Between 1880 and 1910, the proportion of employed women increased from 14.7 to 24.8 percent. In the ten years between 1900 and 1910, the percentage of married women working outside the home more than doubled (from 5 to 11 percent)."[1]

Statistics like these threatened the equilibrium of what Rauschenbusch regarded as the God-given roles of men and women essential to the stability of marriage, family life, and society. His assumptions about gender, absorbed in childhood, were modified only slightly between his earliest writing in the 1890s and his last public speeches in 1917. When he referred to the "two spheres" he meant the system predicated on the duty of all women to marry, have children, and create a home where a husband could find respite from the harsh realities of the work world of men.

Marriage was like the terms of addition; it took two halves to make a whole. A man needed a woman as a woman needed a man; one without the other was incomplete. So ingrained was his conviction about the mutuality of the sexes that Rauschenbusch expressed concern when "the census of 1900 [in Rochester, New York] showed 25,219 men between the age of 25 and 44, the years during which a man ought to be enjoying a home and rearing children, and 7355 of them were still unmarried."[2] His ideal was a nation in which every young man and young woman married and mated during the prime young adult years.

Middle-class strictures on gender that Rauschenbusch had been raised to regard as right and natural were beginning to unravel before the turn of the century. But a statement he made in an unpublished manuscript, "The Righteousness of the Kingdom," reveals that his premise about the reciprocal roles of men and women had changed very little by 1891.[3]

> The two aims of the Christian revolution, the perfection of the individual and the perfection of society, blend and pass into each other; so do the office and faculties of man and woman. Yet the directions of the one aim corresponds to the bent of woman's genius, the other to the inclination of man's ability. The fact that religious work as it now stands is not enlisting the same proportion of men as of women . . . furnishes another presumption that we have left out one term of the Christian synthesis and ventilated the rounded perfection of Christ's revolutionary aim. . . . the combination of the two aims is necessary for the attainment of either.[4]

Gender imbalance in churches was a popular theme among church leaders at this time. Rauschenbusch never tired of urging churchmen to take their rightful place in God's Kingdom through their work and service to the public world. Less well known is that he associated moral decay with new roles for women, a theme he shared with many church leaders, from social progressives like himself to fundamentalists like Billy Sunday. Both men deplored the rising divorce rate, the number of women who failed to marry, the number of married women who failed to have children, the rise of prostitution, the "smut" in novels and the theater, and the immodest dress of "the new woman." They differed, however, on one important point: higher education for women. Rauschenbusch said yes; fundamentalists said no.

Although Rauschenbusch discussed the role of women in "The Righteousness of the Kingdom," this was always secondary to his concern with the role of men.

A rare discussion of women as a separate topic is found in an outline for a book intended to "oppose false doctrine and ideas." His outline for what he entitled *The Woman Problem,* written around 1899, contains a theory about the physiological destiny of women that he rarely stated, but always assumed, even in his later social commentary. Here he stated the belief, common at the time, that women did not belong in the work force because they were limited by menses and childbearing. Men complemented the weakness of women because they were physically capable of working steadily enough to support a family.[5]

The clearest exposition of the gender issues that troubled Rauschenbusch appeared in a speech written for two German Baptist congregations in 1909, entitled "The Social Value of Women." In this document he narrated the story of the evolution of women and the patriarchal family: the slow rise over the last one hundred years to "more wealth, better dwellings, democracy, Christianity, refined, gentler family life" as major components of social progress. He also described the division of work in the modern family between men who worked outside the home and the home as the workplace of women, saying that girls "prefer order, dusting, making things last."[6]

According to this speech, the future of the race depended on the role of women in the home. It was the duty of women, he asserted, to "lift the family further."[7] In closing, he posed some "modern questions about women." These questions were an expression of his own concerns about contemporary women and their changing roles, including competition with men for work, women who ignored housework and disliked manual labor, woman as a competitor instead of a helper to man, women's lack of organizational skills, the economic waste of silly fashions, rivalry between women, and the social harm done by flirty women who intentionally excited the passions of men. His response was to remind women that the value of a mother to her baby boy, to a man, to a husband, and to a father constituted their "true happiness, a noble life."[8]

In early sermons written between 1886 and 1897 when he was the pastor of a German immigrant congregation in New York City, Rauschenbusch used the language of "two spheres" to designate differences between men and women. In those sermons he told women that rearing children was their "monopoly," that childbearing was "inwrought in [them]." As a social theorist during the first decade of the twentieth century, he referred to the "two spheres" less frequently, but he maintained his assumption that the differences were genetic. Just as he believed women were biologically destined to be the "mothers of the race," he regarded women as the more juvenile sex, unfit for public roles because they had led sheltered lives in their workplace, the home.[9] He never abandoned his belief that only family life, as he understood it, could "keep America healthy."[10]

By 1907, when Rauschenbusch wrote *Christianity and the Social Crisis,* the argument that social stability depended on the role of women at home had become essential to his social analysis. The social crisis he described in his book included "the crumbling of the political democracy," "the tainting of the moral atmosphere," and, most important of all, "the undermining of the family."[11] As the "structural cell of the social organism," the family was "the foundation of morality, the chief educational institution, and the source of nearly all the real contentment among men. . . . All other questions sink into insignificance when the stability of the family is at stake."[12] By this time, feminists had begun to question the validity of the "spheres," so Rauschenbusch simply restated his views about "woman's sphere" in terms of "the family" and "the home." Thus he wrote, "The health of society rests on the welfare of the home. What, then, will be the outcome if the unmarried multiply; if homes remain childless; if families are homeless; if girls do not know housework; and if men come to distrust the purity of women?"[13]

Although he modified some aspects of his social theory, his belief that the domestic role of women was fundamental to social stability changed very little over time. In *Christianity and the Social Crisis,* Rauschenbusch had taken his examples of working women from tenement life in the cities, but his concern was all working women. When he argued that economic fear was the cause of family instability, he was as concerned with middle-class family life as he was with economics. The relationship between a steady and equitable economy on the one hand, and stable family life on the other, was central to his assessment of social equilibrium.

Women in the World of Men

Walter Rauschenbusch believed that social and economic policy should enable all women to stay home. In *Christianity and the Social Crisis,* he referred to professional women in a tone of patronizing disbelief: "Some educated girls think they prefer the practice of a profession because the dream of unusual success lures them; but when they have had a taste of the wearing routine that prevails in most professions, they turn with longing to the thought of a home of their own."[14] In the gendered world of men like Walter Rauschenbusch, only unfortunate, poverty-stricken immigrant women had to work. To his way of thinking, it was a sign of progress that there was a large group of middle-class women who did not have to work outside the home.

Rauschenbusch rarely wrote directly about the changing roles of women, but when he did, as in an invited article for *Biblical World* in 1913, he reiterated the issues he had posed four years earlier in "The Social Value of Women." "Some Moral Aspects of 'The Woman Movement'" was an account of the social gains and losses he associated with the new status of women. The article described the inability of women to handle public roles in so many ways that it was hardly the vote of confidence in "the woman movement" he claimed in the summary paragraph.[15]

The article was published in the fall of 1913, a year after both political parties and Theodore Roosevelt's "Bull Moose Party" included a woman suffrage plank in their platforms. It was a year that began with a National American Woman Suffrage Association parade down Pennsylvania Avenue the day of Woodrow Wilson's inauguration. It was also a year in which Rauschenbusch heard Roosevelt say that women should have an equal place with men in government and in politics. By this time, Rauschenbusch would have encountered visible evidence of growing support for significant participation of women in public roles, roles that might change the social order even more than suffrage would. Since women could already vote in some states, Rauschenbusch wondered "what new tremolo stops will have to be pulled on the organ of political eloquence to get those votes? Who knows?"[16] His interest was not primarily woman suffrage; it was the larger issue of the effect of women's new roles on the social equilibrium.

The essay was a masterpiece of understatement. Though he did not say that women do not belong in the public sphere, Rauschenbusch cast doubt on their accomplishments to date. He began on a positive note. "Women have arrived—in industry, in education, in politics. They pervade all domains of life, not passively as adjuncts, but with a sense of equal rights and a feeling of new-found destiny." Then he explained why women were not ready for their "new-found destiny." They were immature because of their "semi-seclusion of the past."[17]

He questioned the fitness of women church leaders by observing that women leaders in groups like Christian Science and Theosophy were as authoritarian as Roman Catholics, a sign of social regression. He followed with stories about the difficulty women had supervising domestic help as an example of their inability to handle labor relations. He was critical of the self-righteousness of women who claimed their new roles on the basis of the moral superiority of women, one of the main arguments used by feminists to support suffrage. Warning against "half-truths and illusions," he said that men should believe that women are morally superior, "But it is a different matter when women think so too. They are not better. They are only made in different ways than men."[18]

At the beginning of his article, Rauschenbusch stated that "When a thing is both right and inevitable we might as well accept it and go ahead."[19] However, after delineating the "evils" that accompanied new freedom for women, he concluded, saying, "I believe in the woman's movement and have always supported it. I trust in its ultimate workings. My point is that all who wish it well must be prepared for the inevitable concomitant evils in it and resist them."[20] Since he had said almost nothing positive about women in new roles, his vote of confidence applied primarily to the "ultimate workings" of "the woman movement" in the future. Unlike much of his social theory, there was nothing progressive in his attitude about women in public roles. Here he rehearsed the same criticisms expressed by many churchmen at the time.[21]

Why, then, his claim of support for "the woman movement"? For one thing, he knew and worked with many women involved in social services in Rochester where he lived.[22] He had read and was acquainted with women like Jane

Addams and Vida Scudder who were involved in social movements. Possibly more important, both of his sisters were college graduates. Emma, three years his senior, was the academic star of the family. Unlike Walter, she held an earned advanced degree. Emma was one of the first women to earn a Ph.D. at the University of Bern (1895).[23] Her dissertation on the English feminist Mary Wollstonecraft, a landmark work published as a book in 1898, can still be found in bibliographies.[24] At the time Walter Rauschenbusch wrote the "woman movement" essay his oldest daughter, Winifred, was a freshman at Oberlin College.

In addition to personal reasons, his philosophy of history required him to assess whether the new freedom of this "social revolution" was a sign of higher ethical standards or of social regression. In this article he seems caught between his personal loyalties, his interpretation of social progress in history, and his anxiety about the impact of new roles for women on society.

As Rauschenbusch understood it, the "woman movement" clearly posed a threat to social equilibrium. The article was a warning to men to prepare for the disequilibrium that would follow if more women took on public roles. Rauschenbusch could support the principle of equality for women as he found it in the actions of Jesus. What he could not support was equality for women in public roles like politics, for which, he believed, they lacked experience and moral maturity. He wrote, "If this social change stopped after readjusting the equilibrium of the sexes, it would constitute an epoch in the history of humanity. Every little brother and sister playing together; every man and maiden mating; every father and mother governing a household in common; every man and woman meeting in society would henceforth act differently on account of this great change. But this change is only the beginning of more changes. The emancipation of half the race must release a vast reservoir of stored energy. What will it do and not do?"[25]

Rauschenbusch's qualified support for "the woman movement" was stated more directly in 1914, in a lecture given at Ford Hall in Boston, a year and a half after he wrote "Some Moral Aspects of 'The Woman Movement.'" At Ford Hall his fear that women might become the dominant sex was stated in the form of rhetorical questions: "Will the woman movement stop with equality? Originally woman was dependent on man as the moon revolves around the earth. . . . But is the earth now going to revolve around the moon?" He noted that women had already become the privileged class in education and that, with the power of the vote, they might even have a political advantage over men. Yet he repeated, "I believe in the woman movement . . . in its ultimate working out."[26]

There was a big difference, Rauschenbusch felt, between the ultimate promise of new equalities for women and the effects of new equality in his time. In this lecture he explained why he believed women, as a group, were not yet ready for public leadership roles. "The feminine virtues in the past were largely due to prohibitions imposed by the social institution of the family. Now women are moving out into freedom and that means a severer test . . . the same test that comes to us at the time of adolescence. I feel toward women at large as I feel toward my own boys as they move out into maturity. I feel proud of them, and get anxious for them, and I pray God He may protect their footsteps."[27] In other words, his concern was that women lacked the experience and moral maturity of men when it came to functioning in public roles.

In a question-and-answer session after the lecture, a man asked, "If you give women the right of suffrage in a society where they already have men to support them, don't they get more than equality[?]" "That is exactly the thing I have been trying to point out," replied Rauschenbusch.[28]

Women, Work, and Sexual Morality

Although Rauschenbusch's understanding of gender changed very little, he expressed himself in a variety of ways he thought appropriate to particular audiences. When he discussed women's changing roles for men's groups, he was remarkably direct about sexual temptation. One lecture in particular, "What about the Woman?," must have resonated with the young men of the YMCA, to whom he spoke. According to his records, he gave the lecture at least twenty times between 1902 and 1912. This was a topic of both professional and personal interest to him, as his two oldest children were in their teens toward the end of this decade.

In this lecture Rauschenbusch directly stated his belief, not mentioned later in the *Biblical World* essay, that "no woman comes to perfect womanhood" without the experience of marriage for love and the self-sacrifice of motherhood. These lecture notes contain the best evidence available of his continuing belief that the two spheres are God-ordained because women were biologically designed for childbearing. Woman "braves sickness and travail, knocks at the gates of death for the sake of love. Man assumes the burdens, family cares, the yoke of lifelong labor."[29] In other words, women matured through the experience of marriage and motherhood and men matured through participation in the work world of men. This was a theory of moral development based on the equal but different duties of men and women.

Stating as it did that sex drives worked for the noblest consummation or the deepest abasement known to man, the lecture was a plea to protect the purity of women so they could fulfill their womanhood. Rauschenbusch told a heart-wrenching tale about the ruin of a woman robbed of her purity, then pleaded with men not to take advantage of "inexperienced girls." Even if there were no other consequences, and even if no one else ever knew, she would never be the same again. Only in all-male company did he depict women as socially inexperienced "girls," easily seduced and unusually vulnerable to the influences of liquor, novels, and the theater.

Appealing to patriotism, he stated that American men were the most chivalrous in the whole world and urged them to be men who protected their women at all costs. The lecture included extensive attention to the negative effects of birth control, the debasement of women who fell into prostitution, and the domestic violence sure to follow known acts of adultery. Confiding that there were times in his life when women had deliberately tempted him, he urged the men to give such women the benefit of the doubt and simply ignore them as he had. Rauschenbusch concluded with a favorite theme, the brotherhood of man. "In truth, the brotherhood of man implies that all women are our sisters. When you join in or laugh at smutty stories, answer bold looks, or join in a low estimate of women, you help lower the moral stand and saturate the atmosphere with sensuality." His closing admonition was, "Love a good girl, marry her as soon as conditions permit. Then be faithful to her as you expect her to be."[30]

Rauschenbusch spoke convincingly about the bliss of sexual desire expressed in a good marriage. Walter and Pauline Rauschenbusch regarded their conjugal relationship as a sweet holy union.[31] But in this lecture he was more interested in elaborating on what happened when men gave in to "the ravenous instinct." Describing the "hereditary evils of illegitimate children," he repeated the fear, common at the time, that a tendency to promiscuity could be inherited. After describing the ravages of venereal disease in graphic detail, he suggested that no man would want to pass this on to an innocent child.[32]

It is tempting to wonder if his concern about sexual temptation was excessive. Yet discussions about sexuality in his writing and speaking indicated that he was utterly sincere in his belief that sexual chastity was a mark of ethical progress, that it would betray the sacred trust of God and the human race if men did not guard the purity of women, the guardians of the future of the race. Widespread promiscuity would lead to social regression.

Rauschenbusch believed that his sexual ethic was both Christian and the highest standard in human history. His conviction that social equilibrium depended on maintaining traditional gender roles lay behind everything Rauschenbusch had to say about social change. Throughout his career, he borrowed from various "scientific" theories to make this point. The form changed but the substance did not. The connection he made between economics, sexual morality, and family was stated most directly in "The Righteousness of the Kingdom."

> Everything that hinders the ready formation of marriages is a cause of social corruption. . . . Industrial pressure acts as forcibly as law to diminish marriages. The maximum number of marriages coincides with the minimum price of grain. Those who artificially disturb and depress the industrial prosperity of the people, bear the guilt of checking marriage and driving the sexual impulse to seek illicit means of gratification. Women yield to temptation and in turn become tempters. And so the evil perpetuates itself.[33]

Rauschenbusch was a social prophet who spoke passionately about poor work conditions and unfair wages, about the social effect of unfair labor practices on democracy. He is rightly praised for sensitivity to the plight of working women and children. But it is equally important to appreciate the class assumptions behind his passion, his belief that all women should be able to conform to middle-class gender ideals. The good society, as he understood it, was one where all women would be able to fulfill their God-given destiny as the "mothers of the race." His concern over the negative effects of a large class of working women was vividly expressed in 1907 in *Christianity and the Social Crisis.*

> Our industrial machine has absorbed the functions which women formerly fulfilled in the home, and has drawn them into its hopper because female labor is unorganized and cheap labor. . . . If the burden of maternity is added at the same time, the strain is immense, and is likely to affect the temper and the happiness of the home. It is thus that our civilization prepares its women for the all-important function of motherhood, for on the women of the working class rests the function of bearing and rearing the future citizens of the republic. Individually Americans are more tender of women than any other nation. Collectively we treat them with cruelty and folly.[34]

When Rauschenbusch wrote about "our present economic order" in *Christianizing the Social Order* five years later, he applauded the limitation of female labor to a ten-hour day as "a great moral achievement . . . in the interest of humanity." He saw this as a breakthrough in an inherited "moral point of view" that would eventually make it possible for everyone to conform to the gender roles and family stability he associated with the middle-class.[35]

His conviction about why men should work was the corollary of why women should not work beyond the home. An imbalance in this formula caused social corruption because, as he had explained in the 1890s in "The Righteousness of the Kingdom," it checked "the ready formation of marriages." When people failed to marry, this drove "the sexual impulse to seek illicit means of gratification." The bottom line in his concern about working women was a fear of "the sexual instinct" run amuck. Premarital sex had the potential to undermine the present level of sexual morality and to destroy the social equilibrium.[36]

Women, Higher Education, and Work

Rauschenbusch supported a college education for women at a time when the conventional wisdom was that college "unsexed" women. By the turn of the century, 40 percent of all college undergraduates were women. Only about 25 percent of college-educated women married. Some who married did not become mothers. But whether college education for women was regarded as acceptable or not, social theorists like Rauschenbusch were concerned about social stability if too many women rejected conventional female roles.[37] Exceptions could be tolerated, even admired, but what would happen if the exception became the rule?

It may seem contradictory that Rauschenbusch supported education for women but regarded the entrance of women into the professions as a dubious kind of progress. In *Christianity and the Social Crisis* he wrote that women entering the professions really wanted a home of their own.[38] The reason for this apparent contradiction lay partially in his theory of social equilibrium. In his 1909 speech "The Social Value of Women," he stated that an equal number of boys and girls "is a provision and necessity of nature, like summer-winter, heartbeat and breathing."[39] If the social equilibrium depended on stable families, how could it be possible on a large scale if there were large numbers of unmarried women?

Rauschenbusch supported higher education for women throughout his career as long as it did not interfere with marriage and motherhood. In 1891 he said that women should be educated so they could be equal partners when they married. A woman who could support herself—if it became necessary—would not have to be a "supplicant" at the mercy of her husband for financial support. Yet women should also be educated for their "real work," motherhood and housekeeping, because if they shunned this role, they doomed the race.[40]

In May 1898, Rauschenbusch wrote an eight-page letter to his wife, Pauline, to accompany his will. In it, he devoted more pages to the education of his daughters than he did to the education of his sons. In case he predeceased Pauline, he wanted her to "make cultured and gracious women of them, who will understand noble and beautiful things and thoughts and let their *special,* their *professional* knowledge be in the world of the household and of motherhood [his emphasis]. Perhaps a dozen years from now women will have ceased to chase wandering lights, but if not, counteract those fallacious tendencies all you can in our girls."[41] Although his children were to learn the manual skills first, he assumed that all of his offspring would have the advantage of higher education, which they subsequently did.

By 1907 he described the contribution of educated women to society as genetic in nature. Better-educated, healthier women uplifted the race by bearing more-intelligent, healthier children. Conversely, a social system where the poorest, least-educated women bear the most children must be changed. "Education can only train the gifts with which a child is endowed at birth. The intellectual standard of humanity can be raised only by the propagation of the capable. Our social system causes an unnatural selection of the weak for breeding, and the result is the survival of the unfittest."[42]

In his published writing about women and work, three themes emerge. The first and most prominent is his reasoning about working-class women; their work is acceptable only when it is an economic necessity. Second, it is acceptable for a middle-class woman to work if she is widowed and has children to support. Third, all women should work but only in their own sphere. Rauschenbusch had no tolerance for upper-class women who had never worked. He regarded women who hired others to care for their homes and family as social parasites, turning their husbands into mere moneymakers forced to support their wives' love of luxury.[43] Some of his harshest criticism was aimed at the predatory nature of women who married for money.

Rauschenbusch's commencement address for women graduates at Simmons College in July 1917 indicates that he never changed his opinion that higher education for women would make them better wives and mothers.[44] Simmons was one of the first colleges to offer liberal arts degrees in women's professions: nursing, teaching and library science. Although the United States had entered World War I only three months earlier, Rauschenbusch asked the young women to think about what would happen when men returned from the war. He told them that the loss of men in the war was a threat because it would raise the value of men and lower the value of women.

The imbalance in the ratio of men to women would lead to a surplus of well-educated single women. And what would they do without "that stimulus to their intimate development which the love relation alone can give"? Here again was the belief that women could not mature morally and spiritually without the experience of marriage and motherhood. He reiterated his observation that the balance of gender roles had already changed, and he observed that women were the greatest gainers during the past generation. He did not expect women to "vacate the place into which they stepped while men were fighting." But he was deeply concerned about the inequity between educated women like his audience and men who went to war who would not be their equals educationally. "One of the problems of the future will be the higher education of men."[45]

In a handwritten draft of the address he said that men would come home from the war looking for family life, love, and prosperity but not meaning in life. They would need a "helpmate" to inspire them. But the address as published in the *Simmons Quarterly* reveals that Rauschenbusch dropped a direct appeal to women to do their duty on behalf of their nation and the Kingdom of God and replaced it with an ambiguous warning that they might gain the whole world but lose their souls. "There will be many wrecked existences, but there will be some brave souls who will work out the eternal truths under the pressure of life, and coöperate with God in the salvation of the nations."[46]

At Simmons, he was as careful to avoid direct offense as he had been a year earlier when he wrote that he had always supported the woman movement. He did not tell the women not to seek work in their chosen fields. By 1917 the rigid gender roles of the nineteenth century were no longer backed by social consensus in theory or in practice. Rauschenbusch was a man caught between generations, struggling with the views of his children, which differed from his.[47] He had become more realistic about new public roles for women, but he also admitted that as he looked to the future—especially the aftermath of war—he feared what might happen. He wondered what would happen if women lacked "that stimulus to their intimate development which the love relation alone can give?" He could not imagine a woman without a man becoming a whole human being. By the same token, he had "tried to imagine what it would mean if a fifth of all men could never hope to call any heart of woman their own," and he did not like what he imagined.[48]

Theologians and Gender

Rauschenbusch was born into a society in which there was little ambiguity about acceptable roles and behavior for men and women. Christopher Lasch remarks of this period that "in no other country in the world was the distinction between the genders so uncompromisingly rigid."[49] This was also true of Germany, where Walter Rauschenbusch spent many of his most formative years.

In times of rapid social change, it is not unusual for disappointed liberals to become more conservative, even reactionary, with age. But this was not the case with Rauschenbusch. He was consistent in being a social progressive who was *always* conservative about gender and the social role of family. Belatedly he acknowledged that an adjustment in the balance between the sexes was taking place. He gave limited affirmation to women in public roles if their behavior met his standards of moral and spiritual maturity. Yet, because he never modified his conviction that all women were biologically destined to become mothers, it was impossible for him to imagine a stable society consisting of anything other than married couples with children.

At Simmons he was clear that the world as a man's world was a thing of the past. He declared, "Outside of the home, this world in the past was a man's world; our art and literature, our methods of organization, and our creative intellectual life and science, were man's domain."[50] After World War I he expected further change in the relationships between men and women. Although he did not advocate a return to the past, he expected lives to be "wrecked" if young women could not marry men who were their equals or if men could find no suitable helpmate to inspire them.[51]

The way theologians conceptualize the social and sexual roles of men and women is important because gender is a basic social classification. Gender roles tell people what society expects of them, what they can expect of others. Whether stated or assumed, gender roles are integral to all social theory and social ethics and have additional force among religious people when the claim is made that these roles are God-given, as Rauschenbusch did in both his social theory and his theology. This is why theologians, pastors, and congregations are often more conservative than society in their responses to changing gender roles.

When gender roles begin to shift, it is socially disorienting for everyone. For men like Rauschenbusch who believed that reciprocality in male and female social roles was a sign of "the true social order," women in roles formerly reserved for men created a sense of social disorientation. Theoretically, he considered the "concomitant evils" of this imbalance dangerous. More personally, it posed the possibility that women might become the dominant sex. If women took on the public roles of men, how would that affect men?

Rauschenbusch was a man of his times whose thinking about gender was more the rule than the exception. But, as a progressive social theorist he could have been more receptive to changing roles for women. In 1913, the year he warned about the evils concomitant with women's new social roles, other social gospel leaders were responding in a more constructive way. Shailer Mathews, who also thought women inadequate to their new roles, edited a series of textbooks intended to educate women about their new political responsibilities.[52] The social gospeler Josiah Strong was openly appreciative of work done by women in new public roles and, compared to Rauschenbusch, generous in his citation of women as both writers and leaders in social betterment.[53] Rauschenbusch rarely sounded an unqualified positive note in his remarks about women.

It would be too easy to look at Walter Rauschenbusch and conclude simply that he was a misogynist. It is unfair to expect him to have had thoughts about gender that very few men of his era were capable of thinking. But it is worth pondering why many popular nineteenth- and twentieth-century theologians, liberal as well as conservative, were unable to imagine a world in which the roles of men and women were less rigidly defined.

Notes

1. Betty A. DeBerg, *Ungodly Women: Gender and the First Wave of American Fundamentalism* (Minneapolis: Fortress, 1990), 25.

2. Walter Rauschenbusch, *Christianity and the Social Crisis* (New York: Macmillan, 1907), 272.

3. Walter Rauschenbusch's manuscript "The Righteousness of the Kingdom" was published as *The Righteousness of the Kingdom,* ed. Max L. Stackhouse (Nashville: Abingdon Press, 1968). My citations are from the book. Stackhouse thinks Rauschenbusch may have written the manuscript while in Germany in 1891.

4. Rauschenbusch, *The Righteousness of the Kingdom,* 114–15.

5. Ronald Paul Huff, "Social Christian Clergymen and Feminism during the Progressive Era, 1890–1920" (Ph.D. diss., Union Seminary, 1978), 184–88.

6. Walter Rauschenbusch, "The Social Value of Women," ms., Walter Rauschenbusch Papers, Box 19, Baptist Historical Society, Rochester, New York, 9.

7. Ibid., 8.

8. Ibid., 12.

9. Many assumptions about the relationship of "family" to the social order and economics in the thought of Rauschenbusch were based on the science of his day. Today many of them have been forgotten or, as in the following quote, are considered cultural myths. "The Darwinian female represented the stabler but also the more juvenile form of the species. Despite her own passivity, she played an active role in the establishment of many a spectacular male modification." Anne Fausto-Sterling, *Myths of Gender: Biological Theories about Women and Men* (New York: Basic Books, 1985), 181. These assumptions about women are found in Rauschenbusch and help account for his deep reservations about women in public roles.

10. See Huff, "Social Christian Clergymen," 184–88, 224, for the way Rauschenbusch related the imperatives of a good marriage and a happy family to a healthy America.

11. Rauschenbusch, *Christianity and the Social Crisis,* 271–79.

12. Ibid., 271–72.

13. Ibid., 279.

14. Ibid., 277.

15. Huff, "Social Christian Clergymen," 191–92. Huff says Rauschenbusch thought he was a supporter of the vote for women on the grounds that women had higher morals than men, but he also observes that Rauschenbusch supported women and felt paternalistic toward them, which Huff terms "two opposing feelings."

16. Walter Rauschenbusch, "Some Moral Aspects of 'The Woman Movement,'" *Biblical World* 42 (October 1913): 196.

17. Ibid., 195.

18. Ibid., 197.

19. Ibid., 196.

20. Ibid., 199.

21. See DeBerg, *Ungodly Women,* 106–17, for a detailed discussion of the way fundamentalists treated the subjects of "vulgar young women" and "marital crimes."

22. See Blake McKelvey, "Walter Rauschenbusch's Rochester," *Rochester History* 14, no. 4 (October 1952): 1–17.

23. Walter Rauschenbusch was awarded a doctor of divinity degree in 1902 by his alma mater, the University of Rochester.

24. Paul M. Minus, *Walter Rauschenbusch: American Reformer* (New York: Macmillan, 1988), 72.

25. Rauschenbusch, "Some Moral Aspects of 'The Woman Movement,'" 195–96.

26. "Is the Woman Movement Going to Save Society?" *Ford Hall Folks* 2, no. 28 (April 26, 1914): 4.

27. Ibid.

28. Ibid., 5.

29. Rauschenbusch, "What about the Woman?" 1–2 (my transcription). The notes for this lecture can be found in the Walter Rauschenbusch Papers, Box 21.

30. Ibid., 17–18.

31. Minus, *Walter Rauschenbusch,* 94–96.

32. Rauschenbusch, "What about the Woman?" 13–17.

33. Rauschenbusch, *The Righteousness of the Kingdom,* 224.

34. Rauschenbusch, *Christianity and the Social Crisis,* 277–78.

35. Walter Rauschenbusch, *Christianizing the Social Order* (New York: Macmillan, 1912), 167.

36. Rauschenbusch, *The Righteousness of the Kingdom,* 244.

37. Peter Gabriel Filene, *Him/Her/Self: Sex Roles in Modern America* (New York: Harcourt Brace Jovanovich, 1974), 23–29.

38. Rauschenbusch, *Christianity and the Social Crisis,* 276–77.

39. Rauschenbusch, "The Social Value of Women," 2.

40. Rauschenbusch, *The Righteousness of the Kingdom,* 242–44. Also Huff, "Social Christian Clergymen," 20.

41. Handwritten letter to Pauline E. Rauschenbusch, May 17, 1898, Walter Rauschenbusch Papers, Box 143, 4 (my transcription).

42. Rauschenbusch, *Christianity and the Social Crisis,* 275.

43. This comes, in part, from personal experience. In *Walter Rauschenbusch,* 95, Minus writes of Walter and Pauline Rauschenbusch, "The chief tension between them was occasioned by a chronic shortage of money." It did not help that Pauline was good friends with Laura and John D. Rockefeller and was frequently a visitor in their luxurious home.

44. From the draft for "The Commencement Address," Walter Rauschenbusch Papers, Box 21. He did not say this directly in the speech as published in the *Simmons Quarterly.*

45. Walter Rauschenbusch, "The Issues of Life," *Simmons Quarterly* (July 1917): 6 (first and second quotes), 8 (third quote). A slightly different draft of the address is in Walter Rauschenbusch Papers, Box 21.

46. Ibid., 9.

47. See Christopher H. Evans, "Gender and the Kingdom of God: The Family Values of Walter Rauschenbusch," in *The Social Gospel Today,* ed. Evans (Louisville: Westminster John Knox Press, 2001), 53–66, for an account of the way Rauschenbusch's family life challenged his public view on gender and family.

48. Rauschenbusch, "The Issues of Life," 6.

49. Christopher Lasch, "Woman as Alien," in *The Woman Question in American History,* ed. Barbara Welter (Hinsdale, Ill.: Dryden Press, 1973), 152.

50. Rauschenbusch, "The Issues of Life," 5.

51. Ibid.

52. William D. Lindsey, *Shailer Mathew's Lives of Jesus* (Albany: State University of New York Press, 1997), 48.

53. See the essay in this volume about Josiah Strong by Wendy J. Deichmann Edwards.

CHAPTER 5

The Social Dimensions of Foreign Missions: Emma Rauschenbusch Clough and Social Gospel Ideology

Paul William Harris

The social gospel is indelibly associated in foreign missions with the rising tide of Western imperialism. In an era when the great powers were partitioning Africa and scrambling for concessions in China, many missionaries inevitably regarded "social regeneration" as, in William Hutchison's words, "a moral equivalent for imperialism."[1] Caught up in the fever, mission spokespersons began to see themselves as agents of Western expansionism, not apologetically but with pride. They not only celebrated evidence of religious conversions but also touted their role in the export of Western learning and social practices. The trend was best exemplified by James Dennis's *Christian Missions and Social Progress,* a massive compendium of all the social horrors and moral abominations that Protestant missions could claim to have alleviated.[2] Although religious conservatives were no more distinguished for cultural sensitivity than liberals, it is easy to understand why the influence of the social gospel on missions has not been regarded as distinctly progressive. Indeed, the era is often seen as falling away from earlier efforts, led most prominently by Rufus Anderson, to concentrate on the development of independent native churches unburdened by excess cultural baggage from the West.

However, the social gospel was a complex and multivocal movement, and we should ask whether it also spawned alternatives to these familiar trends. Was there an anti-imperialist voice in foreign missions just as there was at home? Were missionaries, in other words, capable of constructing cultural relations with other peoples that did not replicate the structural inequalities characteristic of imperialistic relations in the political and economic spheres?[3] The challenge was both practical and ideological, necessitating a fundamental shift in their perspective on indigenous clients. Missionaries long accustomed to ethnocentric condemnation of "heathen" moral corruption would have to move toward solidarity with the downtrodden in their struggles for social justice, in the same way that Walter Rauschenbusch and other social gospelers helped to reframe attitudes toward immigrants during the Progressive Era. His sister Emma tried, and her effort, in both its achievements and its shortcomings, is revealing of the missionary enterprise's openness to a recognition of the social dimensions of religious conversion and to acknowledging women as intellectuals. Emma Rauschenbusch Clough sought to broaden the missionary movement's understanding of the social dimensions of missions to include not only the social consequences of conversion, but also its social origins. In her conception, the social gospel ceased to be a threat to the indigenization of Christianity and became a powerful affirmation of the indigenous sources of conversion movements. She affirmed that natives could be effective actors in constructing their own relationship to Christianity, and in so doing she broke with the conventions of missionary propaganda that depicted converts merely as passive recipients of divine light. Yet her insights were never posed as a direct challenge to dominant ideologies and ultimately had a limited impact.

Rauschenbusch Clough's contribution to the ideology of foreign missions rests on two books that grew out of her experience with the American Baptist Telugu Mission in South India. Her own missionary career was rather brief and serves merely as a prelude to her story. While teaching German in the Chicago public schools, she became involved with the Women's Baptist Missionary Society of the West and developed an interest in missionary work. She was accepted for the foreign field in 1882, at age twenty-two, and spent her first weeks in India assisting with *zenana* work in Madras, which involved visiting high-caste women who were otherwise isolated from any contact with Christian teachings.[4]

Visiting Indian women in these zenanas epitomized the slogan of the women's foreign missionary movement: "women's work for women." Women missionaries in this era worked to forge a separate sphere for themselves within the missionary enterprise, and in so doing they added a social dimension to conceptions of "heathenism." The degradation of women in non-Christian lands came to be seen as stemming from social oppression as well as from the natural depravity of the unconverted heart.[5] Emma Rauschenbusch easily fell into step with this project and began to write of "these secluded heathen sisters of ours." In somewhat less condescending tones than those of the typical missionary, she wrote of the Indian women's "air of nobility" and "minds thirsting for knowledge and truth." Yet there were distinct limits to the kind of proto-feminism that characterized the women's missionary movement. Their notion of sisterhood with non-Christian women did not generally entail a sense of shared oppression by gender; rather it was an effort to share the benefits of the exalted social status that American women already possessed.[6] Observing two men boarding a train while carrying a woman covered by a large cloth to prevent anyone's seeing her, Emma reflected upon "how happy I was. I could look any man honestly in the face, and nobody held a cloth over me."[7]

Rauschenbusch's education was just beginning, however. In August 1883 she transferred to Ongole to take charge of the boys' school and a newly organized class for a group of native assistants known as Bible-women. In Ongole, she began her collaboration with John Everett Clough, leader of one of the largest mass-conversion movements in Baptist mission history. The great ingathering had occurred five years earlier, in 1878, during which Clough and his staff had baptized 9,606 converts, almost all of them from the Untouchable Madigas. By 1883, Clough's church in Ongole had over 20,000 members, making it the largest Baptist church in the world.[8] The Madiga conversion movement had made Clough famous, but it had also roused considerable controversy. The mass baptisms had taken place in the wake of the region's worst famine of the century, during which Clough had played a key role in organizing relief work that had saved thousands of Madigas from potential starvation. Many suspected the converts were merely "rice Christians" seeking material assistance, and they criticized Clough for baptizing so many on such slim evidence of genuine conversion.

Fiercely defensive of his work and his converts, Clough had gained a reputation as a difficult colleague who would brook no interference with his methods. However, he had nothing but praise for Rauschenbusch, particularly her work with the Bible-women. Most important, she showed confidence in the women's abilities and displayed it by giving them responsibility for work in their native villages after a fairly short course of instruction. Unfortunately, the work of supervising such a vast enterprise overtaxed the strength of both Clough and Rauschenbusch.[9] Rauschenbusch's arrival afforded Clough a much-needed opportunity for a furlough to America, but he ended up spending most of the time defending his work. When he came to visit President A. H. Strong of Rochester Theological Seminary, one of his leading critics, he stayed with the Rauschenbusch family. Clough succeeded in winning over both Strong and young Walter Rauschenbusch, who very nearly ended up embarking on a missionary career himself.[10]

Following his return to India, Clough again showed signs of wearing himself out, but it was Emma Rauschenbusch whose strength gave way. In December she retired from the mission and began a lifelong battle against depression and ill health. After leaving the mission, Rauschenbusch decided to pursue further education. She studied for a year at Wellesley and then traveled to Europe for postgraduate work. The Germans, however, did not approve of female doctoral students, and she was denied a degree by the universities at both Leipzig and Berlin. One professor told her frankly that had she been a German woman he would not even have let her sit in on his classes. She had better luck with the Swiss, studying first at Zurich before finally completing a dissertation on Mary Wollstonecraft at Bern.[11]

Rauchenbusch's dissertation, which she subsequently published as *A Study of Mary Wollstonecraft and the Rights of Woman*, sought to salvage Wollstonecraft's historical reputation and thereby challenge the perception that women's rights posed a radical threat to the fabric of society. To that end, Rauschenbusch distinguishes between the historical Wollstonecraft and the image of her that was concocted in a posthumous biography by her husband, William Godwin. Rauschenbusch's Wollstonecraft is not, like Godwin himself, an arch-rationalist product of the Enlightenment but is depicted as a Romantic who rejected neither religion, nor the family, nor her essential feminine nature.[12] Wollstonecraft thus becomes a fitting foremother for moderate, evangelical, female reformers like Rauschenbusch herself. Even thus toned down, however, Rauschenbusch's portrait of the pioneer women's rights advocate clearly announced her own feminism.

The difficulty lies in finding any direct connection between Rauschenbusch's feminism and her later writings about missions. Conceivably, her feminism helped Rauschenbusch to overcome smugness about the oppression of women in "heathen" societies by challenging the assumption that evangelical Christianity had put an end to all of that in the West. However, Antoinette Burton has demonstrated that feminists were as steeped in imperial culture as were other Victorians, and they often used the stereotypical "Indian woman" as a negative reference point against which to measure their own progress.[13]

Meanwhile, Clough's first wife, Harriet, died in May 1893. That July Clough made plans to travel to Vienna for treatment of hearing loss, and he seized the occasion to begin a hasty courtship of Emma Rauschenbusch. They arranged to meet in London and were wed on June 23, 1894.[14] Emma Rauschenbusch Clough returned to India, but she no longer had the strength to resume her former labors. Instead, she turned to authorship and research, applying her recently acquired interest in the new science of ethnology to a study of the Madiga conversion movement.

The results were published in 1899 under the title *While Sewing Sandals: Tales of a Telugu Pariah Tribe*. The book is chiefly significant for tracing the roots of the movement to the years before the famine, locating its source in indigenous religious forms. Unlike most missionary propaganda, which credited conversions to the Holy Spirit and the self-denying zeal of missionaries and which celebrated converts only as decontextualized embodiments of Christian virtue, Rauschenbusch Clough credited the Madigas with real agency in the origins of the conversion movement.[15]

The central character in the book is a man by the name of Yerraguntla Periah. Rauschenbusch Clough discovered that, before his conversion, Periah had a rich spiritual history in the world of Hindu *bhakti*, or devotional sects. He had been initiated as a *guru* in a sect founded by the Yogi Pothuluri Virabramham and had contacts in a number of others. Virabramham was said to have taught that there is one God and he is spirit, and to have prophesied an imminent reincarnation of the deity. His chief disciple further prophesied that this reincarnation would result in the abolition of caste. By disregarding caste, these sects had offered the opportunity for Periah and others like him to move beyond the village worship of demons, spirits, and idols and to make contact with the great tradition of Hinduism. The experience must have been both liberating and empowering, and *While Sewing Sandals* makes a convincing argument that this background, combined with the specific parallels between Virabramham's message and that of the Christian missionaries, was crucial to the development of the conversion movement.[16]

Perhaps most important from John Clough's point of view, these sects practiced an ascetic and proselytizing mode that lent itself to evangelizing work under Periah's leadership. Although loath to concede any doctrinal syncretism in the movement, Rauschenbusch Clough strongly affirmed the methodological syncretism in the collaboration between Clough and Periah. Despite illiteracy and only the most rudimentary knowledge of Christianity, Periah began to evangelize immediately following his conversion, taking advantage of village, kinship, and religious ties. Clough was initially prepared to continue the usual practice of centering the Christian community around his own mission compound, but Periah was anxious to continue his work in the manner of the guru. Instead of bringing his converts to Ongole for baptism, he urged Clough to come to his village of Tallakondapaud and establish that as the center of influence for his work. So in January 1867 Clough borrowed a tent and set out on the first of his many tours. For the next several days he conducted a "glorious" series of meetings in Tallakondapaud that culminated in the baptism of twenty-six Madigas. Several of the converts were associates of Periah in the bhakti sects, and the movement spread rapidly among individuals with such backgrounds, many of whom became part of the core group of preachers who formed the vanguard of the conversion movement.[17]

Rauschenbusch Clough's portrayal of the conversion movement thus differed profoundly from conventional missionary propaganda. Typically converts were depicted emerging from the deep moral corruptions of "heathenism." Although it was common to focus on the exemplary deeds of an individual convert, such converts were regarded as exemplary precisely to the extent that their conversion had thoroughly transformed their characters from degradation to sanctification. The effectiveness of their leadership, insofar as they were regarded as leaders, derived not from an organic relationship to their people but from the force of example, passive as a beacon of light shining in the dark. Before he met Emma, John Clough in fact wrote just such a tract, entitled *From Darkness to Light: The Story of a Telugu Convert,* with the predictable result that the convert in question was almost entirely decontextualized.

In addition to this method of village evangelization, the collaboration between Clough and Periah resulted in what became known as the Ongole method of self-support. Clough wanted Periah to undertake full-time evangelizing and was willing to pay him a salary to do so, but Periah preferred the ways of the guru, who customarily received food and perhaps a small gift from those they instructed. This could only be done, however, where the guru was known, and Clough wanted Periah to strike out more widely. Eventually a compromise was reached in which the indigenous practice was largely retained but was supplemented with quarterly payments distributed at meetings in Ongole.[18]

The story of the Ongole method of self-support makes an important point about the relationship between conversion and dependency. It was generally assumed that, until empowered by the genuine operations of the Holy Spirit on their hearts and by the strict tutelage of the missionaries, recent converts would expect the mission to take care of them. Such attitudes underlay the widespread suspicion that Clough's Untouchable converts acted from mercenary motives, and even the Cloughs acknowledged that many of the converts who flocked into the church after the famine were "inclined to resentment because help was not again brought to them."[19] Missionaries therefore typically assumed that it was up to them to develop native churches that would be self-supporting, self-governing, and self-propagating. Converts would have to be taught the necessity of supporting their own ministers, and only as they learned such responsibility could they be entrusted with managing their own affairs. The paradoxical and unhappy result was a policy that sought to raise indigenous churches on foundations constructed by missionaries according to their own Westernized models.

John Clough struggled with such narrow-minded approaches to the issue of self-support throughout his career. As early as 1872, one of his colleagues took advantage of his absence to reorganize the Ongole church on the model of a Home Missionary Society. The native preachers rebelled against the plan because decentralizing the church organization threatened to sever their personal connections to Clough, whom they regarded as their guru.[20] Clough came to resent deeply the endless agitation to push more and more responsibility for supporting preachers and schools onto the poor Madigas, and he often opted to seek funds in America rather than go after the Untouchable Christians "drumming to get money."[21]

Emma Rauschenbusch Clough, for her part, succeeded in demonstrating that self-support, self-propagation, and self-governance could have genuine indigenous roots. As the movement spread and whole groups of Madigas began converting, Christian organization easily fused with the traditional structures of village governance. In their segregated hamlets, or *palems,* a five-man council of elders called a *panchayat* governed Madigas. Following conversion, the panchayats often became church elders as well, forming the basis for group solidarity that strengthened the Christians in the face of persecution from other castes.[22] Imposing a Western model of self-governing, self-supporting, and self-propagating churches on these Baptist communities could not succeed in making them less dependent on the mission. It could succeed only in undermining their strong foundation in indigenous customs.

Clough himself, although a forceful champion of his own work, never articulated a justification for his methods that transcended the constraints of conventional missionary ideology. That justification awaited the publication in 1914 of *Social Christianity in the Orient.* Although written in the first person in the form of an autobiography, the book was actually written not by John Clough but by Emma, and it constitutes her second important contribution to missionary literature. Rauschenbusch Clough constructed the book by integrating her own research on mission history with reminiscences she had gathered from her husband during the two years before his death in 1910.[23]

It was no easy task for Rauschenbusch Clough to merge her own voice into that of her late husband. While in India she had been drawn to theosophy and a belief in reincarnation, and in 1908 she tried to find another retired missionary to take over the project, fearing that her own "heresies" might creep into the narrative.[24] In addition to fusing her voice and that of her spouse, she also faced the challenge of straddling two genres. On the one hand, the book is a fairly conventional piece of missionary hagiography, celebrating the life and accomplishments of a pioneer. On the other, it incorporated a more sociological understanding of missions that pointed toward later studies such as J. Waskom Pickett's *Christian Mass Movements in India.* Rauschenbusch Clough met these challenges by avoiding controversy and subtly integrating her own insights into the narrative.[25]

Pointed opinions are not entirely absent from the narrative, however. On the issue of self-support, for example, *Social Christianity in the Orient* recounts the days of Clough's midwestern youth when "money was poured in from the Eastern states to plant" schools and churches. It concludes, "To me the agitation concerning self-support . . . seemed a violation of an unwritten contract between the missionary societies and the Asiatic people whom they had drawn under their influence and furnished with desires toward a code of life that included education and social betterment."[26] Clough's role, and that of the mission resources he could infuse into the work, was to transform the conversion movement into something larger than another piece of fabric to be added to the patchwork of Indian religions. His task was to provide the vision and the means for socially uplifting the Untouchable converts and making the movement a real force for social change in caste-ridden India.

Rauschenbusch Clough's greatest achievement in *Social Christianity in the Orient* was her success in explaining how the indigenous origins of the conversion movement carried over into a reform program that helped to raise the status of the degraded Madigas. At the heart of the problem lay the social stigma and disabilities imposed on the Untouchable converts by India's caste system. Insofar as opposition to caste implicitly gave a social dimension to Christianization, foreign missions had functioned as a force for social change in India long before the rise of the social gospel. Concerted opposition to caste dated to at least the 1840s, when abolitionist criticism had forced missionary bodies to become sensitive to any compromise with social oppression.[27] However, the issue of caste took on a new dimension during the era of mass movements because mass conversions had the effect of identifying Christianity with particular caste groups. In one sense, for Christianity to become the religion of a particular caste made it less of a threat to the system as a whole. Recent scholars have argued that conversion movements were merely variants of a process known as Sanskritization, in which caste members mobilize as a group to embrace a different ritual mode that they expect will confer higher status on them.[28] For his part, Clough clearly found it easier to live in peaceful coexistence with other caste groups as he came to accept that the Christian movement in his mission was to be a Madiga movement. *Social Christianity in the Orient* recounts, "As the years passed I grew tolerant and often told the caste people, if they could not, or would not, receive Jesus Christ as their Saviour, to serve their own gods faithfully."[29]

Clough's work with the Madigas manifested the social gospel not simply in the sense that it set itself in opposition to social evils, but that it did so in ways that were more sensitive to social context. Like most social gospelers, Clough approached the problem of social reform as a matter of finding a workable middle ground between revolutionary radicalism and doctrinaire conservatism. In the context of foreign missions, that meant fashioning a reform program that opposed caste but did so in solidarity with authentic indigenous aspirations and not by simply imposing radically alien Western norms. *Social Christianity in the Orient* describes a threefold reform program geared toward freeing the Madiga converts from specific degradations associated with their caste status. Because the program consisted of moral injunctions that any missionary might have imposed on converts, it had never been discussed within the American Baptist Missionary Union in any of the voluminous correspondence maintained during Clough's long career. It was Emma Rauschenbusch Clough who brought these precepts to the foreground and in so doing made the point that Christian ethics were not simply means of making converts behave themselves, but also were a vital component of creating a socially dynamic religious movement.

Two of the key Christian tenets in Clough's reform program required converts to abandon idol worship and to keep the Sabbath. Rauschenbusch Clough explains how adherence to these strictures directly challenged the subordinate role of the Madiga converts in village ritual and economic life. Converts understandably aroused the ire of their higher-caste neighbors when they refused to participate in rituals guarding the whole village from the threat of demons and spirits, and they provoked their patrons and employers when they refused to work on Sundays even during the harvest season. When this led to persecution and economic reprisals, the collective solidarity of the converts demonstrated their determination to make Christianity a force against oppression.[30]

The third element of Clough's reform program was somewhat unusual. This was the prohibition against the eating of carrion, or *tsachina mamsamu*. This reform measure clearly derived its power from the convergent symbolic meanings it held for both Madigas and missionaries. Rauschenbusch Clough learned from the Madigas that eating carrion was the root source of their pollution and hence their degradation, and she recounts their legends of how their ancestors had once eaten a dead bullock and brought the curse of Untouchability upon them. To the missionaries, abolishing the practice spoke to the old saw that "cleanliness is next to Godliness," or, as Clough once put it, "no sooner does the inner man become clean, than he sets about making the exterior clean also."[31] So powerful was this belief among the missionaries that the cleanliness of a palem was often taken as a shorthand indicator of the spiritual state of its inhabitants.[32] Clough's autobiography relates, "I sometimes stood before the men and women of a village where they were weak Christians, and . . . I said to them: 'Oh, men! I am not ashamed to be the Guru of poor people, . . . [but] I wonder why God has chosen me to be the Guru of such *dirty* people.'" Tsachina mamsamu thus became the point of contact between the concepts of purity and pollution of the two religious systems. Although it may have derived from mere squeamishness on the part of the missionary, it was, from an Indian point of view, a clear example of a Sanskritizing reform designed to raise the ritual status of the Christians.[33]

While all of this went on unremarked, other controversies preoccupied Clough in his dealings with the American Baptist Missionary Union. Early on he discovered that the higher-caste community would not tolerate the placement of his converts in government schools, and this led as a matter of course to the establishment of a kind of "separate but equal" school system within the mission.[34] Unlike separate-but-equal schools for African Americans, however, mission schools were not any worse than the schools attended by higher-caste students. Committed to the hope of developing an educated native ministry, the mission maintained a high school despite the fact that few converts were prepared to enter it, and they had no trouble recruiting Hindu students to fill out the classes and bring in additional revenue.[35]

These small steps toward integrated schools fused with Clough's other efforts to cultivate good relations with the local high-caste community, and in 1891 members of those castes petitioned the American Baptist Missionary Union to expand Ongole High School and elevate it into a college. Clough brought the matter personally before the home office, and the board responded enthusiastically to this evidence of "the marvellous change in the attitude of high-caste Hindus toward Christianity." However, Clough's colleagues in the field were nearly unanimous in opposing the scheme. Clough's own son-in-law, who had recently joined the mission and was designated to take over as principal of the high school, wrote that "the proposition to establish a college here now for the benefit of the Telugu Christians, appears to me very much as if the Home Missionary Society should propose to establish a university after the model of Johns Hopkins for the benefit of the Negroes in the South or the Indians in the West."[36] Indeed this debate was echoed a few years later by the now familiar controversy over education for African Americans that pitted Booker T. Washington against W. E. B. Du Bois, and the mission did later experiment with industrial education explicitly modeled on the ideas of Washington.

Despite these parallels between the educational challenges faced by Untouchable converts and those confronting racial minorities in America, explicit discussions of race are strikingly absent from *Social Christianity in the Orient.* In this respect, Emma Rauschenbusch Clough was characteristic of too many white social gospelers in America. Missionaries were occasionally more forthright on the subject of race than their counterparts at home. John Clough often judged new missionaries inadequate for the work because they "distrust the whole of the Christians on account of the few, and ask in many ways . . . more than we have a right to expect." When that happens, missionaries "become proud of our race, proud of our face and proud of our grace" and tend to get taken in by "wily . . . flatterers."[37]

Still, in its celebration of a spirit of solidarity with the victims of social caste, its affirmation of indigenous agency, and its respect for diverse cultural forms, Rauschenbusch Clough's work stands in clear contrast to the kind of paternalism that characterized the racial ideology even of white liberals in the United States. Booker T. Washington himself lamented "the disposition on the part of many of our friends to consult *about* the Negro instead of *with*—to work *for* him instead of *with* him."[38] In this regard, as in so much else, Emma Rauschenbusch Clough went further than almost any of her contemporaries. In her introduction to *Social Christianity in the Orient,* she wrote with uncharacteristic candor: "To-day the Hindus realize that they missed an important opportunity while they held aloof from the Pariahs, and allowed them to reach out after better social conditions under the tutelage of the foreign religion. They have reason to fear that the organic connection between high and low has thereby been weakened, and they are now beginning to cope with the problem along lines distinctly oriental. This marks a phase of the onward tread of a nation."[39] Few missionaries would have been so sanguine about a process of national development that made them expendable.[40]

John Clough's successors did not in fact stand aside to make way for this organic process of change. The Madigas' almost mystical reverence for him may have represented a syncretic fusion of Christian charisma and indigenous sectarian traditions, but it also meant that Clough fundamentally could not be replaced as the leader of the mass movement. Faced with the challenge of replacing someone who symbolized the collective aspirations of the Madiga converts as no one else could, his successors often came to regard Clough as an obstacle to efforts aimed at establishing a truly independent Indian Baptist church. To remedy that problem, the American Baptist Telugu Mission turned in the early twentieth century toward a different version of the social gospel, one that sought to foster self-support and self-governance through more technocratic solutions to social problems.

The downside of this trend toward a spirit of professionalism is that the missionary enterprise might in the process have lost the spirit of prophecy that underlay affirmations of solidarity with indigenous aspirations. To effectively distance themselves from imperialism, missionaries could not simply become innovative service providers. They needed to stand alongside the downtrodden in collective struggle. That insight was literally edited out of Emma Rauschenbusch Clough's contribution to mission ideology. In the process of deleting references to past conflicts among the missionaries, she omitted an insightful passage from the final version of *Social Christianity in the Orient:* "There is a good deal to say in favor of the old days of the pioneers, when each man stood for himself, and sought guidance from God, and went ahead. A sort of uniformity has been gained in the Mission . . . , but they are doing it at the heavy cost of a free reaching out, with the exuberance of a vigorous personality."[41] In the end, the social gospel disappointed Emma both in India and at home. As she buried herself in the work of revision, she watched the presidential campaign of 1912 and wrote to her brother Walter that the way the candidates "prayed & used the language of religion . . . makes me feel queer. . . . I am about as jaded in mind & spirit as I can get to be."[42]

On a personal level as well, the years after her return from India in 1910 were difficult ones. She took an apartment near Walter and his family, but her undisguised contempt for Walter's wife, Pauline, placed considerable strain on all her family relationships.[43] Emma's unhappiness was surely related to the lingering effects of ill health brought on by her years in India, but it may also reflect her difficulty in renewing any sense of purpose and vocation as the project of her late husband's autobiography reached completion. In a sense, having taken on the voice of John Clough, she never regained an independent voice of her own. Many veteran returned missionaries experienced problems of adjustment after leaving the mission field, but it seems safe to assume that these problems were compounded for Rauschenbusch Clough by the degree to which she no longer conformed to the norms for either missionaries or women.

When *Social Christianity in the Orient* appeared in 1914, it received overwhelmingly positive reviews, but only because reviewers generally missed the book's more radical implications. The *Springfield, Massachusetts, Republican* expressed a typical reaction when the reviewer described John Clough as "an educational radical to whose point of view the mission world has later advanced."[44] The self-satisfied tone of these reviews must have taken something away from whatever comfort they gave Rauschenbusch Clough. Debate continued about the problem of adjusting foreign missions' methods and policies to fully recognize, respect, and encourage indigenous aspirations and agency, but Rauschenbusch Clough lacked the institutional base or constituency to remain a part of that discussion.[45]

Women like Emma Rauschenbusch Clough (if others there were) continue to be marginalized by history. Historians have done a great deal in recent years to place the history of Progressivism, women's involvement in social reform, and the social gospel in an international perspective.[46] However, this enriched perspective has barely begun to penetrate our understanding of women's role in the social gospel. Clearly, one reason is that the connections being made are almost entirely between the United States and Europe, while for female social gospelers the major international point of reference may well have been the foreign mission field. The interplay of women, foreign missions, and the social gospel offers rich potential for exploring the boundaries of gender and race, but the territory remains largely uncharted.

Notes

1. William R. Hutchison, *Errand to the World: American Protestant Thought and Foreign Missions* (Chicago: University of Chicago Press, 1987), 91.

2. See James S. Dennis, ed., *Christian Missions and Social Progress*, 3 vols. (New York: Fleming H. Revell, 1902).

3. See the discussion in Paul W. Harris, "Cultural Imperialism and American Protestant Missionaries: Collaboration and Dependency in Mid-Nineteenth Century China," *Pacific Historical Review* 60 (August 1991): 309–15.

4. Walther Rauschenbusch, *Leben und Wirken von August Rauschenbusch* (Cleveland: Peter Ritter, 1901), esp. 228; Dores Sharpe, *Walter Rauschenbusch* (New York: Macmillan, 1942), 39, 48.

5. Patricia R. Hill, *The World Their Household: The American Woman's Foreign Mission Movement and Cultural Transformation, 1870–1920* (Ann Arbor: University of Michigan Press, 1985), 46–47, 77, 131–38; R. Pierce Beaver, *All Loves Excelling: American Protestant Women in World Mission* (Grand Rapids: Eerdmans, 1968), 63, 71; Dana L. Robert, *American Women in Mission: A Social History of their Thought and Practice* (Macon, Ga.: Mercer University Press, 1996), 115–16, 128–30.

6. Emma Rauschenbusch, "What I Saw in Zenanas," *Helping Hand* (October 1883): 77; see also Joan Jacobs Brumberg, "Zenanas and Girlless Villages: The Ethnology of American Evangelical Women, 1870–1910," *Journal of American History* 69 (September 1982): 355–58.

7. Letter by Emma Rauschenbusch, March 19, 1883, *Helping Hand* (July 1883): 77.

8. John E. Clough and Emma Rauschenbusch Clough, *Social Christianity in the Orient* (New York: Macmillan, 1914), 287–90; J. Clough letters, June 24 and July 7, 1878, *Baptist Missionary Magazine* (hereafter *BMM*) (September 1878): 348; Clough letter, August 5, 1878, *BMM* (October 1878): 377; Annual Reports of the American Baptist Missionary Union (hereafter ABMU) for 1878–83, *BMM* (July 1879–84).

9. ABMU Annual Reports for 1885–87, *BMM* (July 1886–88); Emma Rauschenbusch Clough, *The Ongole Bible-Women* (Chicago: Cameron, Amberg, 1896); Emma Rauschenbusch, "New Bible-Women," *Helping Hand* (January 1885): 5; Rauschenbusch letters, *Helping Hand* (May 1885): 36, (January 1886): 5, and (April 1886): 29; J. Clough to J. N. Murdock, May 5, 1887, Coonoor, American Baptist Foreign Mission Society correspondence files, American Baptist Historical Society (hereafter ABFMS files).

10. John E. Clough and Emma Rauschenbusch Clough, *Social Christianity* Manuscript and

Correspondence, John E. Clough Papers, American Baptist Historical Society, Rochester, N.Y.; Clough to J. N. Murdock, June 18 and November 22, 1886, ABFMS files; Sharpe, *Walter Rauschenbusch*, 58–59; Murdock to Rauschenbusch, April 19, 1887, with ms. of Rauschenbusch's reply, Rauschenbusch Family Papers, American Baptist Historical Society.

11. Rauschenbusch letter, *Helping Hand* (November 1889): 6; "One of America's Learned Women," Rochester, N.Y., newspaper clipping (1902), Miscellaneous, Clough Papers.

12. Emma Rauschenbusch Clough, *A Study of Mary Wollstonecraft and the Rights of Woman* (London: Longmans, Green, 1898).

13. See Antoinette M. Burton, "The White Woman's Burden: British Feminists and 'The Indian Woman,' 1865–1915," in *Western Women and Imperialism: Complicity and Resistance*, ed. Nupur Chaudhuri and Margaret Strobel (Bloomington: Indiana University Press, 1992), 137–57.

14. *BMM* (August 1893): 387–88; Clough to Duncan, May 22 and July 31, 1894, ABFMS files; John Clough diary, July 10, 1893, April 26, May 2, May 22, and June 23, 1894, Clough Papers.

15. See Emma Rauschenbusch Clough, *While Sewing Sandals: Tales of a Telugu Pariah Tribe* (New York: Fleming H. Revell, 1899), esp. 117–19.

16. One scholar calls the Virabramham sect "a typical example of messianic syncretism" fusing indigenous beliefs with Christian ideas; see Stephen Fuchs, *Rebellious Prophets: A Study of Messianic Movements in Indian Religions* (Bombay: Asia Publishing House, 1965), 260.

17. Clough, *While Sewing Sandals*, 130–98; Clough diary, January 18 and February 2, 1867, Clough Papers; Clough and Clough, *Social Christianity*, 99–105, 139–45, 188–89.

18. Clough and Clough, *Social Christianity*, 105–7, 355–56; see also Alvin Fishman, *Culture Change and the Underprivileged: A Study of Madigas in South India under Christian Guidance* (Madras: Christian Literature Society in India, 1941), 17.

19. Clough and Clough, *Social Christianity*, 261; see also Clough, *While Sewing Sandals*, 296–97.

20. John McLaurin letter, October 5, 1872, *BMM* (January 1873): 22; "The Mission House at Ongole," *BMM* (January 1874): 1.

21. Clough diary, March 7, 1875, Clough Papers.

22. Clough, *While Sewing Sandals*, 191–93.

23. Note by E. R. Clough in Clough and Clough, *Social Christianity* Manuscript and Correspondence, Clough Papers; Clough to Barbour, February 9, 1909, ABFMS files; Clough and Clough, *Social Christianity*, 394–96.

24. Paul M. Minus, *Walter Rauschenbusch: American Reformer* (New York: Macmillan, 1988), 136–37; note by E. R. Clough in Clough and Clough, *Social Christianity* Manuscript and Correspondence, Clough Papers.

25. J. Waskom Pickett, *Christian Mass Movements in India: A Study with Recommendations* (Lucknow: Lucknow Publishing House, 1933); W. B. Boggs to Rauschenbusch Clough, March 5, 1912, and T. S. Barbour to Rauschenbusch Clough, March 23, 1912, Clough and Clough, *Social Christianity* Manuscript and Correspondence, Clough Papers.

26. Clough and Clough, *Social Christianity*, 353–54.

27. Sushil Madhava Pathak, *American Missionaries and Hinduism: A Study of Their Contacts from 1813 to 1910* (Delhi: Munshiram Manoharlal, 1967), 53; Paul W. Harris, *Nothing but Christ: Rufus Anderson and the Ideology of Protestant Foreign Missions* (New York: Oxford University Press, 1999), 89–93.

28. M. N. Srinivas, "Mobility in the Caste System," in *Structure and Change in Indian Society*, ed. Milton Singer and Bernard Cohen (Chicago: Aldine, 1968), 190; Milton Singer, "Between Tradition and Modernity in Madras," *Comparative Studies in Society and History* 13 (April 1971): 163–65; Agehananda Bharati, "Hinduism and Modernization," in *Religion and Change in Contemporary Asia*, ed. Robert F. Spencer (Minneapolis: University of Minnesota Press, 1971), 74.

29. Clough and Clough, *Social Christianity*, 73.

30. Ibid., 147–69; P. Y. Luke and John B. Carman, *Village Christians and Hindu Culture: Study of a Rural Church in Andhra Pradesh, South India* (London: Lutterworth, 1968), 42–43.

31. Clough to Murdock, journal entry for February 19, 1871, ABFMS files (quote); Clough and Clough, *Social Christianity,* 163–64; Fishman, *Culture Change,* 92; Dharma Kumar, *Land and Caste in South India: Agricultural Labour in the Madras Presidency during the Nineteenth Century* (Cambridge: Cambridge University Press, 1965), esp. 180–82.

32. Leslie A. Flemming, "A New Humanity: American Missionaries' Ideals for Women in North India, 1870–1930," in Chaudhuri and Strobel, *Western Women,* 197–98.

33. Clough and Clough, *Social Christianity,* 164–66 (quote, 166).

34. Clough diary, September 1867, Clough Papers; Clough and Clough, *Social Christianity,* 118–21.

35. Paul W. Harris, "Missionaries, Martyrs, and Modernizers: Autobiography and Reform Thought in American Protestant Missions" (Ph.D. diss., University of Michigan, 1986), 440.

36. Ibid., 457 (first quote), 459 (second quote).

37. J. E. Clough, "Some Needs of the Telugu Misison," *BMM* (May 1895): 131–36.

38. Booker T. Washington, quoted in Ralph E. Luker, *The Social Gospel in Black and White: American Racial Reform, 1885–1912* (Chapel Hill: University of North Carolina Press, 1991), 25.

39. Clough and Clough, *Social Christianity,* vii.

40. Examples of such missionaries from subsequent years, who continued to be pilloried for their views, are discussed in Lian Xi, *The Conversion of Missionaries: Liberalism in American Protestant Missions in China, 1907–1932* (University Park: Pennsylvania State University Press, 1997).

41. Clough and Clough, *Social Christianity* Manuscript and Correspondence, Clough Papers.

42. Emma R. Clough to Walter Rauchenbusch, June 26, 1912, Rauschenbusch Family Papers.

43. Minus, *Walter Rauschenbusch,* 136–37, 191.

44. Reviews of *Social Christianity in the Orient,* Clough Papers.

45. Amanda Porterfield, *The Transformation of American Religion: The Story of a Late Twentieth-Century Awakening* (New York: Oxford University Press, 2001), 53–56.

46. See, for example, Daniel T. Rodgers, *Atlantic Crossings: Social Politics in a Progressive Age* (Cambridge, Mass.: Harvard University Press, 1998); James T. Kloppenberg, *Uncertain Victory: Social Democracy and Progressivism in European and American Thought, 1870–1920* (New York: Oxford University Press, 1986); Ian Tyrrell, *Woman's World/Woman's Empire: The Woman's Christian Temperance Union in International Perspective, 1870–1930* (Chapel Hill: University of North Carolina Press, 1991); Seth Koven and Sonya Michel, eds., *Mothers of a New World: Maternalist Politics and the Origins of Welfare States* (New York: Routledge, 1993); Caroline Daley and Melanie Nolan, eds., *Suffrage and Beyond: International Feminist Perspectives* (New York: New York University Press, 1994).

PART 3

Organization and Professionalization of Women's Social Gospel Work

The Woman's Christian Temperance Union in the Pacific Northwest: A Different Side of the Social Gospel

Dale E. Soden

At 3:00 P.M. on March 1, 1915, using four pens, Governor Moses Alexander signed House Bill No. 142 making Idaho a dry state effective January 1, 1916. Governor Alexander gave one pen to his granddaughter and another to the Reverend Will Herwig, president of the Anti-Saloon League. The two other ceremonial pens went to representatives of the North and South Idaho Woman's Christian Temperance Union, Nettie Chipp and Mollie Vance. To commemorate the moment, *Pathé Weekly* took moving pictures for its newsreel and the WCTU women present sang a song to the tune of "It's a Long Way to Tipperary."[1] Idaho had joined Washington and Oregon, which had both passed legislation in 1914 designed to change the social ethos of a region—a region that had been a frontier only a couple of decades earlier.[2]

The successful campaign for prohibition signaled a remarkable triumph for Victorian and Protestant culture in the face of considerable opposition. Of all the groups that participated in this grassroots effort, none played a larger role than the Woman's Christian Temperance Union. For nearly four decades, thousands of women in the Pacific Northwest had fought against "demon rum" by trying to destroy what they hated most—the saloon. But in addition to their temperance battles, the women of the WCTU worked to realize a vision that clearly should be considered part of the social gospel movement. Since the 1870s, women had collectively spent hundreds of thousands of hours planning, organizing, speaking, lobbying, and working on behalf of legislation, public policy, and public awareness regarding social issues that affected not only their own homes and their own children, but their larger communities as well. Until fairly recently, few historians of the social gospel movement have paid much attention to the work of the Woman's Christian Temperance Union in the United States let alone in the Pacific Northwest. Most treatments of the social gospel have focused on white male liberal Protestant ministers in the North and not on the women who found the temperance union an appropriate vehicle to express their vision of social Christianity. In his classic *Rise of the Social Gospel,* Charles Hopkins neglected to mention the WCTU altogether. More recent analysts of the social gospel have been slightly more attentive to the role of women and to the role of the temperance union, but in general, the Woman's Christian Temperance Union has largely been excluded. In studies of the history of the Pacific Northwest, very little has been written about the Woman's Christian Temperance Union.[3]

It is clear that the WCTU reflected a deep commitment toward applying biblical principles to social problems; alcohol reform provided the focal point and galvanized thousands of women. However, as the larger story is pieced together, we see that women in the WCTU across the country and in the Pacific Northwest attempted to bring about significant social change on a number of fronts. From the establishment of town libraries and coffee houses to working for prison reform and higher wages for working women, members of the WCTU attempted to reform society on the basis of a biblical vision for social justice. Women directed intensive lobbying efforts at the state level to ban cigarettes and "impure literature," and they successfully changed the curricula of public schools in order to educate youth about the evils of alcohol. The WCTU exerted significant pressure on legislators to provide social services for unwed mothers. Women throughout the region rallied on behalf of a social vision that attempted to bring into reality God's Kingdom. Even in the Pacific Northwest, the least churched section of the country, women worked tirelessly to influence public policy and the social ethos of the region. While Prohibition ultimately failed to take hold, without question, these efforts influenced hundreds of thousands of lives. Women in the Northwest insisted that the church and the state be concerned for the welfare of families. They combined piety with a commitment to influencing the social structures of the society in order to make these changes.

Besides acknowledging the specific efforts of women in the Pacific Northwest to foster social reform as part of the larger social gospel effort, it is important to recognize the ways in which the WCTU contributed to the broadening of women's roles in the public realm. The activities of the WCTU thrust hundreds of women into leadership positions, which involved public speaking and political lobbying. In so doing, the organization provided opportunities for many women such as Nettie Chipp and Mollie Vance from Idaho to develop both skills and self-confidence in the political arena. Long before these women obtained the right to vote, they played a major role in shaping the political issues of their respective communities. In this way, the WCTU, and, in a broader sense the social gospel, helped to dismantle the ideology of woman's "separate sphere," which was so widely embraced in the nineteenth century.

While the Pacific Northwest spawned a number of utopian and reform movements in the late nineteenth century, few parts of the country presented a greater challenge to the establishment of the WCTU. The region in the 1870s was far from genteel. Rough and bawdy, wild and open, its communities often embodied a Hobbesian state of nature. Young adult males between the ages of twenty and forty constituted approximately 90 percent of the population in most mining or logging camps. Prostitution, gambling, and alcohol abuse naturally were a part of the social ethos of western communities from the very beginning. The saloon was the most visible gathering place of the community. For example, in 1884, Shoshone, Idaho, boasted thirteen saloons and two churches, but neither house of worship had a minister.[4] From Pocatello and Moscow, Idaho, to Ellensburg, Washington, and Grants Pass, Oregon, western social life focused on the saloon and consumption of alcohol.

The historian Norman Clark has convincingly linked the coming of the transcontinental railroads in the Pacific Northwest in the 1880s with the development of serious social problems associated with alcohol. Clark found the situation in the small community of Kiona, Washington, located on the rail line between Walla Walla and Yakima, to be typical: "Kiona had only one saloon, and four hundred railroad workers came in every night and all day Sunday to drink. The saloon was so crowded that citizens of Kiona could hear noise all over town. There was standing-room-only in the saloon, and the dead-drunks were thrown into the back yard like so many soggy sacks to retch there in full view of the townspeople."[5] In 1892, the Presbyterian synod, meeting in Spokane, defined the character of the region: "The territory . . . is peculiarly liable to the ravages of intemperance. The people live under a high state of pressure in their eager rush after wealth, causing often great nervous depression which calls for the dangerous stimulants supplied by intoxicating liquor."[6] The early economic impulses that brought miners, loggers, sailors, and other entrepreneurs to the region contributed to a social environment that challenged Victorian, Christian, and middle-class assumptions about the way life should be lived. It is into this environment that many women felt called to act publicly even though they did not have the right to vote.

The WCTU in the Pacific Northwest grew out of a larger social reform movement that had its origins in the three decades prior to the Civil War. New England provided a fertile ground for a variety of reform movements including temperance in the early nineteenth century. As the midwestern states came into the Union, the desire for temperance reform as well as anti-slavery activity took root. In this era, a variety of temperance organizations began to spring up throughout New England and the Midwest, among them the Daughters of Temperance, which had been established in 1849. Many of these organizations would provide the initial experiences and ultimately the moral vision for significant numbers of women who would migrate to the Pacific Northwest and lead the temperance movement.[7]

The origins of the WCTU can be traced directly to a remarkable national movement known as the Woman's Crusade of 1874. Women across the country marched, sang, and prayed on the premises of local saloons. For example, in March 1874, many women in Portland, Oregon, rallied against the saloons of their community as part of the Woman's Crusade. Dramatically marching into the saloon district, the women challenged proprietors to see the evil of their ways and customers to reform their habits. Although the crusade failed to generate an infrastructure to sustain the activity, many women across the country were inspired to seek political reform.[8]

In the aftermath of the 1874 crusade, delegates met to establish the Woman's Christian Temperance Union with Annie Wittenmyer serving as the first president. She quickly focused her attention on a strict temperance program that emphasized education through evangelical persuasion. However, by the late 1870s, Frances Willard emerged to challenge Wittenmyer on a platform that would broaden the reach of the WCTU into a number of areas beyond temperance. As president, Willard advocated female suffrage, "social purity," and fair treatment of prostitutes and other women in the courts. She urged the adoption of the eight-hour day and a "living wage" for all workers. As Washington Gladden and Walter Rauschenbusch would later articulate it, Willard's theology centered on the belief that individuals should work for the implementation of God's Kingdom on earth. Willard wanted to link the WCTU with the National Prohibition Party. She also pushed the WCTU to become active in child labor issues as well as to advocate for women who were being oppressed in the industrial revolution. Willard's indefatigable spirit and relentless energy helped grow the WCTU membership from approximately 27,000 in 1879 to over 150,000 members by the time of her death in 1898.[9]

Frances Willard played a significant role in the initial organization of the WCTU in the Pacific Northwest. In 1883, four years after being named president of the WCTU, Willard made a trip to California, Oregon, Washington, and Idaho—the latter two still territories. She hoped that her visit would give support to local efforts and also enhance the prospect of turning the WCTU into a truly national organization. Willard energized women wherever she went and helped establish chapters of the WCTU throughout the region. In Portland, the *Oregonian* reported that thousands had to be turned away when Willard spoke. On June 15, 1883, Willard presided over the organization of the first WCTU chapter in Oregon at the First Methodist Episcopal Church. Six days later, Willard spoke in Olympia and made stops in the following days in Tacoma and Seattle.[10] Everywhere she went, Frances Willard spoke before large crowds. In July she worked her way back down the Columbia River and spoke in Walla Walla on July 12. There Willard accepted an invitation to cross the Columbia and speak to a group of women in Lewiston, Idaho. Unfortunately, Willard was barred from speaking due to an outbreak of diphtheria. Because of communication difficulties, however, she believed that the event had been canceled because of opposition to temperance. In a spirit of defiance she forged ahead and met with women in a private residence; as a result the union was established there and officers were elected.[11] She continued her work in eastern Washington in late July and arrived in Spokane Falls on the twenty-third. Inspired by Willard, women in countless communities organized chapters of the WCTU.[12]

Other women such as Mary Bynon Reese followed Willard into the Pacific Northwest and took up the cause. Reese was born in Allegheny, Pennsylvania, in 1832. In 1874 she found herself caught up in the Woman's Crusade and was arrested with thirty-two other women. Appointed to be a national organizer, Reese traveled to the Pacific Northwest in 1886 and began organizing local unions. She spoke to Nez Perce Indians through an interpreter, and she met with lumbermen in their camps. Reese estimated that she traveled over six thousand miles, "hundreds of which were by wagon, stage and private conveyance, some by canoe with the Indians, and some on horseback through otherwise inaccessible places."[13] Selected as the honorary president of the West Washington WCTU, Reese remained in the Seattle area until her death in 1908. Through the efforts of women like Mary Reese, the WCTU became the strongest woman's organization in the Pacific Northwest.

Two other individuals, Lucia Faxon Additon and Narcissa White Kinney, gained leadership training and opportunities in the public arena from the WCTU long before women achieved the right to vote. Additon lived in Lents, Oregon, and became a leader in the industrial department of the WCTU. A member of the American Academy of Social and Political Science, she wrote extensively and lectured nationwide on issues of labor legislation. In the first decade of the twentieth century, she frequently visited factories and sweatshops across the country. One observer commented that she "has on her tongue's end sermon after sermon on the subject [of sweatshops] that should be thundered into the ears of men of influence until they could find no rest for the body or soul until the evil is abolished."[14] Narcissa White Kenney first became involved in the WCTU in Pennsylvania and by the 1880s became a national lecturer for the organization. She moved to Oregon in 1888 and worked tirelessly to establish community libraries, summer schools, and local Chautauquas. By 1894 she was elected president of the Oregon WCTU and served in that capacity until her death in 1899.[15]

During the late nineteenth and early twentieth centuries, WCTU chapters developed in virtually every county in the three northwest states. Considerable effort went into building a sense of community and purpose around a larger social vision. Taking their lead from the examples set across the country, women in the Pacific Northwest busied themselves with devotional meetings, public lectures, and apron sales to raise money.[16]

Several incidents represent the activities that women undertook to better their world. For example, in 1901, Mrs. H. A. Elder, a local leader of the Temperance Union in Dayton, Washington, testified in a trial on the violation of the Sunday closing laws. She described in detail the way in which temperance women had decided to confront directly the local saloon proprietors who were openly flouting the law. Elder suggests the courage that this must have required because she reported that the women specifically asked the sheriff to protect them. However, apparently he would do so only from a discreet distance. Undaunted, the women made their way to the saloon and found the front door locked; more determined than ever, the women went around to the back, opened the door, and announced that they were there to distribute literature. "In the Columbia [a saloon] we saw men sitting at tables with funny round things in front of them that some one said were poker chips. One bartender hastily snatched empty beer mugs off the bar when he saw us enter, but we saw enough in every case to get sufficient evidence."[17] Apparently the women left their literature and exited without further incident.

Women also organized essay and oratorical contests. These competitions were perhaps less dramatic than the visits to saloons, but they were vital to the development of the women's sense of responsibility and their rightful place in the public sphere. Spokane's daily newspaper, the *Spokesman-Review,* described how much effort went into making these contests significant social events. In one typical case the competition took place at a local church. The organist played a vigorous march as four contestants, each having won a gold or silver medal in previous competitions, proceeded to their places on the platform. After the invocation, one of the women in the WCTU read Psalm 9. Following a vocal solo, a local family played music on the organ, violin, guitar, and mandolin. All four contestants delivered what were described as superb oratorical performances on topics related to temperance and prohibition. Eleven-year-old Charley Mills drew particular praise for his oration, "You Can Stop It if You Will." After the judges deliberated for a half hour, they declared the evening's winner to be Olga Giles for her address entitled "The Martyred Mother."[18] Nearly twenty years later, the 1923 annual report for the Pierce County WCTU in Washington State estimated that for at least ten years prior to the adoption of the Eighteenth Amendment, school children in that county had written more than three thousand essays per year on the harmful effects of alcohol on the human body. Such efforts extended to other social topics as well. The antinarcotic arm of the WCTU remained exceptionally active in the 1920s. The WCTU continued to circulate in public schools copies of the state's tobacco laws. It was reported in 1923 that nineteen Sunday schools had observed anti-cigarette day and that essay contests and traditional oratory contests still proved popular. In that same year, Pierce County organized sixteen public speaking events; a staggering 8,675 temperance essays were submitted throughout the public schools in various competitions throughout the state in 1923.[19]

It was electioneering that pushed women into the public sphere as never before. Year after year from the 1890s on, women throughout the Pacific Northwest organized to fight for candidates and legislation that served their view of God's Kingdom. In Seattle in 1914, the WCTU sponsored "committees of 100" comprised of men and women in business. Working with the Anti-Saloon League, local churches, and local grange halls, the WCTU helped organize billboard campaigns, musical performances, speakers, parades of automobiles, brass bands, and hundreds of young people who marched with torches at night on behalf of Prohibition. Without question, the critical elections of 1914 succeeded because of the efforts of women in general and more specifically the women in the temperance union. In fact a higher percentage of voters (94.6 percent) participated in the 1914 election in Washington State than ever before or since.[20]

If the WCTU encouraged women to break down the separate spheres of influence that had been a part of the Victorian world, the motivation for doing so was a desire for justice that was rooted in the social gospel. Passionate about the principle of equality and committed to a moral vision based on a biblical view of justice, women in the WCTU believed that the eradication of alcohol would lead to a better world. WCTU members composed songs that were intended to inspire a vision of justice and convey a picture of the deep frustrations experienced by women regarding the state of society. The official Idaho state WCTU song expressed a hopeful picture of the future that could be gained if both men and women would commit themselves to changing the state laws. The following verse was typical:

> The drink curse has been doomed at last, Idaho, my Idaho.
> And Satan's ranks are falling fast,
> Idaho, my Idaho.
> Thy people brave have met the foe,
> The Cause is theirs, they fully know,
> And now they say saloons must go Idaho, my Idaho.[21]

In one of the many poems that appeared in publications throughout the region, anger, despair, and social challenge are evident. In words that remind one of the great folk songs of social protest, WCTU members exhorted society to take up the cause.

WHAT WILL BECOME OF OUR CHILDREN

Down in the hell of the city retreat,
Voiced in the jargons of alley and street,
Rum-ridden millions the question repeat,
    What will become of our children?
Born in the wedlock of passion and drink,
Sin-set and sick ere they learn how to think,
Damned to defeat from the cradle's whit brink,
    What will become of our children?
Slaving for sustenance others should earn,
Buying with blood what the dramshops will burn,
Robbed of their birthright to play and to learn,
    What will become of our children?[22]

The WCTU's broader social vision is less well acknowledged than is its direct temperance work. In the last two decades of the nineteenth century, the WCTU developed a remarkable social agenda as well as an organizational infrastructure that affected almost every community in the Pacific Northwest. Interested not only in issues pertinent to women, children, and the home, the WCTU extended its vision into the realms of public health, education, labor, and prison conditions. In doing so, the organization anticipated many of the efforts associated with the social gospel movement and the Progressive period. The connections between these movements remain to be studied.

The WCTU encouraged local chapters to organize themselves into specific departments that would address particular social issues. While not all local WCTU chapters developed the same number of departments, the minutes of these chapters reflect the breadth of their concerns, including press work, social purity, children's work, railroad work, hygiene and heredity, flower mission, temperance and literature, mothers' meetings, the "Y" and parlor meetings, legislative work, suppression of impure literature, evangelistic work, scientific temperance instruction, and prison and jail work.

Like most leaders within the social gospel movement, strategists in the WCTU, substantially influenced by Frances Willard, used a combination of moral suasion and legislative reform. The first approach utilized lectures, sermons, tracts, rational argument, and pleas to the conscience in order to modify mostly male behavior. Women believed fervently in their mission to change the way in which young men and women thought about alcohol specifically and moral purity in general. It was estimated that in 1889, the Oregon WCTU distributed as many as 150,000 pieces of literature at fairs and other gatherings.[23] In LaGrande, Oregon, the WCTU raised a thousand dollars to create a drinking fountain in the center of the city.[24] Many women worked long hours to establish reading rooms in their communities that might help young men thoughtfully reflect on the choices they could make regarding their behavior and moral responsibilities.

Many of these reading rooms evolved into some of the first libraries in small towns across the Pacific Northwest. For example, in 1888 the Boise, Idaho, WCTU proudly opened the first library in the city.[25]

In some communities, WCTU women organized the first kindergartens to help working women care for their children. They also worked to establish reform schools for juvenile delinquents. The Coffee Club proved to be a popular idea in a number of towns throughout the region as women sought to provide an alternative to the saloon for young men looking for a social gathering place. Many local temperance unions worked closely with local law enforcement officials in order to be able to speak to prisoners. Women presented conversion to Christianity as the alternative to a life ruined by drink.

In addition to trying to persuade young men that they should become Christians or at the least change their behavior, WCTU women sought to help young women who were alone or vulnerable to the perils of the city. In many communities, WCTU women initiated the "noon rest," in which they provided help and respite for any woman who was stranded in the city.[26] The WCTU often organized volunteers to meet young women at the railway stations who were in need of assistance. In Spokane, in 1909, Ida Crippen, the superintendent of the eastern Washington WCTU, implored a group of women to take up rescue work among young girls. She said, "Every Christian woman can be a power in the uplifting of her family and neighborhood."[27] In 1913, the WCTU intensified its lobbying efforts on behalf of higher wages for working girls. In that year, the Oregon state president, Ada Wallace Unruh, attempted to live on the four dollars per week that was commonly accepted as the average wage. She found it virtually impossible to survive on such a low wage and argued that there was a "logical relationship between hunger and lack of moral courage."[28] The Portland WCTU lobbied the city to provide a female matron in the local jail to help protect women who might be vulnerable to male prisoners and prison officials.[29] "Mothers' Meetings" were extremely popular throughout the region. Held monthly, the meetings focused on problems associated with raising children. The WCTU chapters frequently spoke out against impure literature and moving pictures and called cigarettes "one of the most serious preventatives to the purity of the youth of our land."[30] In fact, in 1908 the chapter in western Washington intensively lobbied for legislation to raise the age from twelve to eighteen before one could purchase cigarettes.[31]

The WCTU was particularly well known for its commitment to providing homes and shelter for women with children. In 1888 in Portland, for example, the WCTU organized what was known as the Baby Home. The home evolved into a "Refuge Home" for single mothers. According to one contemporary observer, "It offers the shelter of a Christian home—the safeguard of Christian care—to the unfortunate class to whose rescue this enterprise stands committed. This institution is not a reform school; it is not a hospital, and yet in its work for the reformation of lost womanhood it must include these in its ministries.

It does endeavor to guide and control young girls early abandoned to the chance companionship of the street; it does care for the necessities of maternity and helpless infancy born to an inheritance of sin and shame."[32] Lobbying efforts paid off when the state awarded five thousand dollars over a two-year period to the WCTU to help establish the home.[33] In 1922, the Portland chapter of the WCTU established the Children's Farm Home near Corvallis, Oregon. The home provided a place of refuge for needy and abandoned children. By the spring of 1926, five cottages had been constructed; for decades the children's home remained a source of pride for the WCTU.[34]

The Central Portland Union established what was known as the Woman's Exchange and a few years later initiated the Industrial Home, which had a kindergarten, day nursery, and sewing school to support working women. The historian Susan Hincken estimated that in 1905, the Oregon WCTU had distributed 5,000 plants and floral arrangements, 170 items of clothing, plus food. By 1913, the total numbers of items distributed had risen to 13,961 floral gifts, 7,789 pounds of food, and 2,634 garments.[35]

Perhaps what distinguishes the work of the WCTU in the Pacific Northwest from that in other parts of the country is the degree to which women worked with groups hostile to their message. Women in the Pacific Northwest attempted to engage miners, lumbermen, railroad workers, soldiers, and sailors with their message of temperance.[36] For example, the efforts to change the behavior of lumbermen often required the women to go directly into the camps. The county superintendent for Grays Harbor, Washington, "made 50 visits to men and boys from mills and camps who were sick in Hoquiam [Washington] hospital. She distributed 5,000 pages of literature, English and foreign. She gave out four foreign Bibles and nine English testaments. She circulated a small library of nine books to lumbermen, visited two camps . . . [and] gave lodging to seven men leaving the hospital."[37] One report estimated that over 21,000 seamen a year came though Puget Sound ports and the WCTU responded by providing reading material as well as opening their homes to the sailors in an effort to provide a healthy environment.[38] In the 1912 report on work among railway men, it was estimated that the fourteen Oregon temperance unions had distributed more than 3,500 pages of literature and handed out over 300 Bibles.[39] Over the years, the efforts of the WCTU focused more on social welfare activities: caring for the sick and poor and feeding the hungry. Lectures in native tongues directed the message of prohibition and a redeemed life toward the immigrant.

Like many advocates of the social gospel, the WCTU focused intense energy on the state legislatures in order to change countless laws with social implications. Women gathered petitions and developed sophisticated lobbying techniques. Pacific Northwest legislators were besieged by WCTU proposals for age-of-consent laws, child labor laws, an anti-polygamy bill, anti-cigarette legislation, refuge homes, schools for delinquent girls, provisions for female jurors, and, naturally, temperance and suffrage legislation.[40]

One of the most notable successes was the effort to pass legislation requiring school districts to teach what was known as a scientific temperance curriculum. The purpose of such legislation was to instruct students about the nature of alcoholic drinks and other narcotics. Advocates asserted that young men and women needed to learn about the human anatomy in such a way as to understand the impact of alcohol on the body and to gain a moral framework that led to abstinence. Proponents urged that teachers be required to pass an examination on the subject and that the curriculum be taught as thoroughly and diligently as other subjects.

Led at the national level by Mary Hunt, the WCTU's national superintendent for Scientific Temperance Instruction, the movement swept the country in the mid-1880s. Hundreds of thousands of Americans debated the merits of temperance education and in the end, every state in the union approved legislation.[41] In the Pacific Northwest, legislation mandating temperance instruction passed first in 1885 in Oregon and then in Washington and Idaho after WCTU women had circulated hundreds of petitions, sponsored lectures, and kept the issue alive in the press with letters to the editor.[42]

The scientific temperance movement stimulated concern about a number of other health issues associated with the public schools. Women from the WCTU raised awareness about contaminated food; school playground supervision; visits by district health officers, nurses, and dentists; and even designing schools to provide increased ventilation, access to natural light, access to nonalcoholic medicines, and separate gathering rooms during inclement weather.[43]

Ultimately, problems of enforcement led to diminished enthusiasm for making temperance a permanent part of the public school curriculum. However, as Edison Putnam asserted in his study of Prohibition in Idaho, "The significance of the accomplishment is easy to overlook, yet the children who grew to maturity under the influence of temperance education ultimately led Idaho into the prohibitionist camp in the following generation!"[44] Norman Clark drew much the same conclusion about the effect in Washington State. Clark asserted that "when the people of Washington voted for antidrink measures in 1914, 1916, and 1918, they had been exposed to over three decades of formalized, official antidrink instruction."[45]

The great belief that an element of God's Kingdom would come into being with the prohibition of alcohol proved illusory. Prohibition proved unworkable over the course of the next several decades. However, as indicated above, the impact of the WCTU extended well beyond the issue of alcohol reform. In addition, the movement of hundreds of women from the private sphere to the public sphere, while not an explicit objective of the social gospel, must be seen as a significant result of the WCTU's efforts. Without question, thousands of women lobbied, marched, mobilized, and engaged issues of public policy as never before.

The WCTU in the Pacific Northwest appears to have had a course of impact similar to that in other parts of the country. However, it is hard to imagine a more difficult environment or one with more obstacles toward organization. From obdurate miners, lumbermen, and sailors to the lack of an established institutional church, the Pacific Northwest posed particularly difficult challenges to the mission of women in the union. At the time in which Frances Willard came to the region in the 1880s, the area was in many ways a frontier. Yet in spite of these obstacles, women for several decades were motivated by a view of God's Kingdom that led them to try to persuade their fellow citizens to change the habits of their lives and to attempt to alter the political and social structures of their communities. The efforts of these women to implement a biblical view of justice are an important part of the story of the social gospel as well as of the history of the Pacific Northwest.

Notes

1. *Idaho Statesman,* March 2, 1915.

2. Norman Clark, *The Dry Years: Prohibition and Social Change in Washington* (Seattle: University of Washington Press, 1965), 128–43; Edison Putnam, "The Prohibition Movement in Idaho, 1863–1934" (Ph.D. diss., University of Idaho, 1979); John E. Caswell, "The Prohibition Movement in Oregon, Part 2, 1904–1915," *Oregon Historical Quarterly* 40 (March 1939): 76–78.

3. Charles Hopkins, *The Rise of the Social Gospel in American Protestantism, 1865–1915* (New Haven: Yale University Press, 1940); Ronald C. White Jr. and C. Howard Hopkins, eds., *The Social Gospel: Religion and Reform in Changing America* (Philadelphia: Temple University Press, 1976); Sandra Haarsager, *Organized Womanhood: Cultural Politics in the Pacific Northwest, 1840–1920* (Norman: University of Oklahoma Press, 1997), 61–99.

4. Richard White, *"It's Your Misfortune and None of My Own": A New History of the American West* (Norman: University of Oklahoma Press, 1991), 298–327; Carlos Schwantes, *The Pacific Northwest: An Interpretive History* (Lincoln: University of Nebraska Press, 1989), 162–206; Putnam, "The Prohibition Movement in Idaho," 71.

5. Clark, *The Dry Years,* 59–60.

6. Lucy Switzer, "Annual Address," Directory of the Woman's Christian Temperance Unions of Eastern Washington, 1892–93, Washington State Historical Society, Tacoma, Washington.

7. Haarsager, *Organized Womanhood,* 64.

8. John E. Caswell, "The Prohibition Movement in Oregon, Part 1, 1836–1904," *Oregon Historical Quarterly* 39 (March 1938): 235–61; Malcolm H. Clark Jr., "The War on the Webfoot Saloon," *Oregon Historical Quarterly* 58 (March 1957): 4–11; Frances Fuller Victor, *The Women's War on Whiskey; Or, Crusading in Portland* (Portland, Ore.: Geo. H. Himes, 1874); Jack S. Blocker Jr., *"Give to the Winds Thy Fears": The Woman's Temperance Crusade, 1873–1874* (Westport, Conn.: Greenwood, 1985), 7–26.

9. Sharon Anne Cook, *"Through Sunshine and Shadow": The Woman's Christian Temperance Union, Evangelicalism, and Reform in Ontario, 1874–1930* (Montreal: McGill-Queen's University Press, 1995), 32; Ruth Bordin, *Frances Willard: A Biography* (Chapel Hill: University of North Carolina Press, 1986); Nancy G. Garner, "The Woman's Christian Temperance Union: A Woman's Branch of American Protestantism," in *Re-Forming the Center: American Protestantism, 1900 to the Present,* ed. Douglas Jacobsen and William Vance Trollinger Jr. (Grand Rapids: Eerdmans, 1998), 271–83.

10. Olympia Minutes, 1883–1897, Woman's Christian Temperance Union, Washington State Historical Society, Tacoma, Washington.

11. Putnam, "The Prohibition Movement in Idaho," 74.

12. Lucy Gearhart, "The Beginning of the Woman's Christian Temperance Union of Western Washington, 1883–1887," Box 2, Lucy Gearhart Papers, University of Washington Libraries, Seattle, Washington; Woman's Christian Temperance Union, Eastern Washington Chapter Papers, Box 1, Eastern Washington Historical Society, Spokane, Washington.

13. *White Ribbon Bulletin: Official Organ of the Western Washington W.C.T.U.*, March 1908, Washington State Historical Society, Tacoma, Washington.

14. Clipping Scrapbook 86, p. 40 (quote), Clipping Scrapbook 73, p. 89, Oregon Historical Society, Portland, Oregon.

15. "Narcissa White Kenney," *Portrait and Biographical Record of Portland and Vicinity, Oregon* (Chicago: Chapman Publishing Company, 1903), 121–22.

16. Minute Book, 1892, WCTU Puyallup, Washington, Washington State Historical Society, Tacoma, Washington.

17. *Spokesman-Review,* July 22, 1901.

18. Ibid., July 14, 1901.

19. Gearhart Papers, Box 1, 1923 Annual Report of WCTU Pierce County, Washington.

20. N. Clark, *The Dry Years,* 113.

21. *Gem State Signal, Official Organ of the South Idaho W.C.T.U.,* March 1911, Idaho State Historical Society, Boise, Idaho.

22. Ibid., June 1912.

23. Susan Hincken, "The Woman's Christian Temperance Union of Oregon, 1880–1916" (M.A. thesis, University of Portland, 1987), 43.

24. *Spokesman Review,* September 4, 1904.

25. Putnam, "The Prohibition Movement in Idaho," 88.

26. Lucia Additon, *Twenty Eventful Years of the Oregon Woman's Christian Temperance Union, 1880–1900* (Portland: Gotshall Printing Co., 1904), 49.

27. *Spokesman Review,* March 17, 1909.

28. Ada Unruh, quoted in Hincken, "The Woman's Christian Temperance Union of Oregon," 93.

29. Kathryn Baker, "Struggle against Licentiousness: The Social Purity Movement in Portland Oregon" (B.A. thesis, Reed College, 1974), 49.

30. Ibid., 42.

31. *White Ribbon Bulletin* (Western Washington), November 1908.

32. Additon, *Twenty Eventful Years,* 71–72.

33. Baker, "Struggle against Licentiousness," 41.

34. Woman's Christian Temperance Union of Oregon, WCTU Yearbook, 1982, Oregon Historical Society, Portland, Oregon.

35. Hincken, "The Woman's Christian Temperance Union of Oregon," 49.

36. Additon, *Twenty Eventful Years,* 53.

37. *White Ribbon Bulletin* (Western Washington), February 1910.

38. "Eleventh Annual Report of the Woman's Christian Temperance Union of Western Washington—1894," Washington State Historical Society, Tacoma, Washington.

39. Woman's Christian Temperance Union, National Convention Report, Box 6, p. 294, Oregon Historical Society, Portland, Oregon.

40. *Spokesman Review,* March 9, 1916.

41. Jonathan Zimmerman, "'The Queen of the Lobby': Mary Hunt, Scientific Temperance, and the Dilemma of Democratic Education in America, 1879–1906," *History of Education Quarterly* 32 (Spring 1992): 1–30.

42. Putnam, "The Prohibition Movement in Idaho," 261; Hincken, "The Woman's Christian Temperance Union of Oregon," 51.

43. Cook, *"Through Sunshine and Shadow,"* 117.

44. Putnam, "The Prohibition Movement in Idaho," 82.

45. N. Clark, *The Dry Years,* 36.

CHAPTER 7

Shaping a Civic Profession: Mary Richmond, the Social Gospel, and Social Work

Elizabeth N. Agnew

In his book *Work and Integrity: The Crisis and Promise of Professionalism in America,* the philosopher William M. Sullivan traces to early twentieth-century progressivism a model of professionalism that he finds compelling. According to Sullivan, one pillar of progressivism was the notion of a professional career as a "design for living that promised to give individual occupational achievement moral meaning through responsible participation in a civic life." Civic professionals "combin[ed] something of religious dedication with the civic ideals of traditional humanism and the scientific virtues."[1] Sullivan develops his thesis about this strand of American professionalism through an examination of the work of Jane Addams, John Dewey, Louis Brandeis, and Herbert Croly, among others. Another exemplar of civic professionalism, whom Sullivan does not discuss, is Mary E. Richmond (1861–1928), a leader in the nineteenth-century charity organization movement and in the creation of professional social work in the early twentieth century. Like those whose work Sullivan does discuss, Mary Richmond exemplified a "socially responsible sense of calling," characterized by a dual commitment to scientific expertise and citizen participation in a morally and politically integrated civic life.[2]

During her nearly forty-year career as a practical theorist, teacher, and administrator, Mary Richmond drew both explicitly and implicitly on ideals and principles of the social gospel in formulating a civic conception of social work. According to the historian Robert Handy, the social gospel represented a progressive, Christian theological response to the challenges of industrialization, urbanization, and immigration in late nineteenth-century America. Mediating between a conservative, individually oriented strain of social Christianity and radical expressions of Christian socialism, social gospel advocates combined an emphasis on individual responsibility with a commitment to social reform. Their middle-ground approach rested on their beliefs in the social nature of sin and salvation, the centrality of Jesus' teachings, the immanence of God, and the human potential to usher in the Kingdom of God on earth. Handy notes that much of the new social gospel theology was evangelical, but that not all evangelical Christians adopted a progressive social orientation. Conversely, evidence suggests that non-evangelical traditions, such as the Unitarian tradition to which Mary Richmond owed a primary debt, often embodied the tenets and post-millennial outlook of the social gospel.[3]

While social gospel adherents sought to address systemic, social manifestations of sin in light of a "bridge theology" that linked historical Christianity with modern social science, the scholar of religion William McGuire King discusses their simultaneous concern with the experience of individuals. In particular, social gospel theorists focused on the issue of personal regeneration and "the emergence and preservation of meaning in the self."[4] For Mary Richmond, both aspects of the new theology were important. The social gospel's social orientation encouraged Richmond to rethink individually oriented, nineteenth-century practices of charity and to introduce into the emerging profession of "applied philanthropy" a strong commitment to social reform. At the same time, the social gospel's emphasis on individual experience provided her a critical vantage point on the emerging professional ethos of the early twentieth century. The belief in the inextricable link between service and self-realization informed Richmond's critique of bureaucratic, highly specialized, professional work and inspired her holistic model in which casework and social reform, together, fostered the well-being of providers and recipients of service.

Richmond's formulation of social work practices reflected her indebtedness not only to social gospel principles, but also to traditional gender norms. On a personal level, Richmond's accomplishments were testimony to her perseverance and leadership as a woman working primarily with university-trained men in the fields of charity and social work. Richmond channeled her energy into public work, and she neither married nor was a mother. Despite her personal experience, however, Richmond publicly espoused traditional views on women and work. She disavowed the importance of woman suffrage and equal rights, and throughout her career she remained largely indebted to a Victorian ideal of women as dependent wives and mothers. This ideal informed her expectations of women as both recipients and providers of charitable assistance. Like many progressive reformers, Richmond promoted a maternalist ethic, which upheld women's moral, maternal responsibility to care for women and children in need, while also strengthening traditional families.[5] Richmond invoked this ethic to encourage and defend women's participation in trained charitable work, but she maintained through most of her career that women, and particularly married women, should undertake such work as trained volunteers, not as paid professionals. The maternalist ethic complemented the social gospel conviction that Victorian family gender norms would characterize the coming Kingdom of God. Together, the secular and religious strands of Richmond's gender ideology informed her critique of the masculine norms of impersonal, scientific expertise in professional work. Over time, they also helped to increase female participation in social work, albeit while contributing to women's diminished authority and remuneration in the profession.[6]

In developing these claims, I begin with a brief overview of Richmond's early life and her formative encounter with the social gospel in the context of the Unitarian Church. I then discuss her evolving views on religious charity and professional training, including her response to Abraham Flexner's 1915 report on social work's status as a profession. William Sullivan attributes the demise of civic professionalism in the 1920s to the accelerating bureaucratization and specialization of society and work in the wake of World War I. In my conclusion, I discuss Richmond's response to these developments and illustrate her commitment to sustaining a civic vision of social work.

A Life of Preparation

The path by which Mary Richmond came to her professional work distinguished her from many other female reformers of the Progressive Era. These reformers, who were often from middle- and upper-class backgrounds, were of the first generation of women to attend college and were motivated by a mixture of noblesse oblige, gender consciousness, and a desire to find constructive outlets for their talents and educational training.[7] Mary Richmond, by contrast, was orphaned at the age of seven and grew up in near poverty with her maternal grandmother in Baltimore. Physically frail, owing to exposure to the tuberculosis that killed three siblings and both her parents, she was able to attain only a public high-school education before taking up clerical work to support herself and her single female relatives. Richmond gained exposure in her youth to a wide range of radical views and reform causes. Her grandmother introduced her to the radical religious tenets of Spiritualism, as well as to the debates about women's rights, abolition and civil rights for ex-slaves, labor reform, and temperance. Richmond's own positions on these issues as an adult, however, tended to be moderate. She favored temperance and was sympathetic to the cause of labor, but she eschewed socialism. On the subject of women's rights she once stated to a group of students at Bryn Mawr, "I am not one of those who demand 'recognition' for Woman in season and out of season—nothing concerns me less."[8] Furthermore, although her work in urban charity reform took place among significant populations of African Americans, Richmond's essentially benign neglect of race in her analysis of poverty mirrored the stance of many of her reform contemporaries.[9] More influential in Richmond's formation than her grandmother's political views were the plays of Shakespeare, the prose of nineteenth-century American and British novelists and social critics, and the theology and social teachings of the Unitarian Church, which she began attending in her twenties.

Richmond's scrapbook of clippings from the *Baltimore Sun* on the sermons of Dr. Charles Weld, minister of Baltimore's Unitarian church, suggests the impression made on her by the tenets of the social gospel. Dr. Weld preached on the "fatherhood of God and the brotherhood of man," underscored Jesus' role as a moral exemplar for humanity, and held out an expectation of progress in realizing the Kingdom of God on earth.[10] In place of the Calvinist doctrine of total depravity, he preached that humans were "not ruined, but incomplete." Weld emphasized that salvation occurred as people came together in the spirit of Christ, "*not to save their own souls,* but to raise the bottom [of society]," through devoting their lives to destroying "poverty, viciousness, and wrong."[11] He dedicated himself to work on behalf of prisoners and the insane, and he promoted woman suffrage and labor reform. His wedding of social Christianity and principles of sociology corresponded to the liberal religious orientation of many Johns Hopkins University scholars, among them the labor historian John R. Commons and the economist Richard T. Ely. Weld's joint emphasis on personal responsibility and social salvation also resonated with Richmond's views, which had been shaped by literature and her own experience.

In 1889, not long after beginning to attend the Unitarian church, Richmond applied for the job of assistant treasurer of the Baltimore Charity Organization Society (COS). She did so primarily because she needed employment and was bored with clerical work, little realizing that she was taking the first step toward what would become her life's work. Richmond was offered the position, and within two years she became the first woman to be appointed as the general secretary, or administrative director, of the COS. In 1900 she assumed a similar position with the Philadelphia Society for Organizing Charity, and she also began working with colleagues to establish a nationwide network of charity organizations. Then, in 1909, she accepted the position of director of the Charity Organization Department of the newly incorporated Russell Sage Foundation in New York City. Established with a gift of ten million dollars from the widow of Russell Sage, a former New York congressman and entrepreneur, the foundation aimed to promote improved social and living conditions nationwide, through such means as research, education, and financial institutions. During her tenure of nearly twenty years with the foundation, until her death from cancer in 1928, Richmond wrote several of her major works and developed methods for training social workers. In her role as director of the Charity Organization Department, she helped the foundation take the lead in advancing social work as a profession.[12]

Over the course of her entire career, Richmond published numerous books and essays on charitable methods and philosophy, and her magnum opus, *Social Diagnosis* (1917), became the first definitive exposition of social casework methods and their relationship to social reform more broadly.[13] She was instrumental in establishing and teaching in early schools of "applied philanthropy," including the New York School of Philanthropy (today the Columbia University School of Social Work). She also participated in many progressive reform campaigns, especially those addressing the needs of women and children. Indeed, in the words of one colleague, Richmond was "frequently the controlling mind and usually the guiding hand . . . [in] every sound movement for social betterment" during her tenure in Philadelphia.[14] Over the years, Richmond earned the respect and affection of her colleagues and students, and she won national recognition for her contributions to the development of professional social work.

Richmond described herself and her colleagues as pioneers in their work. While they were indeed creative in their efforts to organize and professionalize the work of charity, they were also indebted to the charity organization movement initiated in London, England, some twenty years earlier. They adopted many of its principles and adapted them to the context of urban American life. At a time of growing division between wealth and poverty in America, public assistance for those in need was minimal and was often corrupt and punitive, while private charity was disorganized and ineffective, owing to competition between religious organizations and to indiscriminate almsgiving on the part of the wealthy. Charity organization societies sought to create a more effective response to urban poverty, within the context of a capitalist economy. Specifically, charity leaders combined moral principles and social scientific methods in seeking to reform longstanding traditions of private charitable assistance and "friendly visiting." Rather than provide direct relief, charity organization societies coordinated the activities of all the separate charitable agencies within a given city. Charity agents investigated relief applicants and registered them in a central directory, thus making it possible for cooperating agencies to determine appropriate kinds of assistance for given individuals and families. In conjunction with relief administration, friendly visitors worked closely with family members to encourage thrift, sobriety, diligence, and family responsibility. Over time, American charity leaders increasingly drew on social scientific studies of urban life and environmental factors in poverty in seeking to improve living and working conditions through education, municipal reform, and legislation.[15]

Historians have frequently criticized the American charity organization movement for its paternalistic and even punitive stance toward poverty.[16] Richmond herself was a vocal critic of early American initiatives to organize charity. In 1877, the Reverend S. Humphreys Gurteen had helped to establish the first American COS in Buffalo, New York. The Buffalo COS charter replaced the principle of "love with discernment," espoused by the London charity leader Charles Loch, with a principle rejecting any "sentiment" in the matter and stating that charity should be treated as a business scheme. The Buffalo society embodied this stern philosophy by placing investigative responsibilities in the hands of local police officers, whose aim was to find and punish paupers.[17] In

Richmond's estimation, by 1891 the "narrow and doctrinaire platform" of the Buffalo COS seemed "utterly foolish and inadequate." She nonetheless defended the charitable impulse as "perhaps the best thing we have in the world," and she committed herself to making the tradition of charitable giving more effective.[18]

Religious Motive, Charitable Method

Richmond formally joined the Unitarian Church in the early 1890s, and her embrace of its religious ethic of social responsibility continued throughout her lifelong affiliation with the church. It was in light of this ethic that Richmond focused her critical attention in the 1890s on the charitable practices of churches. Her aim was both to circumscribe and strengthen the role of churches in charity. In the former regard, she sought to persuade religious congregations to stop their practice of general almsgiving, which she believed was often undertaken as a form of bribery to increase church membership. She also hoped to curb the proliferation of religious charities, fueled in large part by sectarian divisiveness and competition. Owing to these practices, she claimed churches were becoming "a menace to the community."[19] Richmond's constructive response to the problems of religious charity entailed distinguishing between motive and method in charity. Churches should furnish the motive, she maintained, while the method, or mechanics, of charitable provision should be left to nonsectarian charitable agencies working in collaboration with a citywide charity organization society.[20] Richmond hoped that this distinction would strengthen churches' authority, albeit within a more limited scope.

To clarify churches' appropriate function, Richmond invoked the image of a mountain stream supplying fresh water to a city's residents through the waterworks of the city. Churches were the "living water" that originated in the mountains and reached the people through the channels of organized charity. The primary responsibility of the churches was personal regeneration, which entailed helping members overcome the "selfishness and inertia of natural man."[21] Through such regeneration, church members would be able to turn their desire to do good away from the "promiscuous dosing of social diseases which passes . . . for charity" and into "really useful channels." Richmond did not speak in terms of sin and conversion, but rather spoke about ignorance and the importance of education in regenerating and redirecting human desire. If churches would cooperate with a city's charity organization society, she believed, it would function like a city's waterworks, collecting and channeling religious motive in ways that would effectively meet the needs of city residents.[22] For charity leaders, the private organization of charity represented an alternative to laissez-faire capitalism, on the one hand, and to socialism, on the other hand. Charity organization also stood as a critique of traditional attitudes toward charity, such as the view that acts of charity allowed Christians to display their virtue. Following the example of other charity leaders, Richmond adopted the motto "Not alms, but a friend" to reclaim the relational connotation of Christian *caritas* from its association with almsgiving and impersonal relief administration.[23]

Over time, Richmond also sought to replace the paternalistic, if not punitive, aspects of middle-class moral uplift with the far richer notion of "charitable cooperation" among and between members of society. To this end, she developed a concentric model of society that effectively elaborated on the social gospel tenet of human brotherhood. At the center of the model was the family. Successive circles accounted for relationships with relatives, neighbors, employers, fellow church members, and civic associates. At the furthest reaches of the social network stood institutions of private and public charity, respectively. This model, which was analogous to the Catholic doctrine of subsidiarity, presumed the efficacy of concentric circles of social support surrounding each family.[24] For Richmond, it represented a moderate, middle way of strengthening social ties through fostering citizens' "enlightened and unselfish individualism."[25]

As an essential complement to this model, Richmond promoted friendly visiting to facilitate the development of existing, if latent, social ties. By intervening in a "self-effacing" manner, friendly visitors sought to "help people help themselves" by helping them to develop life's "natural resources," of which family ties were the foremost example.[26] In addition, friendly visitors helped to oversee and coordinate relief provided to families by relief-giving agencies. In this capacity, friendly visitors played a crucial role in mediating the assistance being offered. Whereas public relief robbed recipients of their "self-respect and proper pride," and private relief was often random and indiscriminate, and potentially pauperizing, friendly visiting in tandem with organized relief made possible a gift relationship.[27] Echoing the social gospel minister Washington Gladden, who believed that the test of charity was whether it made a gift a "vehicle for the communication of the divine life,"[28] Richmond taught that charity was a conduit for moral, if not spiritual, values. As such, its efficacy depended on the quality of relationship between giver and recipient. Optimally, friendly visitors would work with only one or two families and would develop a sustained, mutual friendship that would last for years.

Richmond's manual entitled *Friendly Visiting among the Poor* (1899) rested on the conviction that developing thorough, intimate knowledge of the joys, sorrows, and needs of individuals and families was essential to assisting them.[29] In her subsequent manual, *The Good Neighbor in the Modern City* (1907), Richmond expanded the concept of friendship into a more demanding and impartial ethic, by drawing on the biblical parable of the Good Samaritan. As urban social conditions rendered cross-class friendships increasingly difficult, Richmond appealed to the model of the Good Samaritan to underscore the responsibility of church members to provide care for individuals and, in turn, to refer them to charity societies. She did not, however, stop at this individual response to urban suffering. Church members, she claimed, had a civic duty to participate in preventive and legislative campaigns that addressed labor conditions, urban housing, sanitation, and public health.[30] In this vein, she upheld as an ideal the "Educational Church," in which the role of ministers was to help individual church members develop their spiritual lives through service in the city's urban "laboratory."[31] The church provided a primary impetus to undertake "earnest effort to make the world better," but Richmond also claimed that all such earnest effort was "in the deepest sense religious."[32]

During her tenure in Baltimore, Richmond had imbibed the spirit and knowledge of the new social sciences. As a woman, she stood on the periphery of the Johns Hopkins intellectual community, excluded from university seminars in the emerging disciplines of history, sociology, and political economy, and from the formal application of social scientific theories to the development of the city's charity organization society. Owing to her evident intellectual and administrative ability, and her quiet charisma, however, she earned the respect and assistance of mentors from outside the university community, and under their tutelage she immersed herself in the proliferating literature on charity, sociology, and social reform. In 1900, as she prepared to make the transition from leading the Baltimore COS to becoming the leader of the Philadelphia Society for Organizing Charity, Richmond published an article in which she anticipated the "world's transformation" through the "social" and "spiritual" force of charity. Complementing her religious perspective was her evident indebtedness to the new social sciences. Her concern to make "the loving heart of the world a more effectual instrument of the world's redemption" suggested a shift from a sentimental, emotional conception of charity to one grounded in knowledge of individuals and of social conditions.[33]

Richmond was at once drawn to the new social sciences and the conceptual tools they provided for addressing poverty and yet she was also concerned with the implications of these new academic disciplines. They seemed to challenge the personal basis of charity and its potentially democratic orientation, expressed in the relationships of friendship and citizenship. In particular, Richmond resented the arrogance that too often accompanied expertise. Exemplifying this attitude, a Yale sociologist claimed in 1895 that charity practitioners' initial usefulness to the developing social sciences was giving way to their dependence on universities for instruction "in the laws and principles which govern their work."[34] Richmond criticized the "lofty, professional detachment" of university-trained experts, and, more generally, the "undemocratic and false" national habit of thought that exalted experts at the expense of an educated, lay citizenry and volunteer service.[35]

Richmond's insistence on distinguishing friendly visiting from professional work was one aspect of her challenge to the emerging professional ethos. The historian Burton Bledstein characterizes this ethos in terms of the drive to claim exclusive legitimacy in an area of expertise, to establish a reputation over others, and to increase personal, financial gain.[36] The quandary Richmond faced was that she increasingly realized that high standards of charitable work, and acceptance of this work within the broader public, required training, and yet such training implicitly constituted a turn toward professionalization. Addressing the National Conference of Charities and Correction in 1897 on "The Need of a Training School in Applied Philanthropy," Richmond underscored the difference between the instrumental orientation, evident in the professions of law, medicine, and engineering, and an orientation associated with the eighteenth-century ideal of the "learned professional life." As Bledstein explains, the latter presumed a commitment to good works and public projects, and emphasized the virtues of honesty and civility.[37] Richmond embraced this latter ideal of professional work, endowing it with an implicitly religious conception of professionals as stewards of the people.

A Civic Profession, a Social Vision

Richmond's 1897 address advocated professional training as the basis for defining a professional standard and developing "higher ideals of charitable service." The public to whom charity workers bore an obligation included, in Richmond's view, the recipients of assistance, as well as charitable donors and young trainees, themselves. The latter, she believed, had the right to demand from philanthropy what they had a right to demand from any other profession: "further opportunities for education and development, and, incidentally, the right to earn a living."[38] Richmond's acknowledgment, almost as an afterthought, of the right to earn a living, and her commitment to training volunteers as well as paid workers, suggested her discomfort with potentially self-serving financial motivations in professional work. Similarly, her insistence that the curriculum of the New York School of Philanthropy give priority to practical, experiential training reflected her concern that "applied philanthropy" would become dominated by the theoretical, highly specialized knowledge of academic social scientists. In yet a further challenge to the emerging professional ideal, Richmond promoted a holistic approach, which linked "social casework," as individualized charity work came to be called, with broader initiatives for social reform.

As early as the 1890s, it had become evident to Richmond and her colleagues, through direct experience and through debate with leaders of the social settlement movement, that reformers' efforts were largely ineffective insofar as they attended to the needs of individual families without addressing broader urban conditions. Richmond's colleague Jeffrey Brackett, of the Boston School of Social Work, responded to this dawning realization by criticizing social workers' focus on caring for the "helpless" and "hopeless." He proposed, instead, greater attention to legislation, administration, and education, which he described collectively as the "work of statesmanship." These methods were naturally important to the goals of social work, but in Brackett's eyes they were also clearly instrumental in making the new profession more attractive to men.[39] Richmond saw the importance of both individual casework and political "statesmanship." In her civic model of social work, she joined the perceived maternal and also religious practices of care and humanitarianism with the perceived masculine skills of administration and legislation. Her efforts to integrate religious and social scientific values, or what the historian Daniel Rodgers describes as the distinct progressive languages of "social bonds" and "social efficiency," became a primary contribution of her career.[40]

The particular metaphor with which Richmond explained the connection between individual care and enhancement of social bonds, on the one hand, and social management and advancement of scientific efficiency, on the other hand, came from the world of business. She described individual and social reform in terms of "retail" and "wholesale" measures. Reform began at the retail level, in work with individuals and families. Through this immediate and personal contact, trained professionals and volunteers could gradually gather evidence of systemic social and environmental impediments to human well-being. They could then use this evidence to promote wholesale education, administration, and legislation. Success in securing wholesale measures required, in turn, renewed effort at the local retail level, in order to ensure enactment of legislation or reform measures on the behalf of individuals.[41] This "double movement" or "circle" of reform, as Richmond described it, shaped the successful Pennsylvania child labor legislation campaigns with which she was involved during her tenure in Philadelphia.[42] Similarly, it motivated her research on widows and their children and informed her criticism of progressive reformers who sought state pensions for widowed mothers.

Data gathered from cities across the country in the early years of the twentieth century confirmed for Richmond the extent of widowhood in American society and the need for assistance for single mothers and their dependent children. In contrast to most progressive women reformers, however, Richmond opposed "mothers' pensions" and instead called for personally administered, private charity. Her criticism of bureaucratically administered, one-size-fits-all public assistance was consistent with the value she placed on the "gift relationship." In specific, she stressed that relief must be accompanied by the personal influence of a friendly visitor seeking to inculcate the virtues of hard work, thrift, reliability, sobriety, and sexual morality. Richmond espoused the emerging conviction, moreover, that poverty, in itself, did not merit breaking up a family, but that the absence of the above-mentioned virtues legitimated removing children, whether from the care of both parents, or from a widowed mother.[43] In her discussion of widows, what is noteworthy is that Richmond complemented her endorsement of private, individual assistance with a call for legislation that would fund public campaigns to eradicate tuberculosis and minimize industrial accidents, both of which were leading causes of widowhood. This dual response illustrated Richmond's belief that state and federal governments should address systemic reform rather than provide individual "handouts" that carried no guarantee of "effective living." Insofar as state or federal public assistance served not as handouts but as "gifts" that could "release energy instead of crippling it," Richmond endorsed such measures. Based on this reasoning, Richmond's far-sighted vision for society entailed wholesale provision of public health, old age, and unemployment insurance.[44]

Richmond's participation for more than two decades in family casework and in broader reform initiatives culminated in her five-hundred-page magnum opus, *Social Diagnosis.* Drawing on a model of "social medicine" espoused by a Harvard physician and social ethicist, Richard C. Cabot, and utilizing techniques from the fields of law, psychology, and history, Richmond formulated a method whereby social caseworkers could gain thorough knowledge of the personal and social dimensions of individuals seeking assistance. She intended her method to be useful to practitioners in charitable agencies, hospitals, schools, courts, sanitariums, and prisons. Richmond presented "social diagnosis" both as a scientific process and as an art that required devotion to a "larger whole," rather than "narrow insistence upon technique alone."[45] The bridge that she hoped to create between scientific and artistic perspectives in social work mirrored her efforts to unite social reform and individual care, and her commitment to join professional work and volunteer service. At stake was the effort to leaven scientific, secular, instrumental techniques with humanistic, religious, relational ideals. Richmond's holistic conception of social work, however, rendered it vulnerable to criticism by Abraham Flexner, the largely self-created arbiter of American professions who first earned a reputation by overseeing the Carnegie Foundation's nationwide study of medical education published in 1910.

In 1915 Flexner delivered an address to the National Conference of Social Work, in which he admitted his lack of expertise in the field but nonetheless expounded on why social work was not a profession. Citing six "objective" criteria, Flexner granted that social work was learned, self-organized, and altruistic (indeed maybe *too* altruistic to be taken seriously as a profession); however, he claimed that it failed as a profession because it displayed insufficient intellectual authority, had indefinite ends, and lacked a clear educational discipline.[46] Rather than being among the "established and recognized professions," social work was a "mediating" profession.[47] Despite claiming that he had no desire to discourage social workers, Flexner faulted them for being "somewhat too self-confident," given to "excessive facility in speech," and prone to perceive vigor as synonymous with intelligence. Using the masculine pronoun, Flexner said that a social worker's recognition of his dependence should induce "caution, thoroughness and moderation," and make him "less cock-sure than the professional man whom he calls in."[48]

Flexner's address underscored the divergence between a practice of social work shaped by religious values and traditional feminine norms of caring, on the one hand, and a model of professional work derived from clinical medicine, on the other hand. Whereas Richmond remained faithful to social work's roots in a tradition of voluntary service and found inspiration in the social gospel in articulating a professional ideal of civic cooperation, Flexner showed his indebtedness to a medical model of professionalism based on ideals of self-sufficient action and autonomous, rational knowledge. Similarly, the maternalist dimension of Richmond's social work philosophy and the value she assigned experiential and personal knowledge fell short of Flexner's traditionally masculine standards of scientific knowledge. Flexner did not explicitly address gender, but in contrast to his use of the male pronoun in his speech, his assessment of social work clearly reflected his awareness that its practitioners were primarily women, and that its principles included traditionally feminine values. In this vein, he criticized social workers for claiming too much authority in relation to (male) professionals in courts and hospitals, and he faulted their lack of autonomy and expertise, as well as their attempts to join the intellectual "brotherhood" of the professions.[49] Having dismissed social work as a profession, Flexner nonetheless concluded his address by praising its "professional spirit" and "unselfish devotion."[50] Moreover, he noted its success in making up for shortcomings in the "recognized" professions: "[i]t pieces out existing professions; breathes a new spirit into them; and binds them together in the endeavor to deal with a given situation from a new point of view."[51]

Richmond formally responded to Flexner at the national conference in 1917, and she did so diplomatically, conceding some of his points and challenging others. Social workers, she granted, were "middlemen" to the extent that they were "merely matching folks and disabilities"; however, she rejected the implication that a caseworker was little more than a "telephone girl at the switchboard who pulls out one plug and pushes in another." Rather, the skills of casework included "discovering the social relationships by which a given personality had been shaped; the ability to get at the central core of difficulty in these relationships; and the power to utilize the direct action of mind on mind in their adjustment."[52] These were the skills of social diagnosis, and at their center was a concept of personality for which Richmond was indebted to the social gospel. Ironically, her defense of social workers' "skill of our own" played into the culture of professionalization that she otherwise resisted.[53] Through the 1920s, however, Richmond continued to draw on her liberal religious convictions in advocating a participatory, civic vision of social work.

"Personality," the Social Self, and the Critique of Bureaucracy

According to William McGuire King, social gospel theologians interpreted an "enthusiasm for humanity" and its corresponding commitment to social reform as outward expressions of a profound inner experience of God.[54] They described this inner experience in terms of "personality" and the potential for self-integration through working to create meaning within a broader social environment. The opportunity for individuals to find their own personal center of meaning through a commitment to social service was one goal of social gospel adherents. A second goal was to enable others to discover personal fulfillment and authentic human relationships by seeking to transform oppressive social conditions in which they lived and worked.[55] Richmond's emerging philosophy of social work reflected her embrace of both goals of social action. On the one hand, her emphasis on self-effacing service expressed the Christian paradox, to which social gospel theologians alluded, that only through losing one's life in service to Christ did one find one's life. Service to others, said social gospel writers, went hand in hand with self-realization and an inner experience of God.[56] On the other hand, Richmond's description of social workers' "reverence for personality" referred to their concern about the quality of life of those that they served. Such reverence, Richmond believed, complemented social workers' commitment to social and legislative reforms that would create more tenable living and working environments, and thus would contribute to more meaningful human life.[57] Her conviction about the social context of personality fostered her skepticism about both the mental hygiene movement and the emerging bureaucratic approaches to welfare.

The language of personality had roots in social gospel theology, but it also resonated with the mental hygiene movement and the turn toward psychiatric technique in social work. As she drew on this language to defend social workers' "skill of our own" against Flexner's criticisms, Richmond found herself having to distinguish social casework from a psychoanalytic orientation for which she had little enthusiasm.[58] Social casework, she argued, "radiate[d] outward along all the lines of a client's social relations," seeking better adjustment between the individual and the society. In contrast, the fields of psychiatry and psychiatric social work began with a diseased personality and "bore in and in."[59] Richmond was fifty-six years old when she expressed the latter distinction, and it is likely that the growing interest in mental processes and in Freudian psychology ruffled her Victorian sensibilities. She believed, moreover, that "adjustment" must be a two-way process, requiring change in both individuals and society. She noted in a personal letter in 1916 that striking a "just balance" between the "mental" and "material" aspects of reform was crucial, and would be "the hardest trial ahead of us."[60] In her view, the new psychiatric orientation in casework contributed little to striking such a balance.

The advent of World War I both strengthened the appeal of psychiatric social work as an area of specialization and hastened the growth of bureaucracy in the profession. Not only did the war increase demand for services to soldiers suffering shell shock and other traumas of battle, but it also created a new area of service among thousands of working-class and middle-class families who faced the challenges of home-front living in the absence of spouses, fathers, and sons.[61] Perceiving an opportunity to expand social casework, Richmond helped to create a nationwide Home Service Division of the American Red Cross in 1917, with the goal of training volunteers to assist families. She was wary, however, of establishing a permanent national bureaucracy, and thus she called for the division to disband after the war. At the same time, she and several colleagues turned their attention to restoring professional unity and self-determination, by forming the Committee on Professional Organization.

This committee was concerned not only with growing internal divisions and divisiveness over social work goals and methods, but also with the threat of external bureaucratic control based on scientific management principles.[62] For some years, businessmen had argued that federated fund-raising would increase income, reduce waste, and enforce efficiency among social work agencies. Well-organized campaigns to sell war bonds served as a model and inspiration for federated "community chests," whose numbers began to accelerate rapidly after the war, jumping from 12 to 363 between 1919 and 1930.[63] In Richmond's view, federated finance was an "ingenious, well-intentioned, and mistaken" plan that allowed businessmen to determine the standards for social work. Despite having little or no training in social work, businessmen required social service agencies to comply with federation guidelines in exchange for endorsement and assistance with fund-raising. Not only did the new federation leaders insist on almost exclusive allegiance to psychiatric techniques, but they also controlled hiring and wages in social work agencies. While the perceived threat to professional self-determination was Richmond's foremost concern, she was no doubt aware of the gender implications: federation directors hired men for the lucrative administrative positions in agencies and relegated women to casework, with its routinization, dependency, overwork, and minimal salaries.[64]

In 1922, Richmond's narrow defeat for the presidency of the National Conference of Social Work confirmed the ascendancy of practitioners dedicated to the mental hygiene and financial federation movements. That same year the Russell Sage Foundation published *What Is Social Case Work?*, Richmond's implicit challenge to the growing specialization and divisiveness within social work, and her mature vision for the profession. This vision reflected Richmond's indebtedness to the joint individual and social premises of social gospel theology, which she now couched in terms of her "democratic point of view."[65] Social workers' recognition of human interdependence, their willingness to appreciate human differences and to treat people according to their differences, and their conviction that human beings all had wills and purposes of their own and were not "dependent and domesticable animals" had their roots, she said, in the "spiritual conviction of the infinite worth of our common humanity."[66] To be true to their mission, Richmond claimed that social workers needed the "freedom to do good work and . . . to make discoveries through intensive service." She proposed that caseworkers have the opportunity to take sabbaticals in order to study the implications of their work for broader reform initiatives.[67] "Social discoveries," she claimed, should be a "by-product of successful case work," and she called on caseworkers to bear "faithful witness to the need for social reforms wherever their daily work reveals the need."[68] Richmond's commitment to the "long view" and her expectation that social workers would act as stewards of the community reflected both the postmillennial hope and the human responsibility expressed in social gospel theology. Richmond herself, moreover, embodied its dual commitment to personal and social regeneration by devoting her final years to researching and seeking to reform marriage laws, in response to casework evidence showing the detrimental effects of child marriage in America.

Conclusion: Sustaining a Civic Ideal

William Sullivan argues in *Work and Integrity* that the 1920s marked the failure of Progressives' hopes to reorganize professional life on civic principles. Professionals, he says, could no longer successfully bridge a "metropolitan culture of expert competence" and "provincial worlds which still adhered to the inherited moral ideals of character." Nor could they provide a compelling sense of civic life as an alternative to the increasingly separate realms of bureaucratic work and leisure consumption.[69] As William McGuire King notes, the bridge began to dissolve in large part because the relationship between the social gospel and the social sciences became increasingly strained after World War I.[70] Richmond witnessed the ascendancy of bureaucratic expertise, and yet in the last decade of her career she maintained her commitment to a civic vision of social work. In her final public address in 1927, she told her colleagues: "Study and develop your work at its point of intersection with other community services and social activities of your community. Learn to do your daily tasks . . . from the basis of the whole and with that always in mind. After all, society is one fabric, and when you know the resources of your community both public and private . . . you are able to knit into the pattern of that fabric the threads of your own specialty."[71] Her health rapidly failing owing to cancer, Richmond did not attend the National Conference of Social Work the following summer, at which the theologian Reinhold Niebuhr echoed her own religious perspective. In his address entitled "Religious Imagination and the Scientific Method," Niebuhr said, "[w]e need the scientific approach to all life's problems, and a religious perception of the total meaning of things, and a commitment to what is best in life and best in the world itself."[72]

Richmond's civic ideal remained steeped in the Victorian culture into which she was born. The value she placed on marriage and family, on community, and on meaningful work, together with her critique of the challenges posed to these by the emerging corporate economy, reflected a Victorian conception of civic participation in which home, religion, work, and politics were united in an ideological whole.[73] And yet Richmond's vision was not simply "provincial." Her indebtedness to the social gospel, which for decades provided a bridge between Christianity and the new social sciences, pushed her beyond a simple focus on moral character and traditional almsgiving and encouraged her formulation of a profession of social work that took social reform and social justice seriously. At the same time, the social gospel's values informed her critique of narrow, instrumental, and sometimes self-serving practices and attitudes in professional work. The female gender norms of the social gospel, together with the maternalist reform ideology, contributed to her critique and constructive vision, while also increasing social work's female constituency.

By the 1920s, the civic vision that Richmond endorsed was increasingly distinct from the specialization, corporatization, and psychiatric orientation that had come to dominate professional social work. In our current age of challenge and promise in American professionalism, however, both scholars and social work practitioners are rediscovering Richmond's legacy.[74] Representing perspectives ranging from neoconservative political thinkers to feminist social work practitioners, the renewed interest in Richmond's holistic approach, encompassing both individual and social dimensions of reform, may be testimony to her own belief that a profession that does not know its history is "a shambling and formless thing."[75]

Notes

I am indebted to the participants of the second annual Social Gospel Conference at Colgate Rochester Divinity School in the spring of 1999 for their challenging and insightful comments on an earlier version of this essay; to Wendy J. Deichmann Edwards and Carolyn De Swarte Gifford for their incisive editorial suggestions; and to Jeffrey Fry, my colleague in the Department of Philosophy and Religious Studies at Ball State University, for his thoughtful comments on drafts of this chapter.

1. William M. Sullivan, *Work and Integrity: The Crisis and Promise of Professionalism in America* (New York: HarperBusiness, 1995), xvi (second quote), 65 (first quote); see also chap. 3, "A Metropolitan Maturity: The Progressives' Struggle for a Civic Professionalism."

2. Ibid., xvi (quote), 64–65.

3. Robert T. Handy, ed., *The Social Gospel in America, 1870–1920: Gladden, Ely, and Rauschenbusch* (New York: Oxford University Press, 1966), 5–9. Although Handy claims that the "new" theologians distinguished themselves from earlier liberal Unitarians, the latter were indeed among those who embraced social gospel tenets. Charles H. Hopkins is one historian who regards Unitarians as an important force, together with other denominations, in shaping and disseminating social gospel ideals. See his work *The Rise of the Social Gospel in American Protestantism, 1865–1915* (New Haven: Yale University Press, 1940), 4, 318. As the present essay will discuss, sermons delivered in Baltimore's Unitarian church attest to the influence of the social gospel.

4. Handy, *Social Gospel*, 8 (first quote); William McGuire King, "An Enthusiasm for Humanity: The Social Emphasis in Religion and its Accommodation in Protestant Theology," in *Religion and Twentieth-Century American Intellectual Life*, ed. Michael J. Lacey (New York: Cambridge University Press, 1989), 55 (second quote).

5. See Seth Koven and Sonya Michel, eds., *Mothers of a New World: Maternalist Politics and the Origins of Welfare States* (New York: Routledge, 1993), 6.

6. On gender norms in the social gospel see Janet Forsythe Fishburn, *The Fatherhood of God and the Victorian Family: The Social Gospel in America* (Philadelphia: Fortress, 1981). In *The Altruistic Imagination: A History of Social Work and Social Policy in the United States* (Ithaca: Cornell

University Press, 1985), 81, John H. Ehrenreich notes that women comprised nearly 80 percent of social and welfare workers in 1930, thus contributing to the low status of the profession.

7. See Kathleen D. McCarthy, *Noblesse Oblige: Charity and Cultural Philanthropy in Chicago, 1849–1929* (Chicago: University of Chicago Press, 1982), and Mina Carson, *Settlement Folk: Social Thought and the American Settlement Movement, 1885–1930* (Chicago: University of Chicago Press, 1990).

8. Mary Richmond, "Criticism and Reform in Charity," in *The Long View: Papers and Addresses by Mary E. Richmond* [hereafter *LV*], ed. Joanna C. Colcord and Ruth Z. S. Mann (New York: Russell Sage Foundation, 1930), 53.

9. See Margaret Tillson Pittman-Munke, "Mary Richmond and the Wider Social Movement: Philadelphia, 1900–1909" (Ph.D. diss., University of Texas, Austin, 1985), 67.

10. See Dr. Weld's sermons "Personal Honor" and "The Doctrine of the Trinity" (quote from the former) reported in the *Baltimore Sun* ca. 1890 and found in the Mary E. Richmond Archives, Butler Rare Book and Manuscript Library, Columbia University (hereafter MERA).

11. Charles Weld, sermon entitled "No Total Depravity" (first quote) and "The Top and Bottom of Society" (second and third quotes), MERA.

12. See David C. Hammack, "A Center of Intelligence for the Charity Organization Movement: The Foundation's Early Years," chap. 1 in *Social Science in the Making: Essays on the Russell Sage Foundation, 1907–1972*, by David C. Hammack and Stanton Wheeler (New York: Russell Sage Foundation, 1994), 3, 20.

13. Richmond's other works include *Friendly Visiting among the Poor* (1899), *The Good Neighbor in the Modern City* (1907), *A Study of Nine Hundred and Eighty-five Widows* (1913), *What Is Social Case Work?* (1922), *Child Marriages* (1925), *Marriage and the State* (1929), and *The Long View* (1930), a posthumous collection of essays and public addresses.

14. Ethel Rupert, "Philadelphia, 1900–1909," *The Family* 9, no. 10 (February 1929): 330–31.

15. See Frank D. Watson, *The Charity Organization Movement of the United States: A Study in American Philanthropy* (1922; New York: Arno Press, 1971), 54–60, 90–97, 150–56. Richmond outlines the components of charity organization in "What Is Charity Organization?" *LV*, 136–43.

16. See, for instance, Roy Lubove, *The Professional Altruist: The Emergence of Social Work as a Career, 1880–1930* (Cambridge, Mass.: Harvard University Press, 1965); Michael B. Katz, *In the Shadow of the Poor House: A Social History of Welfare in America* (New York: Basic Books, 1986); and Lori Ginzberg, *Women and the Work of Benevolence: Morality, Politics, and Class in the Nineteenth Century United States* (New Haven: Yale University Press, 1990). In "Philanthropy as Social Control in Late Nineteenth-Century America: Some Hypotheses and Data on the Rise of Social Work," *Societas* 5, no. 1 (Winter 1975): 49–59, Marvin E. Gettleman specifically blames Richmond for sanctioning social control not only over the poor, but also over the well-to-do, by controlling their almsgiving, and over the middle class, by providing professional social work training and thus blunting radical socialist critiques of capitalism. Richmond's contemporary, the settlement leader Jane Addams, publicly criticized charity workers as intrusive, moralistic, and punitive, and her enduring cultural prominence no doubt has lent weight to the similar line of critique among contemporary historians. See Jane Addams, "The Subtle Problems of Charity," *Atlantic Monthly*, February 1899, 163–78.

17. S. Humphreys Gurteen, "Beginning of Charity Organizations in America," *Lend a Hand* 13, no. 5 (November 1894): 355–58.

18. Mary Richmond to Mr. Frank D. Watson, February 23, 1911, MERA (first and second quotes); Mary Richmond, "The Friendly Visitor," *LV*, 40–41 (third quote).

19. Mary Richmond, "Our Relation to the Churches," *LV*, 116–17; idem, "The Church and Personal Service," *Charities Record* 8, no. 1 (February 1895): 85 (quote); and idem, *Friendly Visiting among the Poor: A Handbook for Charity Workers* [hereafter *FVP*] (1899; reprint, Series in Criminology, Law Enforcement, and Social Problems, Publication no. 2, Montclair, N.J.: Patterson Smith, 1969), 168–73.

20. Richmond, "Our Relation to the Churches," 115.

21. Richmond, "The Church and Personal Service," 86 (first quote); idem, *FVP,* 170 (second quote). Richmond echoed Francis Peabody's description of the "thirsty fields [that] wait for the stream of service which descends from those heights of prayer [high on the mountain of the ideal]," in "The Problem of Charity," *Charities Review* 3, no. 1 (November 1893): 6.

22. Richmond, "Our Relation to the Churches," 116 (first quote), 117 (second quote).

23. See Richmond, "Criticism and Reform in Charity," 43–45. The motto is often credited to Octavia Hill, a London charity reformer. In "The Training of Charity Workers," *LV,* 93, and "What Is Charity Organization?" 141, Richmond distinguishes the organization of *charity* as a personal practice from the organization of *charities* as an institutional process.

24. Mary Richmond, "Charitable Cooperation," *LV,* 186–202.

25. Richmond, "Criticism and Reform in Charity," 45.

26. Mary Richmond, "The Philanthropic Advertiser," *LV,* 110 (second quote); idem, "The Settlement and Friendly Visiting," *LV,* 125 (first and third quotes).

27. Richmond, *FVP,* 144; idem, "The Philanthropic Advertiser," 110 (quote); and idem, "Adequate Relief," *LV,* 328.

28. Washington Gladden, quoted in Mary E. McDowell, "The Settlement and Organized Charity," *Proceedings of the National Conference of Charities and Correction Held in Grand Rapids 4–10 June 1896,* ed. Isabel C. Barrows (Boston: Geo. H. Ellis, 1896), 123–24.

29. Richmond, *FVP,* 180.

30. Mary Richmond, *The Good Neighbor in the Modern City,* 4th ed., Russell Sage Foundation Series (Philadelphia: Lippincott, 1909), 13–27.

31. Mary Richmond to Edward Devine, March 7, 1901, MERA.

32. Richmond, "The Church and Personal Service," 85.

33. Richmond, "What Is Charity Organization?" 132. This first appeared in *Charities Review,* a publication of the New York Charity Organization Society.

34. William H. Brewer, "The Relation of Universities to Charity and to Reform Work," in *Proceedings of the National Conference of Charities and Correction Held in New Haven 24–30 May 1895,* ed. Isabel C. Barrows (Boston: Geo. H. Ellis, 1895), 145.

35. Mary Richmond, "Case Worker and Client," *LV,* 391 (first quote); idem, "The Retail Method of Reform," *LV,* 220 (second quote).

36. Burton J. Bledstein, *The Culture of Professionalism: The Middle Class and the Development of Higher Education in America* (New York: Norton, 1976), 159–93.

37. Ibid., 172–73.

38. Mary Richmond, "The Need of a Training School in Applied Philanthropy," *LV,* 100 (second quote), 104 (first quote). For further discussion of these ideas see Richmond, "The Training of Charity Workers," 87–92.

39. Jeffrey R. Brackett, "Report of the Committee on Training of Social Workers," in *Proceedings of the National Conference of Charities and Correction Held in Philadelphia 9–16 May 1906,* ed. Alexander Johnson (n.p.: Press of Fred J. Heer, 1906), 451.

40. Daniel T. Rodgers, "In Search of Progressivism," *Reviews in American History* 10, no. 4 (December 1982): 123–27.

41. Richmond, "The Retail Method of Reform," 216–18.

42. Ibid., 216.

43. Mary Richmond, *A Study of Nine Hundred and Eighty-five Widows* (New York: Russell Sage Foundation, 1913), 34–45.

44. Richmond distinguished between "handouts" and "gifts" in a letter to Joseph Lee, April 10, 1916, MERA; she stated her support for "health insurance and other wise measures of prevention," in "The Mine Fields," *LV,* 467. See also Judith Sealander's discussion of Richmond in *Private Wealth and Public Life: Foundation Philanthropy and the Reshaping of American Social Policy from the Progressive Era to the New Deal* (Baltimore: Johns Hopkins University Press, 1997), 116–17.

45. Mary Richmond, *Social Diagnosis* (New York: Russell Sage Foundation, 1917), 370. The scientific practice of "social diagnosis" was rooted in the "art" of friendship, which Richmond discussed some twenty years earlier in "The Art of Asking Questions," *LV,* 105–7.

46. Abraham Flexner, "Is Social Work a Profession?" in *Proceedings of the National Conference of Charities and Correction Held in Baltimore 12–19 May 1915* (Chicago: Hildmann Printing Co., 1915), 576–77 (quote from 577), 584–88.

47. Ibid., 585.

48. Ibid., 588–89 (quotes from 589).

49. Ibid., 580 (quote), 586. According to Clarke Chambers, in 1915 roughly 2,800 of 4,000 social workers in New York City were women. See his "Women in the Creation of the Profession of Social Work," *Social Service Review* 60, no. 1 (March 1986): 7–8. A contemporary social work practitioner and professor, Karen S. Haynes, asks, "Why did we allow a predominantly female profession to be so directed by a male medical model of what . . . autonomous practice should look like?" Haynes, "The One Hundred-Year Debate: Social Reform versus Social Treatment," *Social Work: Journal of the NASW* 43, no. 6 (November 1998): 506.

50. Flexner, "Is Social Work a Profession?" 590.

51. Ibid., 586.

52. Mary Richmond, "The Social Case Worker's Task," *LV,* 399.

53. Ibid.

54. King, "An Enthusiasm for Humanity," 53.

55. Ibid., 53–58. The term "personality" appears throughout these pages.

56. See, for instance, Mary Richmond, "The Long View," *LV,* 469.

57. References to "reverence for personality" are found in Richmond, *What Is Social Case Work?* [hereafter *WSCW*] (New York: Russell Sage Foundation, 1922), 158, 259–60.

58. Richmond, "The Social Case Worker's Task," 399.

59. Richmond, *WSCW,* 131–33 (quote 133).

60. Letter from Richmond to Mr. Joseph Lee, April 10, 1916, MERA.

61. On the "psychological turn" in social work see James Leiby, *A History of Social Welfare and Social Work in the United States* (New York: Columbia University Press, 1978), 183–85.

62. Signs of disunity are evident in the "Experimental Draft of a Code of Ethics for Social Workers," 11–13, MERA.

63. Leiby, *History of Social Welfare,* 172.

64. Mary Richmond, "To Those Still on the Job," *LV,* 443 (quote); Daniel J. Walkowitz, "The Making of a Feminine Professional Identity: Social Workers in the 1920s," *American Historical Review* 95, no. 4 (October 1990): 1058–59.

65. Richmond, *WSCW,* 248.

66. Ibid., 249 (second quote), 257–58 (first quote 258).

67. Ibid., 251–52 (quote 251).

68. Ibid., 225.

69. Sullivan, *Work and Integrity,* 95.

70. King, "An Enthusiasm for Humanity," 63.

71. Mary Richmond, "The Concern of the Community with Marriage," in *Family Life Today: Papers Presented at a Conference in Celebration of the Fiftieth Anniversary of Family Social Work in America Held in Buffalo 2–5 October 1927,* ed. Margaret E. Rich (Boston: Houghton Mifflin Company, 1928), 76.

72. Reinhold Niebuhr, "Religious Imagination and the Scientific Method," *Proceedings of the National Conference of Charities and Correction Held in Memphis 2–9 May 1928* (Chicago: University of Chicago Press, 1928), 54–55.

73. Elaine Tyler May, *Great Expectations: Marriage and Divorce in Post-Victorian Culture* (Chicago: University of Chicago Press, 1980), 20–21.

74. William Sullivan discusses both the promise of professionalism in making possible a civil and meaningful public realm (*Work and Integrity,* 15) and also the challenges to professionalism in seeking to balance technical expertise with civic purpose (ibid., xix). The general theme of crisis and promise is interwoven throughout his book.

75. Mary Richmond, "The Biography of a Social Worker," *LV,* 556. Works that address Richmond's renewed relevance for social work and reform include George W. Liebmann, *Six Lost Leaders: Prophets of Civil Society* (New York: Lexington, 2001); Joel Schwartz, *Fighting Poverty with Virtue: Moral Reform and American Urban Poor, 1825–2000* (Bloomington: Indiana University Press, 2000); James Billups, "The Moral Basis for a Radical Reconstruction of Social Work," in *The Moral Purposes of Social Work,* ed. P. Nelson Reid and Philip R. Popple (Chicago: Nelson-Hall, 1992), 100–119; and Carolyn Morell, "Cause *Is* Function: Toward a Feminist Model of Integration for Social Work," *Social Service Review* 61, no. 1 (March 1987): 144–53.

PART 4

Women and Social Gospel Theology

Dorothy Day and the Social Gospel Movement: Different Theologies, Common Concerns

Robert Trawick

Dorothy Day is a persistent presence in American life, often un-recognized but continuing to challenge. The institutions she helped to found, the Catholic Worker houses, are still scattered throughout the American landscape and continue to offer spiritual and physical sustenance to those in need. The fierceness of her conviction and the honesty of her appraisals not only of society but of herself have led many to consider her an American saint, a woman of unsurpassed religious dedication and conviction.[1]

It is disturbing, then, how often surveys of American religious history omit Dorothy Day altogether. When she is mentioned, she is most commonly placed alongside figures more traditionally understood as social gospel theologians,[2] such as Gladden, Rauschenbusch, and Ely, her work somehow seen as a Catholic addition to a largely Protestant stream of social Christianity.[3] Yet while Day shares many of the convictions of the Protestant clergy traditionally understood as the leaders of the social gospel movement, she stands in some degree apart from all of them. Her politics, her gender, and her religious affiliation are all anomalies of a sort if we are to consider her a social gospel theologian.[4]

Whether or not Day is best understood as a part of the social gospel tradition depends, of course, on how we define that tradition. There are dangers in generalizing about the diverse theologians who make up that tradition, but some commonality must exist if the label is to have any meaning. Certainly the theologians of the social gospel tradition share, along with Day and the more politically oriented progressives, a distress at the dislocations caused by the industrialization of American society and the gospel of wealth that underwrote capitalist expansion. Using that measure, Day is one with Gladden, Rauschenbusch, and Ely. But she is also one with the Wobblies, with industrial unionism, with the political forces of the left who made this their cause.

So defining the social gospel based upon its practical concerns with the burgeoning industrial society of the late nineteenth century seems to capture too wide a spectrum of adherents. Certainly not all of the reformist tendencies of that period sprang from religious motivation, and of those that did, not all shared the theological perspective of those religious thinkers generally annexed to the social gospel movement. The distinctiveness of the social gospel theologians was precisely their theology, a recognition that has allowed a somewhat more accurate definition of the social gospel. It cannot be so broad as to capture all of the social reform that swept this country around the turn of the twentieth century and continued well into the modern era.

Concentrating on theology has also allowed scholars to break down some artificial barriers that have long kept too many who truly belong to the tradition from being recognized. Scholars of the past several generations have begun to reassess some of the traditionally understood characteristics of the social gospel as in some way accidental. The essays in this volume continue that work. So the commonality of race, gender, and geography that earlier generations adduced in the social gospel movement has been eloquently questioned and significantly discredited.

Defining Theological Characteristics of the Social Gospel

There remains the question of what continues to bind together the various theologians and practitioners of the social gospel. Hopkins's work on the social gospel, while it does not partake of the new intellectual history that has so broadened our perspective, does give a reasonable picture of the theological glue that binds. As Hopkins notes, "the primary assumption was the immanence of God."[5] The notion of a God so active in history, the prominence of providential thinking was a source of much discomfort to later theologians. Although the theological importance of Providence has continued to animate the work of a few contemporary theologians,[6] its overall lack of a place in today's theological discourse is glaring, especially when compared to the social gospel school. It remains a central piece of social gospel thought.

This dominance is further revealed in that most distinctive trope of social gospel theology, the Kingdom of God. Certainly the expectation of God's ultimate triumph, even within history, is not novel. All types of millennialist thought, from that of Joachim of Fiore in the twelfth century to that of Joseph Smith in the nineteenth, have enriched and confused Christian teaching for generations. But social gospelers used the Kingdom of God idea primarily as a rebuke of very contemporary social attitudes. Social gospel theology always looked to a teleology that was at least in part this-worldly, a transformation of the existing social structures.

The Kingdom of God is such a dominant force in social gospel theology that it deserves some explication before we move to the comparative task of assessing Dorothy Day's relationship to this theological school. Rauschenbusch's conception of the Kingdom remains among the most concise and valuable. Of the Kingdom he writes, "It is something that is here on this earth; that quietly pervades all humanity; that is always working toward the perfect life of God. It cannot be lived out by you alone—you have to live it here with me, and with that brother sitting next to you. We together have to work it out. It is a matter of community life."[7]

The biblical foundation of the Kingdom is crucial. For Rauschenbusch, as for so many social gospel theologians, the dominant metaphor for social life is Paul's organic metaphor, the church as a body: "For as in one body we have many members, and all the members do not have the same function, so we, though many, are one body in Christ, and individually members of one another. Having gifts that differ according to the grace given to us, let us use them" (Romans 13:4–6 RSV).

Rauschenbusch believes that "Paul's philosophy of the Christian church is the highest possible philosophy of human society. The ideal society is an organism and the christianizing of the social order must work toward an harmonious co-operation of all individuals for common social ends."[8]

If we can define anything as characteristic of social gospel theology, it is this hope. It is not, however, simply the employment of the language of the Kingdom of God, but rather the defining of that term which makes it a mark of commonality, and at least among the theologians most widely associated with the social gospel, the definition of Kingdom of God took distinctly Protestant forms. As such, among the features that define the traditional social gospel theologian—white, male, urban, Protestant—the last named cannot be jettisoned.

Among the typically Protestant characteristics of the social gospel definition is its reliance on biblical sources. The interest of Rauschenbusch and others in biblical studies is perhaps a product of their historical location in a period of flourishing historical criticism. But it is also a strain that runs deep in Protestant theology, and the longing for the early church, certainly tempered in social gospel theology with more accurate perceptions of the realities of that church, connects these theologians with their Reformation forebears in indissoluble ways.

It is not just the centrality of biblical sources that marks the Protestantism of this theology. The Kingdom of God theme, interpreted under the rubric of the New Testament, was also interpreted in ways that pointed to a Protestant social majority. The theology, which in many ways was a radical break from the complacency of nineteenth-century mainline Protestantism, nevertheless was confident that the social institutions and makeup of the Victorian era could be "Christianized," that is, transformed rather than displaced. It has long been understood that Rauschenbusch, Gladden, and others had an optimistic view about the power of individual moral transformation and viewed it as the central piece of social change.[9] That the social structures of the time would be adequate for bringing about the Kingdom if they were so transformed is apparent in Gladden's words from *The Nation and the Kingdom*: "Philanthropy, the principle of compassion and kindness, has been largely organized into the social life of the nation. The defective and dependent classes are now wards of the state. A considerable part of the life of civilized society is controlled by the Christian principle, and we have come to a day when it does not seem quixotic to believe that all social relations are to be Christianized."[10]

Certainly the optimism of social gospel theology has been caricatured in later interpretations of the movement. Rauschenbusch was deeply aware of the pervasiveness of sin in ways that later neo-orthodox critics misunderstood or chose to ignore. Yet Rauschenbusch too felt that forces already in place within the life of the country would lead to social regeneration. Moderately socialist though he was, he writes from the position of the Protestant majority that was relatively well served by those institutions.

Catholic Social Christianity and the Catholic Worker Movement

Mel Piehl, in his history of the Catholic Worker movement, notes that the social location of the Protestant ministers who have traditionally been given the title of social gospel theologians was at once a great strength and a profound weakness. By coming from the mainstream of American religious life, even as they criticized it, many social gospel theologians "could sometimes affect society in substantial ways." However, notes Piehl, "the tie to the community of power also tended to tame the ideas of the social gospel and confine its audience to those Americans who shared a particular experience and vocabulary."[11]

It is precisely at this point, the social location of many of the social gospel theologians, that the separation between their social movement and that of Dorothy Day and the Catholic Worker movement is most apparent. Social gospel theologians worked for the poor, and at times with the poor, but their distance from the communities of the working class is at times glaring. Much has been made, and for good reason, of the lack of real ties between the social gospel movement and the labor movement. Washington Gladden, almost alone among the traditionally understood leaders of the social gospel movement, stands out for his attempts to bridge the gaps between Protestant Christianity and organized labor, a group that at the turn of the twentieth century could accurately claim to speak for large numbers of the working poor. Rauschenbusch, on the other hand, is at his most vulnerable when facing charges that he lacked any real social connection to the working classes represented in the labor movement, particularly after his move from his Hell's Kitchen parish.[12]

Gladden and Rauschenbusch conform to the traditional model of social gospel leadership: white male clergy. It may well be that their very positions as voices of authority in American Protestantism represented a gap between them and the poor that was in some degree unbridgeable. Certainly, other Protestant movements, particularly those led by women, seem to have had more success in creating solidarity. One thinks, for example, of Jane Addams's Hull-House, an institution whose similarities to Day's Houses of Hospitality are interesting. It could be that Protestant women had an advantage over the male clergy in establishing connections with their constituency, a possibility that demands further exploration.

However, if their separation from the white male clergy, traditionally understood as the leaders of the social gospel, may have aided Protestant women in connecting with the urban poor, their Protestantism still constituted a type of barrier. The great bulk of the white urban poor, of the American working class during the social gospel era, were Catholic, and the connections between Catholics and Protestants in the early twentieth century were tenuous and often fraught with controversy and even danger. One Protestant minister, Samuel Loomis, noted in 1887, "The Catholic Church is emphatically the workingman's church. She rears her many edifices in the midst of the densest populations, provides them with many seats, and has those seats filled."[13] Many social gospel theologians echo the concern that the working class was largely unserved by their churches. When Gladden laments that the white working classes are not in the churches, he is only half-right. They were in churches, but more often than not Catholic ones.

Dorothy Day's religious journey was a long and restless one, and she did not find herself in the Catholic church until her early adulthood. Her Catholicism was one of choice rather than of birth, though she herself would probably speak of a spiritual if not a familial compulsion to Catholicism. She did not initially share the social location of many late nineteenth- and early twentieth-century Catholics. She was not poor prior to her connection with Catholic Worker and she had, up to the founding of the Catholic Worker movement, addressed the issues of worker's rights from largely the same vantage point as men like Gladden and Rauschenbusch.

Indeed, while a radical from her early days, and a dabbler in revolutionary socialism, she too had her transformative experience as Gladden had with the North Adams strike and with his Columbus, Ohio, congregation and Rauschenbusch with his Hell's Kitchen parish. In 1932 Day, then a journalist, had witnessed the Hunger March on Washington by the nation's unemployed, which was supported by many industrial unions, to demand the passage of an Unemployment Insurance Bill. Day had been genuinely shocked to see the conditions of the marchers and their treatment as a hostile army by the United States govern-ment.[14] Upon returning home she wrote, "Far dearer in the sight of God, per-haps, are these hungry ragged ones, than all those smug well-fed Christians who sit in their homes, or in fear of the Communist menace. . . . How little, how puny my work has been since becoming a Catholic. How self-centered, how ingrown, how lacking in a sense of community."[15] Soon after observing the march, Day published the first issue of *Catholic Worker* and began the movement that bears its name.

It is interesting, in comparing the biography of Day to those of prominent clerical leaders of the social gospel, that Day was able to establish a connection with her congregants that ministers such as Gladden and Rauschenbusch seem to have been unable to do. If sympathy for the poor abounds in social gospel theology, empathy seems for some reason impossible. We have already suggested that the social location of Protestant clergy represented a form of authority that was difficult to break down. With Gladden, who seems at times particularly aware of his distance from the workers, a political location may also have played a role. Gladden, while a champion of the rights of union workers, remained throughout his life suspicious of socialism. He knew the primary texts of so-cialism perhaps better than any social gospel theologian other than Rauschen-busch and was never able to reconcile his own faith with what he saw as an in-tractable atheism in socialist theory. For Day, having come to Catholicism after embracing radical politics, the connection between the two was never intrac-table. Indeed, along with a very few other radical socialists Day assumed that the church of Jesus and the goals of socialism were not essentially at odds.[16]

Even given Day's more radical political background, however, her biography does share some common reference with the biographies of major social gos-pel leaders. The movement with which she has become most identified shares significant features with the social gospel movement as well; both are prima-rily concerned with the dislocation caused by the industrialization of Ameri-can society and certainly both have some form of utopianism, of realized eschatology, at their center.[17] It is in the attempt to realize that goal that funda-mental differences appear between the two groups. Three features of Day's the-ology and the Catholic Worker movement that it spawned stand in contrast to the characteristics of the social gospel movement: its lay leadership and the di-rect connection of the movement with the working class, its relationship to government and consequent eschewing of political avenues for reform, and its connection with American culture.[18]

Distinguishing Catholic Worker from the Social Gospel

If we are to rely on the traditional historiography of the social gospel movement, the first distinction to be made between it and Catholic Worker would be that the social gospel movement was largely a clergy-led affair, while Catholic Worker was entirely led by laity. In part, this distinction rests on an unnuanced reading of social gospel history, reflecting a lack of attention to the very sorts of social gospel activity to which this collection of work is a witness. Nonetheless, even as we recover those elements of the social gospel tradition lost to history, the movement continues to be identified with its dominant clergy. If the social gospel tradition did have a significant element of grass-roots leadership, nevertheless, in Catholic Worker there was a disconnection between the movement and the hierarchy of the church that was not prominent in the social gospel tradition.

As Piehl notes, it is somewhat surprising that of the great examples of social Christianity in the early part of the twentieth century, it would be the Catholic movement that would take its force entirely from the laity, given the dominance of Luther's dictum of "the priesthood of all believers" in Protestant theology.[19]

It is tempting to view Catholic Worker as partaking of the more modern social reform method of empowerment and as breaking from what some have identified as a paternalism in the social gospel approach to class issues. I would argue that such a characterization is not only anachronistic but misses the essentially Catholic character of the decision. Catholic Worker was almost exclusively a lay movement because its leader was a layperson and because her religious convictions led her to identification with the working class in more intimate ways than most social gospel theologians would attempt.

Nowhere is Day's identification with the poor and her acceptance of her place among the poor more evident than in her theological commitment to poverty. Her relationship with poverty is an ambiguous one, as she notes. "Poverty is a strange and elusive thing. I have tried to write about it, its joys and its sorrows, for twenty years now; I could probably write about it for another twenty years without conveying what I feel about it as well as I would like. I condemn poverty and I advocate it; poverty is simple and complex at once; it is a social phenomenon and a personal matter. It is a paradox."[20]

Her poverty was voluntary, unlike that of the people with whom she would become united, but once accepting it she broke down any hierarchical understanding of the direction of works. Her approach to social Christianity was never top down, but always looked to a radical egalitarianism, an approach to theology with distinctly Catholic precedents. Day herself points us towards the life of Saint Francis as a model for this type of social action. She writes, "We have tried to imitate Saint Francis in his holy poverty. Our aim has been to combat the atheism of the day by our devotion to the liturgical movement; to combat the bourgeois spirit by the Franciscan spirit; to oppose to class-war technique the performance of works of mercy."[21]

Voluntary poverty was not just a face of the Catholic Worker movement and Day's theology. It gets to the heart of her theological convictions, convictions nurtured by centuries of Catholic tradition. The theological center of Day's vision was a form of personalism learned at the feet of Peter Maurin, her spiritual mentor, and made to impinge on every aspect of Catholic Worker activism. She spoke of personalism as a "constructive socialism," and described it as "human beings enter[ing] into a direct relationship with one another and liv[ing] a life of genuine fraternity."[22] This personalist strain in her thought, resonating with traditional Catholic theology, gives her theology that distinctive vision of the relationship between religious reform and the state that further distinguishes her from traditional social gospel thought.

Her view of the body of Christ, her preferred metaphor to the social gospel language of Kingdom, is colored by her direct connection with the poor, evidenced in her own voluntary poverty, and while it has affinities with the social gospel position it is nevertheless distinct. If the social gospelers looked to a Kingdom that would transform the existing power structures of the country, Day's vision draws more on the monastic spirit of withdrawal from the world and at the same time ministering to it, the double movement that had characterized the early mission of the Franciscans.

Day's theological forebear here is Saint Augustine, and her vision of the body of Christ shares much with Augustine's City of God. The City of God is a city of sojourners, a small band removed from the temptations of the earthly city and having little traffic with it. Yet, the very disassociation with the world allows a prophetic distance that gives the City of God its transforming power even against the Earthly City. She writes, "The association of such groups would have to resist the dictates of an organized center, accumulation of power, and a political superstructure. The focus of such groups, or cells, is not a political but a religious motivation."[23]

This is not to say that she had no motivation to transform existing social structures, but her movement, still best represented by the Houses of Hospitality that dot the country, was focused more on the religious succoring of the people, a direct action that took up most of her resources. Such an orientation, while not foreign to the motives of the social gospel ministers, does represent a different focus. By the time that Day had begun her ministry in the 1930s, many of the remnants of the social gospel movement had become more interested in transformative work in the political arena.[24] This interest in the sphere of politics is represented by the movement of theologians, such as Reinhold Niebuhr, who had been raised in the social gospel tradition, to Christian realism and a demand that Christians undertake the moral compromises needed in a world not yet ruled by the law of love.

Day's position, writes Piehl, "remained closer to the classical position that religion as such belonged to a sphere separate from politics, and that the most authentic kind of Christian life meant rejecting power."[25] Of course, the separatist position is never to be read as inactivity. Day's political schooling, long before her conversion to Catholicism, had been in the anarcho-syndicalist school, best represented in American culture by the Industrial Workers of the World with whom she was associated throughout her life. Anarcho-syndicalism as a school of thought believed, among other things, that political institutions were inherently oppressive and that the functions of government could be more justly performed by cooperative groups of workers. The anarcho-syndicalist school was never an inactive one, and its anarchy was not a door for chaos but a demand for personal regard for the other and action on behalf of the other. Describing her anarchist political position, Day noted that "our concept of anarchism is a religious one and it stems from the life of Jesus on earth who came to serve rather than to be served and who never coerced. There was no question of force."[26]

This sort of distancing from the state places Day in a different category not only from the Protestant social gospel theologians, but even from other Catholic representatives of social Christianity. Father John Ryan, working during the same period as the social gospel reformers and sharing many of their goals and methods, was a frequent participant in high-level debates about social legislation, a position that reveals a strategy far different from Day's.[27] Writing about the difference between Day's movement and other Catholic social reform movements, George Kelly notes, "Some Catholic social movements, even the nonviolent kind, lack spiritual motivation or a communal prayer life, so that the pressing goal is the Kingdom of Man, not Christ. The Catholic Worker Movement has never suffered from these defects, because its goals and methods and spirituality are truly Catholic."[28]

Perhaps the most significant difference between Day's Catholic Worker movement and the social gospel movement was one already mentioned, and which the distinctions noted above only serve to heighten. The relationship of Catholicism to American culture was simply different from the relationship of Protestantism to American culture, and the problems faced by the movements were dissimilar. If the social gospel, as noted above, was threatened most by its connections to the structures of power, the Catholic Worker movement was threatened, at least in terms of effectiveness, by its distance from those structures. The movement, in drawing on the inspiration of Francis and other Catholic sources, was "introduc[ing] into American culture religious-social ideals little known in the United States."[29]

Certainly, the vision of America at its best as representing some form of a new Jerusalem was deeply embedded in American social consciousness, so that when Rauschenbusch, Gladden, and others looked to the image of the New Testament church as the ideal for social relationships, they were not introducing a notably foreign element into American religious life. Protestant thought, and much American religious symbolism, had partaken of that concept for some time. But the monastic ideal, the voluntary poverty, the complete separation from the methods of the state, these were elements that did not have as strong a lineage in the United States.

Protestant thought has not lacked for sectarianism along these lines, as the Anabaptist movement and its descendants show us. But that separatism was not fundamentally American. If there was some religious distrust about the role of the state, it was always ambiguous and dominated by the more prominent strain of Christianizing the state in the theocratic ways present in Protestantism at least since the outbreak of Reformed theology. Day's theology is older, and perhaps less liberal on this point, and it did not immediately resonate with American culture. As Piehl notes, "In its emphasis on humility, poverty, and contemplative Catholic spirituality, the Catholic Worker looked like something from a bygone age—and certainly a time before 1776."[30]

If Day's theology and the Catholic Worker movement are not finally to be judged as pieces of the social gospel tradition, it remains nonetheless the case that her voice is an important one for students of religious reform in America. And the similarities between the social gospel movement and Catholic Worker are not to be overlooked. Day belongs beside Rauschenbusch and Gladden in any complete survey of religiously motivated social reform in the early part of the twentieth century.

Day's influence extended far beyond this time period, and for those committed to the tenets of the social gospel, it is tempting to claim her work as part of that tradition, if only to prove its continued relevance. Theological liberalism in general and the social gospel movement in particular have suffered their fair share of academic abuse in the latter half of the century. Day's continued commitment and effectiveness through World War II, the civil rights movement, the Vietnam War, and the antinuclear movement would be valuable examples of the vitality of the social gospel tradition, if she truly belonged there.

But in the final analysis, it seems to do some violence both to the social gospel tradition and to Day's own theological commitments to thus categorize her work. There is no need to co-opt Day's work as social gospel. It remains a unique social vision in American religious history. Deeply Catholic, yet drawing as well from anarcho-syndicalist politics, Dorothy Day's vision is sui generis. That she stands in importance alongside Rauschenbusch, Gladden, and the social gospel tradition is undeniable. That she is a crucial figure in the history of religious reform movements is likewise an unassailable position. But she remains distinct from the social gospel tradition in both theological emphasis and method, if nevertheless showing great sympathy for many of its goals.

Notes

Special thanks to my wife, Amanda S. Trigg, who provided invaluable research assistance for this essay.

1. Day herself would have resisted such a label. She said, "Don't call me a saint. I don't want to be dismissed that easily." Quoted in Robert Ellsberg's introduction to Dorothy Day, *By Little and By Little*, ed. Robert Ellsberg (New York: Knopf, 1984), xviii.

2. See, for example, the discussion of Dorothy Day in George C. Bedell, Leo Sandon Jr., and Charles T. Wellbron, *Religion in America*, 2d ed. (New York: Macmillan, 1982). A fine overview of Day appears in a chapter entitled "Missions, Humanitarianism and the Social Gospel."

3. Washington Gladden was a pioneer of the social gospel, preaching from his pulpit in Ohio.

Walter Rauschenbusch is often considered the leading theoretician of the movement, giving shape to its theology in his *A Theology for the Social Gospel.* Richard T. Ely belongs among these figures for his pioneering work in connecting theology with economics.

4. Of course, the gender-specific readings of the social gospel movement are being challenged, to which the work in this volume attests.

5. C. Howard Hopkins, *The Rise of the Social Gospel in American Protestantism, 1865–1915* (New Haven: Yale University Press, 1967), 320.

6. See, for example, the work of Langdon Gilkey, especially *Naming the Whirlwind: The Renewal of God-Language* (New York: Bobbs-Merrill, 1969).

7. Walter Rauschenbusch quoted in Robert T. Handy, ed., *The Social Gospel in America, 1870–1920: Gladden, Ely, and Rauschenbusch* (New York: Oxford University Press, 1966), 266.

8. Walter Rauschenbusch, *Christianizing the Social Order* (New York: Macmillan, 1913), 366.

9. Mel Piehl, *Breaking Bread: The Catholic Worker and the Origin of Catholic Radicalism in America* (Philadelphia: Temple University Press, 1982), 32.

10. Washington Gladden, *The Nation and the Kingdom* (Boston: American Board of Commissioners for Foreign Missions, 1909), 4.

11. Piehl, *Breaking Bread,* 33.

12. John R. Aiken and James McDonnell, "Walter Rauschenbusch and Labor Reform: A Social Gospeller's Approach," *Labor History* 11, no. 2 (1970): 131–50.

13. Samuel Loomis, *Modern Cities and Their Religious Problems* (New York: Pilgrim Press, 1887), 99.

14. Philip S. Foner, *Women and the American Labor Movement* (New York: Free Press, 1982), 308.

15. Dorothy Day, *The Long Loneliness* (New York: Harper and Row, 1963), 232–34.

16. For example, Father Haggerty, the intrepid Catholic priest, was very influential in the early days of the Industrial Workers of the World. Haggerty's own biography seems to belie the possibility of keeping a foot in both camps, however. He died defrocked as well as largely forgotten by his anarcho-syndicalist brethren.

17. The Kingdom of God is not Day's preferred metaphor. She relies much more heavily on the organic metaphor of the church as the body of Christ. As we have seen, this was not absent from the work of the social gospel, but it was secondary to the idea of the Kingdom of God. Certainly, a distrust of government inherited from those in her anarcho-syndicalist background may have caused Day to be more guarded in using Kingdom language.

18. I am indebted here to Piehl's invaluable work on the distinctions between the two movements.

19. Piehl, *Breaking Bread,* 135.

20. Day, *By Little and By Little,* 109.

21. Ibid., 71.

22. Day quoted in William D. Miller, *Dorothy Day: A Biography* (San Francisco: Harper and Row, 1982), 382.

23. Ibid.

24. Piehl, *Breaking Bread,* 137.

25. Ibid., 138.

26. Day quoted in Miller, *Dorothy Day,* 382.

27. Father John Ryan (1869–1945) spent much of his career as a professor at the Catholic University of America. Also a member of the National Catholic Welfare Conference, Ryan was instrumental in mediating between American Catholics and the government on many significant pieces of social legislation, including parts of Franklin Roosevelt's New Deal program.

28. George A. Kelly, *The Catholic Church and the American Poor* (New York: Alba House, 1976), 128.

29. Piehl, *Breaking Bread,* 136.

30. Ibid., 137.

CHAPTER 9

Jane Addams, Walter Rauschenbusch, and Dorothy Day: A Comparative Study of Settlement Theology

R. A. R. Edwards

Recent works of social criticism find a variety of commentators worrying over the state of America's soul. Robert Wuthnow's *Loose Connections: Joining Together in America's Fragmented Communities* (1998) and Robert Putnam's *Bowling Alone: The Collapse and Revival of American Community* (2000) spring immediately to mind. These are new voices in an old conversation about the supposed decline of civic life in America. Robert Bellah has been pondering the fate of the common good for some time. In both *Habits of the Heart* (1985) and *The Good Society* (1992), he and his coauthors argued that Americans today have difficulty understanding the older traditions, both biblical and republican, that once informed public life. This difficulty, they concluded, means that Americans cannot see the "truth that the individual is realized only in and through community."[1]

Most recently, Bellah offered a more explicitly theological analysis of the problem, stating that "[t]he dominance of Protestantism, for historical reasons, in what I will be calling the American cultural code is responsible for many of our present difficulties. We badly need an infusion of . . . the Catholic imagination if we are to overcome those difficulties." Why has our Protestant cultural code failed us? It is, according to Bellah, "virtually inarticulate about the common good" because of its emphasis on the relationship between the individual believer and the savior. "The downward spiral," as Bellah puts it, "begins with the statement, 'If I'm all right with Jesus, then I don't need the church.'" Or, one might add, civil institutions. An alternative Catholic code, speaking of the sacramental life, would open up access to a vocabulary and a body of thought that speak both eloquently and persistently about the importance of the common good.[2]

This characterization of Protestantism would probably have come as a shock to social gospelers. They have been understood as Christian, and largely Protestant, reformers, wanting to transform both personal lives and the social order. The creation of a godly social order was their defining goal. Could Protestantism really have been as shallow a cultural code as Robert Bellah would now have us believe? Perhaps not the entire tradition of Protestantism; that would clearly seem like a far too sweeping indictment. But historians would have us revisit our judgement of nineteenth-century reformers, and even some social gospelers, as unambiguously religious. Richard Wightman Fox asks us to reconsider the social gospel. We have, he argues, "accept[ed] at face value the social gospelers' status as 'religious' figures and their churches as 'religious' institutions, without asking the prior question: To what extent had religion already been transformed in liberal Protestantism by secular assumptions and commitments?"[3]

If Fox is right and Protestantism had already become secularized by the early twentieth century, this would suggest that Americans increasingly lacked a theological perspective from which to think about the ways that private religious beliefs might translate into public actions. They lacked insight into the ways one's private beliefs might and do matter to the commonweal, with serious social consequences.[4] If Bellah is right, we should look to theology, and particularly to Catholic theology, for a source of renewed commitment to the common good.

The Progressive Era offers a good place to begin to look for answers to our questions. Here reformers such as Jane Addams (1860–1935) actively rejected theology even while espousing Christianity as they tackled social problems. An important exception, Walter Rauschenbusch (1861–1918), tried to put theology back on the progressive agenda with *A Theology for the Social Gospel* in 1917 but his efforts failed. The social gospel continued but with Protestants increasingly emphasizing the "social" over the "gospel." By the 1930s, a return to settlement work with a theological sensibility would be embarked upon not by Protestants but by Catholics, when Dorothy Day (1897–1980) cofounded the Catholic Worker movement, with Peter Maurin, in 1933. Exploring the philosophies of these three thinkers will allow us to better understand the role of theology in social reform efforts. These three will also provide us with a kind of case study to test Bellah's assertion that the shape of national culture is determined by its cultural code and his conclusion that it matters a great deal whether that code is Protestant or Catholic.

Before turning to Addams, we must first look at the late nineteenth-century religious landscape. By this time, traditional Calvinism, once a major influence in North American theology, was in its death throes. In spite of the efforts of Jonathan Edwards, Calvinism had, over the course of the eighteenth and nineteenth centuries, allowed itself to become distracted by increasingly peripheral theological issues, most notably infant damnation.[5] It was losing adherents rapidly by the late nineteenth century. At this point, new scientific theories, most notably Darwin's theory of evolution, began to make profound inroads into social thought.[6] Some Protestant ministers, following the lead of Henry Ward Beecher, responded by giving social Darwinism a theological spin, imbuing it with the spirit of predestination.[7] The result was an increasingly shallow celebration of progress, with the existing social order understood to embody God's divine plan. As Henry Ward Beecher put it, observing the crowded New York of the 1870s, "Looking comprehensively through the city and town and village and country, the general truth will stand, that no man in this land suffers from poverty unless it be more than his fault—unless it be his *sin.*"[8]

Into this insipid religiosity burst the social gospel. Its proponents argued against the use of Christianity as a prop for the reigning social order. The social gospelers sought to reinvigorate Protestantism with a new vision of God and his Kingdom. Preachers like Josiah Strong and Washington Gladden insisted that God's Kingdom could not be advanced on earth unless Christians stepped forward to take responsibility for their society. Christian faith demanded a sense of stewardship from its believers. Individual salvation became inextricably linked with social salvation.[9]

Jane Addams's social work spanned the years of the rise of the social gospel. Addams undoubtedly came into contact with those active in the movement. She moved in similar circles and participated in some of the same conferences, including the World's Parliament of Religions, held in Chicago at the World's Columbian Exposition in 1893, and the second annual Christian Socialist Fellowship Conference, held in Chicago in 1907. While she shared their social concerns, Addams differed sharply from social gospel leaders on the question of the role of Christian theology in politics. Indeed as Kathryn Kish Sklar rightly states, "Although Hull House residents have generally been interpreted as reformers with a religious motivation, it now seems clear that they were instead motivated by political goals. . . . In, but not of, the social gospel movement, the women of Hull House were a political boat on a religious stream."[10] As a political reformer, Addams accordingly rejected theology in the process of building a social philosophy of her own, while continuing to believe that the spiritual life was nonetheless an important part of the call to social action. Her solution was a philosophy that entailed a religion without a theology, a faith without a creed.

Addams's life history holds some of the clues as to why such a solution would have appealed to her. Addams recalled in particular a childhood struggle with the notion of predestination. She went to her Quaker father about it: "he said that he feared that he and I did not have the kind of mind that would ever understand foreordination very well and advised me not to give too much time to it; but then he proceeded to say other things of which the final impression left upon my mind was that it did not matter much whether one understood foreordination or not, but that it was very important not to pretend to understand what you didn't understand and that you must always be honest with yourself inside, whatever happened."[11] The lesson, to achieve moral integrity and avoid dry scholasticism, was not lost upon her. It provided her with a formula for approaching the world that would prove in the long run to serve her well.

Yet she initially struggled to apply the lesson to her own life and was hindered in her efforts after her college years by the death of her father. His loss shook her deeply. In an attempt to reconnect herself to the larger world after his death, she joined her local Presbyterian church. She had experienced no great conversion but rather found herself "longing for an outward symbol of fellowship . . . some blessed spot where unity of spirit might claim right of way over all differences."[12] Even here, Addams was groping toward something other than organized religion. She entered one church but clearly wanted a sense of unity that extended beyond one denomination. She wanted to reconcile her "childish acceptance of the teachings of the gospels" with an "almost passionate commitment to the ideals of democracy."[13] Sensing that her answer did not lie in an organized church, she continued her search. The solution came to her during her second trip to Europe, in 1887–88: she would open a social settlement. Ellen Gates Starr, Addams's companion on this European trip, was similarly inspired by the idea. Upon their return to Chicago, they found a house on Halsted Street. On September 18, 1889, the pair moved in and Hull-House opened its doors.[14]

As Christopher Lasch suggests, Addams's personal search reflected her generation's ongoing difficulties with the theologies of organized religion. What struck him most forcefully in considering the correspondence of the young Addams and Starr was their "theological confusion . . . their utter inability to grasp the points of Christian doctrine that earlier would have been taken for granted."[15] Both Addams and Starr still felt a religious impulse, but that impulse was experienced in a "theological void." Lasch concludes, "It was the waning of theology . . . that created the cultural climate out of which the social settlement emerged."[16] The social settlement provided these young women a way out of their theological confusion by offering "a secular outlet . . . for energies essentially religious."[17]

Addams herself acknowledged her religious impulses as she opened Hull-House. In "The Subjective Necessity for Social Settlements" (1892), she explored the pressures in society that seemed to call for the creation of social settlements; one of these was a burgeoning Christian renaissance, calling Christianity back to its early humanitarian roots.[18] Addams described this Christianity less as a religion than as a way of life. As Addams understood it, Jesus's message was simply "that the truth is one."[19] The humanitarian impulse of Christianity, Addams stated, revealed a "desire to make social service . . . express the spirit of Christ."[20]

Addams explained her position in more detail.

That Christianity has to be revealed and embodied in the line of social progress is corollary to the simple proposition that man's action is found in his social

relationships in the way in which he connects with his fellows, that his motives for action are the zeal and affection with which he regards his fellows. By
this simple process was created a deep enthusiasm for humanity, which regards
man at once as the organ and object of revelation, and by this process came
about that wonderful fellowship, that true democracy of the early Church.[21]

Her religious inclinations reveal themselves here. Addams interpreted religious
feeling as a "deep enthusiasm for humanity." Of course, orthodox Christian
theology, the kind that Addams's generation was having increasing trouble com-
prehending, defined religious feeling quite differently. Religion was hardly a deep
enthusiasm for humanity—it was a deep enthusiasm for God. Yet Addams's
unorthodox definition was one other members of her generation would readily
have understood. It quite aptly reflected the "secularized religiosity" of those
years.[22]

True Christianity, according to Addams, resulted in "true democracy." This
democracy was revealed in the early church in the fellowship of believers, itself
attained by the Christian belief that human beings were "objects of revelation."
The most important revelation of all, Addams indicated, was that Christianity
was "revealed and embodied in the line of social progress." The conflation of
the secular and the sacred is here complete. There is no difference between the
two in Addams's version of Christianity. Christianity is embodied in social
progress and social progress is embodied in democracy. Addams used Christian rhetoric to bolster faith certainly, but faith in democracy, not in God.

By removing the theological content from Christianity, Addams was left with
a collection of words and images that she could use to lend apparent religious
support to the pillars of her social thought, the interdependence of social classes
and the democratic way of life. Practicing Christianity would lead to social democracy, because Christians loved humanity deeply and looked to human beings
as objects of constant joyful revelation. Seen from this viewpoint, it becomes clear
that Addams used, in a fairly unreflective way, religious words to describe essentially secular concerns. Catherine Peaden has come to the same conclusion. Looking at Addams's rhetoric, she writes, "Although Addams grew less and less conventionally religious through her lifetime, Christian discourses remained a central
feature of her rhetoric, from the morality at the core of all her texts to the use of
Christian symbols and parables. However, this Christian strand of her discourse
came more and more to rest in an Arnoldian conception of culture as a replace-
ment for religion and more and more intersected romantic rhetoric."[23]

Addams was certainly not the originator of such an a-theological Christianity. Historians have well documented the decline of orthodox religion in these
years; Henry Ward Beecher serves as the usual whipping boy in such narratives.[24]
And it is not my intent to substitute Addams as the story's whipping girl. Rather,
I have focused on Addams as a way of studying how even social reformers most
interested in recovering authentic religion were unable to escape the drift of their

culture's increasingly secularized style of religion. The analysis that T. J. Jackson Lears provides in *No Place of Grace* is most helpful here. He argues persuasively that Addams and Starr began Hull-House in order to escape their own suffocating class advantages. That is, if they perceived their middle-class advantages as stifling, they acted to save themselves by opening a social settlement. If their personal problems could be solved in such a way, why could the lives of the working class not be made similarly richer through the avenue of personal choice?

Lears analyzes the Hull-House interest in the labor question from this perspective. Worker education became a cause both Addams and Starr took up with enthusiasm because they believed it would enable workers to better understand and appreciate their work conditions, even though such understanding would not necessarily improve or change them. Addams described the advantages of worker education in this way: "If a child goes into a sewing factory . . . understand(ing) the design she is elaborating in its relation to art and decoration, her daily life is lifted from drudgery to one of self-conscious activity, and her pleasure and intelligence is registered in her product."[25] This kind of approach to the labor question would see education used to accommodate workers to their role in the emerging corporate order.[26] By seizing on personal adjustment as the solution to social problems, Lears argues, even a reformer like Addams lost sight of social justice. According to his interpretation, she advocated therapeutic adjustment to the emerging capitalist system; Hull-House did not challenge the emerging social order at all. In his opinion, an act that seemed radical—living among the poor, albeit in the comfort of a middle-class home—turned out to be socially conservative.

Addams's spirituality must be understood within this wider context of secularizing religiosity. It is particularly important to do so now because recent studies of Addams's spiritual life have tended to obscure, rather than clarify, this crucial connection between secular religion and corporate capitalism. Jean Bethke Elshtain, in her article "A Return to Hull House," argues that Addams "viewed her work through the prism of Christian symbols and injunctions, purposes, and meanings."[27] But this characterization disregards the way that Addams redefined Christianity to better suit her own political and theoretical concerns.

In her biography *Jane Addams and the Dream of American Democracy: A Life*, Elshtain continues to downplay the redefinitions at work in the heart of Addams's Christian discourse. Elshtain states that Addams's religious sensibilities reflected "the generic liberal Protestantism of her day" and acknowledges that "Addams associates Christianity with social progress and with a deepening of human affection."[28] But she asserts that this is not as much of a break with orthodox Christian belief as it first seems. Elshtain argues that Addams merely put new wine in old wineskins. "The good news of the Incarnation and Resurrection had been siphoned off, and Addams had refilled the wineskin with a social message,"

Elshtain writes, "an account of Christianity's origins that offered the poor what she thought they needed: a serviceable story that promised comfort for the time being, strength for the journey, and hope of social transformation in the here and now."[29] It is difficult to see, however, how refilling the wineskin with a social message and leaving out the incarnation and the Resurrection leaves us with Christianity at all. Elshtain seems curiously unwilling to interrogate Addams's account here. She avoids Fox's question ("To what extent had religion already been transformed in liberal Protestantism by secular assumptions and commitments?") altogether, so determined is she to offer us, in the words of Christine Stansell, "not a political intellectual but a Protestant saint."[30]

But this characterization only begs the question: what kind of Protestantism is this? Though she wants to keep Addams in the pantheon of religious reformers, even Elshtain finally admits that Addams's real faith was democracy. "Perceiving Jesus of Nazareth as a forerunner of the Founding Fathers," she explains, "she recast him as a proto-democrat bearing a saving message with egalitarianism at its heart. . . . Thin though this theology may be, its message of democratic inspiration has been embraced by thousands of Americans over the years."[31] Elshtain allows that this theology, thin as it may be, was typical of the American social gospel movement and that Addams's work reflects the movement at its best and most attractive.[32] But, if this is the case, Fox's question becomes even more central for us. Democracy and theology are not the same thing. Democratic inspiration is not just another kind of religious commitment. Wrapping secular concerns in religious rhetoric is not merely about putting new wine into old wineskins. An important substantive shift has taken place. Though Elshtain, for whatever reasons, does not want to grapple with it, Fox's question is the right one to ask. It must be answered if we are to understand both the culture that produced the social gospel and the reform efforts it undertook.[33]

Elshtain recognizes the thinness of theology that Addams offered. This thinness is at the very heart of the historical issue here, for it was the "waning of theology rather than the persistence of piety"[34] that shaped the culture out of which the settlement movement emerged. Christian rhetoric continued to be used and deployed in this time, but it should matter a great deal to cultural and religious historians whether Jesus was understood by historical actors as a deity or a democrat. Painting Addams as a kind of Protestant saint, emphasizing her Christianity while refusing to unpack the meaning of this term to late nineteenth-century reformers, is to misapprehend Addams and her times on a fundamental level.

Changing the terms of the argument from religiosity to spirituality is another way of misapprehending Addams and of avoiding Fox's question. Eleanor Stebner's book The Women of Hull House seeks to understand the Hull-House generation as spiritual rather than religious.[35] To Stebner, Addams was the model ecumenist. Stebner concludes that Addams showed us how religiosity can find a place in public life only by abandoning doctrine and dogma and focusing instead on the "action of loving one's neighbor and learning to live together in recognition of the humanity of all."[36]

Whereas Stebner herself has nothing but approval for the victory of spirituality over doctrinal religion, her own book suggests that this is indeed a pyrrhic victory. It also does not in fact lead to as much inclusiveness as she would like to believe. As Stebner's own portrait of Hull-House reveals, the woman with an increasingly devoted religious life, Ellen Gates Starr, was the one woman Hull-House had the most difficulty accommodating. Starr became an active Roman Catholic, keeping a Latin breviary, a crucifix, and a prie-dieu laden with candles in her room.[37] Stebner reports that Starr's "increasing religious devotion . . . negatively affected her standing at Hull House."[38] Because Starr "blatantly communicated the connectedness of her religious and political convictions," younger residents came to regard her as "fanatical."[39] Starr's "unyielding sense that she was living as God desired" alienated her from the other settlement women.[40] Gioia Dilberto, one of Jane Addams's recent biographers, concurs with this portrait of Starr. She concludes that Starr's "passionate religious faith . . . [was] out of step with the cool professionalism of the other residents."[41] Stebner's own interpretive assertions aside, only a particular type of spirituality, only a Christianity that operated "within a theological void," was fully welcomed at Hull-House.[42]

This kind of a-theological spirituality was of course perfectly in step with the process of accommodation that Lears described. Elshtain and Stebner both wish to recover Addams as a reformer with a distinctly Christian sensibility, but Addams's faith can best be described as the reduction of Christianity to a therapeutic faith in human potential. And this faith was perfectly suited to accommodating corporate capitalism, which itself increasingly relied upon a therapeutic worldview.[43]

Walter Rauschenbusch has been viewed as part of this same process. Both Susan Curtis and Janet Fishburn interpret the social gospel as a path of adjustment to the emerging culture of consumption.[44] Curtis goes so far as to call it "a consuming faith," by which she means to draw attention to both the honest belief of most social gospelers and their increasing adaptation of secular and commercial language.[45]

While this context is arguably the correct one in which to understand the emergence of the social gospel, Rauschenbusch was more than an apologist for middle-class prosperity and an advocate of self-culture.[46] Curtis argues that the "men and women who dominated that movement in the 1920s were satisfied with an ideology of self-realization, a diminution of private anxieties, and an improved standard of living for many Americans."[47] Her argument builds admirably along the path that Lears suggests, but Rauschenbusch does not seem to fit this scheme. Indeed, it has been argued that Rauschenbusch anticipated

Reinhold Niebuhr by attempting "to combine political radicalism with theological conservatism" in his *A Theology for the Social Gospel* (1917).[48]

Rauschenbusch here wanted to reconceptualize sin as a social condition, capable of being institutionalized between classes. An entire class could fall into a public form of sin stemming from the "power of social transmission, from the authority of the social group in justifying, urging, and idealizing wrong, and from the decisive influence of economic profit in the defense and propagation of evil."[49] Such an expanded definition of sin did not suggest that individuals were no longer to be held personally responsible for their part in such matters. For Rauschenbusch, sin had both private and public dimensions. As Lasch argues, Rauschenbusch "sensed that orthodox theology, notwithstanding its puzzling habit of holding individuals accountable for sins that were nevertheless in some sense collective, provided a better understanding of sin than a liberal theology that attributed it to ignorance or 'cultural lag.'"[50] To sin was still actively to reject God, either in one's private life or in one's public life. The unexamined life could lead one to hell.

Christians should reject sin by working for the coming of God's Kingdom, and the two most important aspects of the Kingdom were love and labor. "Being the realm of love, the Kingdom of God must also be the commonwealth of cooperative labor," Rauschenbusch asserted, "for how can we actively love others without serving their needs by our abilities?"[51] We do not serve out of joy or a deep enthusiasm for our fellow men, as Addams would have it; we serve because it is our religious duty. Whether we are happy to love our neighbor is beside the point; we *must* love our neighbor.

Rauschenbusch understood that the social gospel and theology needed each other. The social gospel, Rauschenbusch declared, "requires more faith and not less. It offers a more thorough and durable salvation. It is able to create a more searching sense of sin and to preach repentance to the respectable and mighty who have ridden humanity to the mouth of hell."[52] For Rauschenbusch, the social gospel needed theology in order to clarify what was meant by "sin," "salvation," and "faith." To bandy about the terms in Addams's fashion would reduce them to platitudes, repeated out of sentimentality rather than understanding. Theology also needed the social gospel, in order to focus its attention on the "great ethical problems of social life."[53] From this perspective, only "when religion and ethics are viewed as inseparable elements of the same single-minded and whole-hearted life" is Christianity most Christian.[54]

Rauschenbusch did not succeed in restoring orthodox theology to the social gospel. In part he was hindered in his project by his own beliefs in human perfectibility and progress.[55] Rauschenbusch spoke of "the immense latent perfectibility in human nature."[56] A belief in progress is at its heart incompatible with the very prophetic tradition that Rauschenbusch was trying to recover. A belief in progress is hopelessly secular in its appeal and it insists on judging God according to human standards. That is, it makes the "mistake of identifying the Kingdom of God too closely with any particular form of human society."[57] This last is a crucial error, as Lasch so cogently points out, and even Rauschenbusch in the end was unable to resist its temptations. Because Lasch explains the consequences of limiting God in this way, it is worth considering his argument in full.

> [Rauschenbusch's] concessions to the Enlightenment, however, make it hard for him to explain why the victims of injustice should submit to the authority of a democratic God who shared their own standards of right and wrong yet presided over a world in which those standards were consistently flouted and betrayed. Only the knowledge that some higher set of standards prevailed and that these, at least, were not flouted with impunity could give hope to the hopeless or enable them to see themselves as moral agents, not merely as victims.[58]

Here it becomes clear what the stakes are for both theology and social action. For Christianity to tie itself to humanitarianism, as Addams had done and as Rauschenbusch was in the end unable to resist doing, was a devastating move. It meant that religion would lose the ability to address social problems in a way that would allow the hopeless and oppressed to keep faith, both in God and in themselves. As Fox suggests, liberal Protestantism had already absorbed too many secular assumptions to retain its force as an independent body of knowledge for crafting social reform efforts. And as Bellah would predict, it would fall to Catholics to try to revive a theologically informed attempt at social reformation, in the person of Dorothy Day and the Catholic Worker movement.

Day began her public life as a radical activist, working as a reporter for leftwing journals like *The Call* and *The Masses*. Her conversion to Catholicism in 1926, following the birth of her daughter Tamar, transformed her life. She broke her ties with the radical, and largely atheist, political community of New York and searched for a way to combine her politics with her newly found faith. She succeeded in 1933 when she cofounded the Catholic Worker movement.

The details of Day's conversion and the history of the Catholic Worker movement have been covered well elsewhere; the stories need not be repeated here.[59] The significance of Day to this discussion lies in her social philosophy. Unlike the other thinkers considered here, Day refused to compromise her religion with links either to humanitarianism or to a faith in progress. Instead, Day based the Catholic Worker philosophy squarely on theological grounds. The two key theological concepts for her were the mystical body of Christ and the mystery of the incarnation. These were standard Catholic teachings; nothing about them necessarily entailed radical politics or social revolution. Yet Day used these orthodox ideas to arrive at very unorthodox social and political positions, including a commitment to radical egalitarianism, Christian anarchy, and voluntary poverty. Day's thought best exemplifies Garry Wills's contention that "much serious religion tends, today, to be politically radical and theologically conservative."[60] Wills suggests the connection between the two positions lies in the overlooked meaning of radical as rooted; radicals go back into history, to the

roots, and find there meaning and urgency. In this way, Day returned to orthodox Catholicism and found there the Catholic Worker movement.

The teaching of the mystical body of Christ shaped her perceptions of the path
she followed. Day believed that the mystical body provided "a sense of solidarity . . . whereby we are members one of another."[61] She argued that if we fail to
recognize this connectedness, "our religion is an opiate, for ourselves alone, for
our comfort or for our individual safety."[62] This doctrine bound us together and
forced us to confront our unity and interdependence.

Day saw the mystery of the incarnation as leading to the same conclusion.
Intimately tied in her mind with the mystical body, the incarnation refers to the
mystery of God made human and, more deeply, suggests the possibility of a
suffering God. The life of a follower of this incarnated God was to be like his,
full of suffering, "guided by the folly of the Cross."[63] The cross, as Day understood it, was both folly and triumph, failure and redemption. The incarnation
sanctified human life as it called people to lead a truly strenuous life.

Day wove these two Catholic teachings together to arrive at her social philosophy. She drew the conclusion that as Christ became human in the incarnation, so too humanity shares in Christ's life in the mystical body. Therefore,
Christ becomes present to us in one another. Day exclaimed, "It is not a duty to
help Christ; it is a privilege."[64] In the same way, it is a privilege for us to serve
one another, she believed. Our service was offered, she reasoned, "[n]ot for the
sake of humanity. . . . Not because these people remind us of Christ . . . but
because they are Christ, asking us to find room for Him, exactly as He did at
the first Christmas."[65] God has our salvation "hinge on the way we act toward
Him in His disguise of commonplace, frail, ordinary humanity."[66] The only
question that remained for Day was how to act on this insight.

Day grounded her answer initially in traditional terms. She believed that the
guides to right conduct were the corporal and spiritual works of mercy.[67] Day
soon added her own principles by which the Catholic Worker houses would be
organized. She believed that the works of mercy could best be performed from
a position of voluntary poverty. Voluntary poverty may be understood in part
as an attempt to follow Christ. Catholic Workers felt "a respect for the poor and
destitute as those nearest to God, chosen by Christ for his compassion."[68] But
the impulse went further; it extended beyond service to witness and penance.
Day argued, "[T]o pledge yourself to voluntary poverty for life so that you can
share with your brothers is not enough. One must live with them, share with
them their suffering too. Give up one's privacy, and mental and spiritual com-
forts as well as physical."[69] The works of mercy cannot be performed from a
distance and one cannot secure the interests of people without sharing them.
Involuntary poverty was a sign of institutionalized sin to Day but voluntary
poverty was a spiritual weapon, a way of life to be sought after as a "pearl of
great price."[70] To serve the poor, one must be poor. It would seem at first glance
to be a fool's errand, but Day saw it as partaking willingly in the folly of the cross.

An understanding of the cross as an apparent paradox resolved in the person of Jesus, a theologically informed position, provided Day with a position safe from the temptations of progress. She was undaunted by a life of apparent failure.

> What we do is very little. But it is like the little boy with a few loaves and fishes. Christ took that little and increased it. He will do the rest. What we do is so little we may seem to be constantly failing. But so did He fail. He met with apparent failure on the Cross. But unless the seed fall into the earth and die, there is no harvest.
> And why must we see results? Our work is to sow.
> Another generation will be reaping the harvest.[71]

Day's theology enabled her to anchor her faith in a long-term vision. She understood that even if she did not see results, the work itself was not at all in vain.

In comparison to Day's firmly grounded Christian hope, Addams's rootless Christianity seems decidedly optimistic,[72] believing naively that Christianity "has to be revealed and embodied in the line of social progress" and claiming a faith in "the zeal and affection with which [a person] regards his fellows." We have already seen in both Addams and Rauschenbusch the very real danger of equating Christianity with social progress.

And why should one regard one's fellows with affection? Addams believed that such a feeling was "natural." She wrote, "In time it came to seem natural to all of us that the Settlement should be there. If it is natural to feed the hungry and care for the sick, it is certainly natural to give pleasure to the young, comfort to the aged, and to minister to the deep-seated craving for social intercourse that all men feel. Whoever does it is rewarded by something which, if not gratitude, is at least spontaneous and vital and lacks that irksome sense of obligation with which a substantial benefit is too often acknowledged."[73] Here Addams's optimism makes itself most clear. Her assertions that her work merely harnessed natural instinct would be rejected by both Rauschenbusch and Day. To Rauschenbusch, giving up an institutionally sanctioned class advantage is not natural. To Day, meeting a bum and treating him like an "ambassador of God" is not natural. Both are rather acts of faith, acts furthermore that may or may not be rewarded in any tangible way.

The Catholic Worker movement can best be understood as practicing a kind of "religious politics," as Mel Piehl puts it.[74] The movement is deeply concerned with politics; it wants to create a new society by putting into daily practice the teachings of the gospel. In fact, Piehl argues, it is the Workers' "adherence to traditional Catholicism that has been most misunderstood" since its beginnings.[75] Secular thinkers and many Protestants, he suggests, have considered this religious politics either "baffling" or an "irrelevant hindrance to the movement's admirable social views."[76]

From the above discussion, however, it becomes clear that this religious politics, this commitment to both radical social change and orthodox religious teachings, is what gives the movement its staying power. The Catholic Worker movement survives precisely because it makes "its ethical vision a corollary of religious faith, rather than redefining religion in purely ethical or social terms."[77] It refuses, in other words, to walk down the path that both Addams and Rauschenbusch in the end chose to follow. The Workers refuse to make religion more compatible with secular ideas of progress or democracy. They understand, as Stephen Carter puts it, that "religion, properly understood *is* a very subversive force."[78] The Workers prefer faithfulness to expediency, like the prominent 1950s Worker Ammon Hennacy, and accept that they may appear, by the world's standards, to be constantly failing, like their founder Dorothy Day. It is exactly "by losing power rather than gaining it [that] the Catholic Worker has kept in the forefront of its social vision a thoroughly religious sense of what all human life should be about."[79]

This may be the toughest lesson this historical case study reveals for those interested in restoring theology to a place in social reform efforts. Such a move requires accepting both limits and failures. It means abandoning a belief in progress. It means that religious people, more so than others, cannot afford to compromise their beliefs to accommodate secular standards. Such a move, in the end, however tempting, is fatal to the very qualities that make religious belief most attractive in the first place. Addams's a-theological religion was well suited to accommodate the transformation of Hull-House from the workplace of committed, passionate volunteers like herself into the purview of professional and secular social workers. Rauschenbusch's belief in progress meant that the social gospel would be unable to sustain its critical examination of American society; it is difficult to offer a compelling critique of a society that is perceived to be consistently improving merely with the passage of time. Of the three, only Day succeeded in establishing a tradition that, nearly seventy years after its founding and twenty years after her death, remains true to its roots.

None of this suggests guaranteed success. The Catholic Worker movement is small even today and can hardly declare victory in its work to build a new society in the shell of the old. The fact of the matter is faith guarantees nothing. And that is the point, one we have increasingly lost sight of, one Addams's generation helped to obscure. As Elshtain suggests, "The social gospelers of Addams's era aimed to retool Christianity, so to speak, so as to make it do lots of practical work."[80] Even more than this, Addams wanted faith to produce results, just as it had produced joy for the early Christians. But the power of the theological perspective lies not in its promise of results; rather, it lies in its promise of insight. We need this insight now more than ever. As the political theorist Michael J. Sandel notes, the technology that increasingly links people in distant lands—satellite hookups, television, the Internet—does not necessarily make them neighbors. "Converting networks of communication and interdependence into a public life worth affirming," he writes, "is a moral and political matter, not a technological one."[81] I would add simply that it is also a theological matter. Theology promises to help avowed believers make tangible connections between their faith and their actions. As this historical study suggests, only by retaining theology as a separate body of thought can this promise be fulfilled. If believers compromise their religious ideas to fit in with the prevailing social or political order, they will in the end lose their religion altogether. And it will in turn lose its ability to offer them any insight into social or political life.

Notes

I would like to thank the editors for their help and their patience. Thanks as well to those who read earlier versions of this essay and helpfully offered comments and suggestions, especially Robert Westbrook, Laure Pengelly, Joseph Fornieri, and Harry O'Rourke.

1. Robert Wuthnow, *Loose Connections: Joining Together in America's Fragmented Communities* (Cambridge, Mass.: Harvard University, 1998); Robert Putnam, *Bowling Alone: The Collapse and Revival of American Community* (New York: Simon and Schuster, 2000); Robert Bellah et al., *The Good Society* (New York: Vintage, 1992), 5 (quote).

2. Robert Bellah, "Religion and the Shape of National Culture," *America* (July 31, 1999): 9–10 (first quote), 12 (third quote), 13 (second quote).

3. Robert Wightman Fox, "The Culture of Liberal Protestant Progressivism, 1875–1925," *Journal of Interdisciplinary History* 23, no. 3 (Winter 1993): 645.

4. I do not mean to suggest that theology alone can provide this insight. Secular sources, like philosophy, can also provide insight into the question of how we should live. But for people who profess themselves adherents of a particular set of religious beliefs, only theology can rightly do this work for them. Insofar as millions of Americans claim to be religious, their inability to draw insight from the body of thought known as theology is a serious problem.

5. For a discussion of the decline of Calvinism in America, see Joseph Haroutunian's *Piety versus Moralism: The Passing of the New England Theology* (New York: Henry Holt, 1932).

6. For more on the impact of Darwinism on American religious thinkers, see James Turner's *Without God, Without Creed* (Baltimore: Johns Hopkins University Press, 1985).

7. Janet Forsythe Fishburn, *The Fatherhood of God and the Victorian Family: The Social Gospel in America* (Philadelphia: Fortress, 1981), 59.

8. Beecher as quoted in Sydney Ahlstrom, *A Religious History of the American People* (New Haven: Yale University Press, 1972), 789. Emphasis in original.

9. See C. Howard Hopkins, *The Rise of the Social Gospel in American Protestantism, 1865–1915* (New Haven: Yale University Press, 1940), and Donald K. Gorrell, *The Age of Social Responsibility: The Social Gospel in the Progressive Era, 1900–1920* (Macon, Ga.: Mercer University Press, 1988).

10. Kathryn Kish Sklar, "Hull House in the 1890s: A Community of Women Reformers," *Signs* 10 (1985): 663. For more on the political work of the Hull-House community see Robyn Muncy, *Creating a Female Dominion in American Reform, 1890–1935* (New York: Oxford University Press, 1991).

11. Jane Addams, *Twenty Years at Hull House* (1910; New York: Signet, 1981), 30.

12. Ibid., 68.

13. Ibid.

14. This familiar story is covered in detail by Addams herself in *Twenty Years at Hull House*.

15. Christopher Lasch, *The New Radicalism in America, 1889–1963: The Intellectual as a Social Type* (New York: Knopf, 1965), 10–11.

16. Ibid., 11.

17. Ibid.

18. Addams, "The Subjective Necessity for Social Settlements," in *The Social Thought of Jane Addams,* ed. Christopher Lasch (New York: Bobb-Merrill, 1965), 29.

19. Ibid., 40.

20. Ibid.

21. Ibid., 40–41.

22. T. J. Jackson Lears, *No Place of Grace: Antimodernism and the Transformation of American Culture, 1880–1920* (New York: Pantheon, 1981), 73.

23. Catherine Peaden, "Jane Addams and the Social Rhetoric of Democracy," in *Oratorical Culture in Nineteenth-Century America,* ed. Gregory Clark and S. Michael Halloran (Carbondale: Southern Illinois Press, 1993), 193.

24. See Ahlstrom, *Religious History,* especially chaps. 46 and 47.

25. Addams as quoted in Lears, *No Place of Grace,* 80.

26. Lears, *No Place of Grace,* 79–80.

27. Jean Bethke Elshtain, "A Return to Hull House," *Cross Currents* 38 (Fall 1988): 260.

28. Jean Bethke Elshtain, *Jane Addams and the Dream of American Democracy: A Life* (New York: Basic Books, 2002), 35 (first quote), 96 (second quote).

29. Ibid., 76.

30. Christine Stansell, "What a Woman Could Do," *New York Times Book Review,* January 27, 2002, 16.

31. Elshtain, *Jane Addams,* 72.

32. Ibid., 97.

33. Joel Schwartz's *Fighting Poverty with Virtue: Moral Reform and America's Urban Poor, 1825–2000* (Bloomington: Indiana University Press, 2000) makes an attempt to understand this culture and its reform work. His portrait of Addams and Rauschenbusch is so heavy-handed, however, that one must view this as only a first effort to come to grips with the place of Addams and Rauschenbusch in this story. For instance, he accuses Addams of dishing out "condescension masquerading as compassion" (118) based mostly on what seems to be a highly selective reading of her work. And his treatment of Rauschenbusch relies almost exclusively on a manuscript that Rauschenbusch "discarded" in his lifetime and was only published posthumously after its discovery in 1968 (109).

34. Lasch, *New Radicalism,* 11.

35. Eleanor J. Stebner, *The Women of Hull House: A Study in Spirituality, Vocation, and Friendship* (Albany: State University of New York Press, 1997), 20.

36. Ibid., 82.

37. Gioia Dilberto, *A Useful Woman: The Early Life of Jane Addams* (New York: Scribner, 1999), 191, 245. Starr went on to become a Benedictine oblate in 1920 and entered the Convent of the Holy Child in Suffern, New York, where she lived until she died in 1940. In an article written after Starr's death, Eleanor Grace Clark characterized Starr's life as an example of a "kind of Catholic living." She claimed that "Ellen's task was never to lose sight, nor if possible ever to let others lose sight of, the holy purpose of their service which was, in her view, simply to please God" ("Ellen Gates Starr, OSB [1859–1940]: An Account of the Life of the Co-Foundress of Hull House," *Commonweal* 31 (March 15, 1940): 447, 444).

38. Stebner, *Women of Hull House,* 92.

39. Ibid.

40. Ibid., 94.

41. Dilberto, *A Useful Woman,* 246.

42. Lasch, *New Radicalism,* 11.

43. See Lears for more on this point. See also William Leach, *Land of Desire* (New York: Vintage, 1994), especially chaps. 7 and 8.

44. Susan Curtis, *A Consuming Faith: The Social Gospel and Modern American Culture* (Balti-

more: Johns Hopkins University Press, 1991), and Janet Forsythe Fishburn, *The Fatherhood of God and the Victorian Family: The Social Gospel in America* (Philadelphia: Fortress, 1981).

45. Curtis, *Consuming Faith,* 12.

46. Fishburn, *Fatherhood of God,* 64, 120.

47. Curtis, *Consuming Faith,* 14.

48. Christopher Lasch, *The True and Only Heaven: Progress and Its Critics* (New York: Norton, 1991), 380n.

49. Walter Rauschenbusch, *A Theology for the Social Gospel* (New York: Abingdon Press, 1917), 67.

50. Christopher Lasch, "Religious Contributions to Social Movements: Walter Rauschenbusch, the Social Gospel, and Its Critics," *Journal of Religious Ethics* 18 (Spring 1990): 10.

51. Rauschenbusch, *Theology for the Social Gospel,* 55.

52. Ibid., 11.

53. Ibid., 15.

54. Ibid., 14.

55. Lasch, "Religious Contributions to Social Movements," 9.

56. Walter Rauschenbusch, *Christianity and the Social Crisis* (New York: Macmillan, 1907), 422.

57. Lasch, "Religious Contributions to Social Movements," 8. See also Turner, *Without God, Without Creed.*

58. Lasch, "Religious Contributions to Social Movements," 21.

59. See Mel Piehl's *Breaking Bread: The Catholic Worker and the Origin of Catholic Radicalism in America* (Philadelphia: Temple University Press, 1982), James Fischer's *The Catholic Counterculture in America, 1933–1962* (Chapel Hill: University of North Carolina Press, 1989), and William Miller's *Dorothy Day: A Biography* (New York: Harper Collins, 1982) and *A Harsh and Dreadful Love: Dorothy Day and the Catholic Worker Movement* (New York: Liveright, 1973).

60. Garry Wills, *Bare Ruined Choirs* (Garden City, N.Y.: Doubleday, 1972), 250.

61. Dorothy Day, *The Long Loneliness* (1952; New York: Harper and Row, 1981), 147.

62. Dorothy Day, "Aims and Purposes" (originally in the *Catholic Worker,* February 1940), in *By Little and By Little: The Selected Writings of Dorothy Day,* ed. Robert Ellsberg (New York: Knopf, 1983), 91.

63. Day, *The Long Loneliness,* 247.

64. Day, "Room for Christ" (originally in the *Catholic Worker,* December 1945), in *By Little and By Little,* 97.

65. Ibid.

66. Ibid.

67. The corporal works of mercy are to feed the hungry, to give drink to the thirsty, to clothe the naked, to shelter the homeless, to ransom the captive, to visit the sick, and to bury the dead. The spiritual works of mercy are to instruct the ignorant, to counsel the doubtful, to admonish sinners, to bear wrongs patiently, to forgive offenses willingly, to comfort the afflicted, and to pray for both the living and the dead.

68. Day, *The Long Loneliness,* 204.

69. Ibid., 214.

70. Day, "The Pearl of Great Price" (originally in the *Catholic Worker,* July–August 1953), in *By Little and By Little,* 112.

71. Day, "Aims and Purposes," in *By Little and By Little,* 92.

72. For a rich discussion of this distinction, see Lasch's *The True and Only Heaven,* 530. In brief, he argues that progressive ideologies are based on optimism, which is little more than "a higher form of wishful thinking." It "rests on a denial of the natural limits on human power and freedom, and it cannot survive for very long in a world in which an awareness of those limits has become inescapable." Hope, on the other hand, "asserts the goodness of life in the face of its limits. It cannot be defeated by adversity" (ibid.).

73. Addams, *Twenty Years at Hull House,* 88.

74. Mel Piehl, "The Politics of Free Obedience," in *Revolution of the Heart,* ed. Patrick G. Coy (Philadelphia: Temple University Press, 1988), 180.

75. Ibid., 182.

76. Ibid.

77. Ibid.

78. Stephen L. Carter, *The Culture of Disbelief: How American Law and Politics Trivialize Religious Devotion,* (New York: Basic Books, 1993), 43.

79. Piehl, "Politics of Free Obedience," 212.

80. Elshtain, *Jane Addams,* 73.

81. Michael J. Sandel, *Democracy's Discontent: America in Search of a Public Philosophy* (Cambridge, Mass.: Belknap Press, 1996), 340.

CHAPTER 10

The Ecumenical Woman's Missionary Movement: Helen Barrett Montgomery and *The Baptist,* 1920–30

Kendal P. Mobley

Helen Barrett Montgomery (1861–1934) presents a problem for the definition of the social gospel. If she is a social gospel figure, then the definition of the social gospel must be expanded to include a missionary movement built around gender-based concerns that extended far beyond the crisis of America's industrial age. If, on the other hand, she is excluded, what is one to make of her early career as a social reformer and of all of the ways her thought intersects with the tenets of the social gospel? This essay compares the theology of the ecumenical woman's missionary movement, which Montgomery represented, and key elements of the theology of social gospel. Drawing upon some of Montgomery's lesser-known denominational writings—many of them produced in defense of the missionary cause during the height of the fundamentalist-modernist controversy—this essay raises the question of whether the social gospel should be redefined to make room for a gender-based theology focused on the emancipation of women.

Montgomery was a pioneering social reformer in late nineteenth-century Rochester, New York. She was instrumental in the founding of the Women's Educational and Industrial Union, an agency devoted to protecting the rights, health, and safety of women laborers in Rochester. Montgomery was a frequent and popular lecturer in the city, and local newspapers often reported her views on social and political questions. She became the first woman in Rochester's history to be elected to the school board and was instrumental in bringing reform to the public schools. At the urging of Susan B. Anthony, she chaired the committee that raised the funds to open the University of Rochester to women.

In the early twentieth century, Montgomery emerged as one of the most influential intellectuals of the ecumenical woman's missionary movement, whose organizing principle was a gender-based theology of mission expressed in the slogan, "Woman's Work for Woman."[1] Her six books and other publications on behalf of the Central Committee on the United Study of Foreign Missions testify not only to her scholarly accomplishments,[2] but also to her ecumenical, missionary, and feminist concerns.[3] She authored some of the best selling mission study books in American history. Her well-known book *Western Women in Eastern Lands* sold about 100,000 copies and inspired the Golden Jubilee celebrations of 1910–11, a traveling missions conference that toured thirty-four cities and raised more than one million dollars in celebration of the fiftieth anniversary of organized women's work in foreign missions. Montgomery spoke 209 times on the tour.[4] She helped launch the World Day of Prayer and maintained close ties with the Interdenominational Conference of Woman's Boards; its successor, the Federation of Woman's Boards of Foreign Missions; and the Joint Committee on Women's Union Colleges. Montgomery, Lucy W. Peabody, and Clementina Butler worked together to establish the Committee on Christian Literature for Women and Children in the Mission Fields.[5]

There is a third dimension to Montgomery's life that is key to understanding her remarkable career—her lifelong service and leadership among Baptists. She was for more than forty years a Sunday school teacher in the Lake Avenue Baptist Church of Rochester. And, although she outgrew the exclusivism that made her a "[s]tiff little Baptist" in her youth,[6] she remained committed to and involved in the Northern Baptist Convention (now the American Baptist Churches in the USA) and its principles. In 1914 Montgomery became the first president of the newly organized Woman's American Baptist Foreign Mission Society—a merger of two predecessor organizations, the Eastern and Western societies. She held the office for a decade, except for 1921–22, when she served as the first woman president of the Northern Baptist Convention, becoming the first woman elected to the presidency of any national Protestant denomination—and that during the height of the fundamentalist-modernist controversy.[7] In 1924, her translation of the New Testament was published by the Northern Baptist Convention's Judson Press to commemorate the centenary of the American Baptist Publication Society. Her advocacy of ecumenical missions never mitigated her strong commitment to Baptist life.

These three dimensions of Montgomery's life—personal involvement in social reform, advocacy for world mission on the ecumenical level, and lifelong leadership and service among Baptists—shared a single, overarching purpose in Montgomery's mind: the emancipation of women through the power of the gospel of Jesus Christ. In fact, while Montgomery was a remarkable woman in many ways, her pathway into the woman's ecumenical missionary movement was typical of millions of women who shared her Victorian values: a determination to live a life of Christian usefulness expressed in lifelong service to the local church and the denomination, expanding activity in gender-based domestic social reform, and support for or participation in gender-based missionary activity abroad.

The ecumenical woman's missionary movement itself was no small matter. Dating from 1893, the organized movement came to include about forty denominational women's foreign missionary boards supported by millions of women.[8] These women raised funds, studied the movement's theology of mission, and volunteered for missionary service. From 1860 to the end of 1911 the women of the United States raised over $42 million for foreign missions,[9] and despite the forced consolidations of women's boards with male-dominated denominational structures that began in 1909, the financial contributions of women continued to grow. By the 1920s there were six thousand local women's mission societies contributing three million dollars per year to foreign missions.[10]

Women and girls learned the theology of the movement at annual summer schools for mission study in places like Northfield, Massachusetts; Chautauqua, New York; and Winona Lake, Indiana. They began in 1904 with one school and 235 registered students, and by 1917 there were twenty-five schools with 11,693 women and girls.[11] The curriculum at these schools focused on the annual mission study book published by the Central Committee on the United Study of Foreign Missions, which published a book every year from 1900 to 1938. The combined sales of the first ten ecumenical mission study books produced by the central committee totaled about 700,000 copies.[12]

Perhaps most remarkable is the way women responded to the missionary call once the way was opened to them. Although women were a part of the earliest American foreign missionary efforts, they were not appointed in significant numbers until the autonomous women's boards were organized, beginning in 1860. By 1910, 55 of a typical 100 missionaries commissioned by the denominational boards were women,[13] and by 1925 there were 4,824 single American women and 4,661 married American women on the foreign mission field.[14]

The central focus of the ecumenical woman's missionary movement on the emancipation of women, its organizational distinctiveness, and its sheer size are significant factors setting the movement apart from the social gospel as it has been traditionally understood. But there is the additional factor that the ecumenical woman's missionary movement was focused on the world beyond the borders of the United States. These women, while they were often quite critical of what they viewed as the sub-Christian survivals of oppression against women in Western culture, regarded American womanhood as a model of emancipation for the rest of the world. Indeed, while Montgomery herself often chastised the West for exporting its sins to the rest of the world, many of her assertions regarding other races, cultures, and religions are often regarded as imperialist and racist by twenty-first-century standards.

Although the ecumenical women's missionary movement and the social gospel are not identical in terms of historical development, there are several significant points of convergence.[15] Gary J. Dorrien has observed that the social gospel presented a particular theology of Christianization, the key element of which was social salvation. Both he and Susan Hill Lindley have emphasized that the social gospelers believed that the aim of Christianity ought to be the earthly realization of the Kingdom of God. Helen Barrett Montgomery and the ecumenical woman's missionary movement shared these goals and expressed them in very similar language, only with an emphasis on what such a realized eschatology would mean for the emancipation of women worldwide.

Janet Forsythe Fishburn has characterized the social gospel primarily as a reform movement that also happened to engage in theological revision; she regards it as a movement with a definite social structure of leaders and followers, political goals, and a limited life span. To Fishburn the social gospel movement existed in the space between church and society. Montgomery's movement was just as interested in social and political reform, though it focused primarily—but not exclusively—on the non-Christian world.

Rosemary Skinner Keller has observed how, as a social gospel consciousness evolved among women, they stretched the social boundaries of the woman's sphere and continually redefined domesticity to include ever-broader and worldlier concerns. She emphasized how these social gospel women were motivated by their own personal salvation experiences to pursue the salvation of society and to rebel against their own traditions when they found them too limiting. One can see in Helen Barrett Montgomery the same determination, born out of a deep personal piety, to live a useful Christian life of service to God and humanity, and to revise human traditions where they conflicted with her vision of the near and coming Kingdom of God.

Susan Hill Lindley has noted that the social gospelers shared a basic perception of the goodness of American ideals without denying America's problems and believed that these problems stemmed not from the ideals but from a failure to realize them. This is exactly how Montgomery regarded American society because she believed that insofar as America was free and democratic, the country was manifesting the essential principles of the New Testament. In short, while Montgomery preferred to identify herself with the global cause of the women's ecumenical missions movement, the social Christianity of her movement was certainly related to and informed by the social gospel.

From Woman's Mission Advocate to Denominational President

In 1921, at the Northern Baptist Convention annual session meeting in Des Moines, Iowa, Helen Barrett Montgomery presented to the denomination a gift of more than $450,000,[16] the results of a two-year "Jubilee" fund-raising campaign related to the golden anniversary of the Woman's American Baptist Foreign Mission Society. The original goal had been $365,000[17]—$1000 for every golden day in the golden year[18]—but the women oversubscribed the offering.

Montgomery was sixty years old and quite well known both within the Baptist world and beyond it, and the Baptists moved in the same business session to elect her the first woman president of a major denomination in the United States.[19] In her comments in an open letter following the meeting, she claimed her election as an affirmation of women's role in the denomination, saying: "First of all I want to thank you in the name of the women of our churches for the honor that you have conferred upon them in the election of a woman as presiding officer. I know that I stand in a representative capacity, and that what has been done was done in recognition of the part that the organized women of the denomination have had in the denominational development."[20]

Montgomery went on to link the advancement of women with what she saw as the Baptists' role as Christianity's leaders in democracy. In this way, she associated the emancipation of women with the core of Baptist identity. She wrote: "I am glad that recognition should have been first given in such conspicuous fashion by those who are proud to be called Baptists. We always have led in democratic movements; I am glad that we led in this" (August 13, 1921, 874).

That was a significant statement coming from Montgomery. In her mind it placed Baptists on the cutting edge of a worldwide movement toward democratization ignited by Christianity. In *Western Women in Eastern Lands,* she wrote "this reaching out of women for fuller freedom and juster opportunities is confined to no race nor country." It springs from "the gradual penetration into the common consciousness of certain principles which Christ enunciated and of which the New Testament is full. These principles are (1) the supreme worth of the individual, (2) his direct responsibility to God, (3) the obligation of unselfish service laid on all irrespective of sex, (4) human brotherhood, (5) divine fatherhood. . . . The Gospel is the most tremendous engine of democracy ever forged. It is destined to break into pieces all castes, privileges, and oppressions. Perhaps the last caste to be destroyed will be that of sex."[21] Here was a theme to which Montgomery would return again and again in her writings: the connections among the missionary advance of the gospel of Jesus Christ, the progress of democracy, and the emancipation of women worldwide.

Helen Barrett Montgomery and *The Baptist,* 1920–30

From 1920 through 1930, Montgomery published forty-nine items in *The Baptist,* a weekly journal of news and comment owned by the denomination. The paper was intended to express and confirm a growing denominational consciousness among the constituency of the young Northern Baptist Convention, which had been established in 1908 at Oklahoma City, Oklahoma. The growing tension of the fundamentalist-modernist controversy was exerting a strain on that hard-won denominational unity, and it quickly became a central topic of debate in the pages of *The Baptist* in the 1920s.

Montgomery had an item published in the very first issue, and her name was listed as a contributing editor until *The Baptist* stopped listing contributing editors in mid-September 1922. Although the style and content of Montgomery's items published in *The Baptist* vary widely, many of them show how she was struggling to maintain a shrinking middle ground between the fundamentalists and the modernists—the ground upon which the woman's missionary movement was based.[22]

The Northern Baptist Convention seemed to be moving in two directions at once—one modernist, ecumenical, and optimistic, the other fundamentalist, sectarian, and defensive. The modernists adopted soul competency as their precept and championed education and social activism,[23] but the fundamentalists questioned the modernists' commitment to the Bible and personal evangelism. The fundamentalists adopted biblical inerrancy and theological orthodoxy as their principles. They wanted denominational mission efforts to be focused almost exclusively on evangelism and church planting.

On the other hand, modernists' doubts about the necessity of personal evangelism and their questions about the authority of the Bible threatened to undermine the basis of the woman's missionary movement because the movement had always engaged in its educational and reform activities with evangelical presuppositions and goals. Thus, while the modernists supported the missionary activities of women, they did so on the basis of what many women would have considered a faulty and destructive theological perspective. Montgomery's items published in *The Baptist* illustrate how she struggled within her own denomination to defend its commitment to the balanced missionary approach she had worked a lifetime to build.

Since education and social reform constituted the most important missionary activities supported by the women's societies, the fundamentalist attack on "liberalism" was in fact an attack on the work of the woman's missionary movement as well. Yet neither the fundamentalists nor the modernists had the balance necessary to maintain the tension between evangelism and civilization that the woman's missionary movement had achieved, nor were the real concerns of women foremost in the thought of either side of this male-dominated controversy.

Furthermore, the fundamentalists wanted to circumscribe the role of women generally by following a strict, literal reading (their opponents said it was a misreading) of the Epistles on women's submission in home and church. This effort was in direct conflict with the most basic assumption of "Woman's Work for Woman": that Jesus Christ is the "great Emancipator of woman" (August 25, 1923, 944).

The 1920s saw the height of the fundamentalist-modernist conflict among Northern Baptists. As a denominational leader—indeed, as the convention president from 1921 to 1922—Montgomery needed all of her political skills to steer a middle course and focus the attention of the convention on Christian mission. Her articles for *The Baptist* during this difficult period show how much she had in common with both sides in the conflict.

Like the fundamentalists she was conservative in her views of the Bible, Christian doctrine, and Christian piety. She believed in personal evangelism. She believed in the salvation of the individual by grace through faith in Christ. She maintained an orthodox Christology. At the same time, she expressed deep concern for the unity of her denomination, for its principles of freedom, and for its ideals of democracy; and she feared the consequences of creedalism.

With the modernists she defended modern education and the social implications of the gospel. She longed for the reformation of society and the liberation of women all over the world, and she saw education as central to both of these goals. Thus she was a proponent of education in general and of Christian education in particular—especially the education of women. All of these views come through clearly in her writings for *The Baptist,* and although she was critical of both the fundamentalist and the modernist position, her clear preference for the modernists was evident as well.

Montgomery's highest commitment was to world mission. In her view, this was the overriding issue—the most basic "fundamental" of all. She viewed the Northern Baptist Convention as an instrument for missionary endeavor. The unity of the denomination would advance world mission while denominational conflict would impede it. Consequently, she fought to keep the fundamentalists and the modernists united for the sake of world mission. "Can we not unite in the great work that is ours to do, and postpone discussions?" she asked in her open letter to the convention. "Can we not agree to disagree about many matters, while we unite in the one great matter, the evangelizing of the world in obedience to our Master?" (August 13, 1921, 874).

Montgomery turned to the two resources that, in her experience with the ecumenical women's missionary movement, had produced much unity: prayer and mission study. She wrote: "I wish that instead of coming together to discuss fundamentals before the next Convention, we might spend a quiet day of prayer in preparation of our hearts for the convention." Next, she wanted the convention to focus on the work of missions rather than debate doctrine. "There are missionaries, who have a great story to tell," she wrote. "Let us give them time to tell it. Why can not we have the whole Convention pursuing the study of our mission text-books under great leaders, instead of having the classes held in a corner between sessions?" (August 13, 1921, 874). Evidently, her suggestions carried weight, for these two ideas were incorporated into the next annual meeting of the convention (May 20, 1922, 514).

Finally, she appealed to the convention members' responsibility to be faithful stewards of Baptist principles, such as the autonomy of the local church, soul competency, the separation of church and state, and religious liberty. Yet in this appeal to principle was also couched a challenge to Baptists, as "the recognized democrats of the Protestant world" to rise above disputes over doctrine and join together for the sake of mission. She challenged them "to prove that without abandoning our democracy we can learn to stand shoulder to shoulder in the cooperative prosecution of the great tasks of the kingdom" (June 17, 1922, 625).

For Montgomery, Baptist principles were not merely helpful in promoting mission; rather, she viewed "the standard of a free church in a free state" as an essential part of the content of Christian mission in Europe, where "[o]ne hundred million people . . . as a result of the war, have religious liberty for the first time." Thus, she challenged Northern Baptists to examine their own faithfulness to the Baptist tradition: "Have we, ourselves, a firm hold of the principle of toleration and religious freedom so that we can help them to establish it? Are we free from intolerance and bigotry? Pray God that we may purge ourselves of any root of bitterness and rise to the fullness of this great opportunity" (June 17, 1922, 625).

Montgomery's Criticisms of Fundamentalists and Modernists

In a piece that seems to have been aimed at both sides of the fundamentalist-modernist controversy, Montgomery discussed a book called *Ce Qu'on a Fait de l'eglise, etude d'Histoire Religieuse* (What they have made of the Church, a study of religious history), written by five anonymous Roman Catholic priests who documented and then criticized the progressive domination of the Roman Catholic Church by its hierarchy. To those modernists who sought to end the distinctions between denominations and create one organically unified Christian church, she held up Roman Catholicism as "a powerful institution ever becoming more powerful, bureaucratic and corrupt, until even the pope himself is held fast in the toils of the Roman *Curia*." Then, in a clear swipe at the fundamentalist movement, she wrote: "We too have those who would suppress free thought and free speech in the supposed interest of the truth. Truth does not need such support. There are those who believe that the only way to preserve the great Christian fundamentals is to write them out in statements and definitions to which all believers must be forced to subscribe. There are those who in their advocacy of the faith take up the weapons of abuse, denunciation and aspersion of motives. To all such the story of the great disappointment which the history of an absolute church has brought to the hearts of her true lovers, ought to appeal with force" (June 19, 1920, 735).

Like most Baptists, Montgomery valued soul competency very highly. A moral corollary of this idea is the conviction that truth carries within itself the power to persuade the rational individual. Montgomery worked from the Baptist commitment to soul competency to justify a missiology that incorporated a strategy of Christian civilization as well as evangelization. In a free marketplace of ideas, she believed, the inherent superiority of Christianity as a basis for civilization would inevitably become clear. In her view cleanliness, orderliness, compassion, purity, intelligence, rationality, prosperity, health and well-being, science, and progress were the natural and unique social consequences of Christianity. Other religions, in her view, manifested themselves in disorder, impurity, ignorance, irrationality, superstition, poverty, disease, backwardness, and squalor. Where Christianity was free to grow and develop openly and unconstrained alongside other religions, it would clearly demonstrate its inherent superiority. She frequently marshaled evidence highlighting these contrasts.[24]

Montgomery never tired of reminding the Northern Baptists of their commitment to freedom, and she urged them to champion civil liberties in general for all people. In a 1920 article, for example, she made an implicit comparison of the 1837 murder of the abolitionist Elijah P. Lovejoy at the hands of a proslavery mob in Alton, Illinois, to the "Red Scare" fueled to a great extent by the actions of U.S. Attorney General A. Mitchell Palmer in 1919 and 1920. Palmer's boldest move came on January 2, 1920, when government agents in thirty-three cities arrested thousands during what came to be known as the "Palmer raids."[25] Later that same year Montgomery wrote: "In these days when government spies abound, when intolerance 'doth much more abound' and the baiting of political heretics is one of the major sports, in days when the liberty of the press and freedom of thought and action are threatened as they have not been before for generations, it is a good thing to remember at what cost our liberties were bought, and to highly resolve that the free institutions which we have inherited we will defend with unselfish boldness, and the freedom of thought which we claim for ourselves we will accord to others, even to those whose opinions we abhor" (August 21, 1920, 1039).

Her commitment to freedom led Montgomery to side with the modernists and against the fundamentalists on a key issue: she supported freedom in education. "Education is the breath of life to a democracy," she said to the Northern Baptist Convention meeting in Indianapolis in 1922. In a statement that must have thrilled the modernists, she proclaimed: "We Baptists must become enthusiasts for education. . . . Let us correct any faults that may exist, but let us not so frighten our people with wild and unfounded criticism that they withhold their generous support and patronage from our schools" (June 17, 1922, 626).

Montgomery believed the elevation of women through education was essential not only to Christianity, but also to democracy. Speaking before the Baptist World Alliance in Stockholm in 1923, she said: "Most of the great civilizations of the past have builded themselves upon a foundation of ignorant and repressed womanhood and motherhood. . . . Civilizations builded on such foundations could not stand; they carried within themselves the seeds of death." This is true, Montgomery thought, because the degradation of women and mothers means the degradation of children, and ultimately, of the whole culture. "For it is to *mothers* that we commit absolutely the training of the coming generation for the first six most significant and impressionable years of life." The key to the future of any nation is its women, according to Montgomery. Through the education and emancipation of women, Christians could "build the coming kingdom" (August 25, 1923, 944).

Indeed, her major works show clearly that her confidence in the felicitous influence of Christianity for the emancipation of women was a cornerstone of Montgomery's apologetics. She believed the liberating effects of Christianity, experienced through Western-style education, law, and custom, were clear evidence that Christianity was superior to the other religions of the world.

Montgomery's Commitment to Personal Agency

Another recurrent theme in Montgomery's writing for *The Baptist* is an admonition to personal agency. Although she never wavered from a commitment to personal evangelism, she maintained that one's personal faith in Jesus Christ as Lord could not legitimately be separated from a personal commitment to social activism.

Montgomery's high view of the Bible as the authoritative word of God comes through clearly in *The Baptist*. Even though she never advocated a particular view of biblical inspiration, she longed for people to experience the Bible as God's word in their own lives. In discussing her hopes for revival among the Syrian churches of south India, she remarked: "When the awakening comes, it will be because the Scriptures are again known and loved by the common people" (January 8, 1921, 1680). This was a deeply egalitarian sentiment—a democratic trust in the ability of the common person to read and interpret the Bible without the aid of creed or hierarchy. She believed in the moral power of truth to compel the rational individual to appropriate action.

Prayer is a vital part of a healthy Christian life, according to Montgomery, not just because of its benefits for the Christian but because of its effect upon the world. Montgomery viewed prayer as the Christian's "mightiest weapon of supreme strategy," calling it "a real force, a practical agency by the use of which we cooperate with God for the regeneration of the world" (February 10, 1923, 46). She compared it with the radio signal—something that was relatively new in her world—and its power to transmit the vibrations of the human voice. "Shall it be thought a strange thing if prayer has even wider vibrations? If one could really see, he might behold fine waves vibrating from the soul of the true Christian in prayer, waves that are registered in the throne of God." Montgomery regarded prayer as a power that could be utilized according to certain laws. "We can, if we will, develop this prayer power, but like electricity it has laws. One must work for and not against the laws, if power is to be produced" (February 10, 1923, 47).[26]

This view of prayer implied a strong belief in human agency—the power of human beings, under the grace of God, to affect the world around them profoundly for good or ill. This faith in human agency consecrated by God's grace formed a postmillennial theme in Montgomery's mission theory, and it was clearly revealed in her views on prayer: "When we pray, we open channels for the grace and power of God to run sweetly along. By prayer we cooperate with him to build the kingdom of God. Prayer is a force as real as steam, electricity, water power, the X-Ray; as mysterious as light, heat, radium. Because we do not in obedient faith use it, the kingdom halts." Montgomery suggested that Christians could, if only they would "believe and work," bring forth the Kingdom of God: "we can strengthen all the good in the world; we can help to remove intolerable burdens; we can hasten the day when nations as well as individuals shall bow to the Lordship of Jesus; we can hasten the day of his coming!" (September 24, 1921, 1081)

For Montgomery, the Christian life could not be divided neatly into sacred/secular dualisms. Her postmillennial evangelical piety led her into social and political activism and, combined with her concern for the elevation of women, developed into the missiology of "Woman's Work for Woman."[27] Just before the passage of the Nineteenth Amendment, she wrote: "the great organizations of Christian women, the home and foreign mission societies, should as soon as may be add a committee on legislation to their other activities. Some one woman should be selected in each circle, whose duty it will be to keep watch on the course of state and national legislation, to circulate petitions when those are needed, to induce the women to write letters or send telegrams when these may be powerfully utilized." The purpose of this political activism was, in her view, to influence legislators on those questions that were most important to the lives of women and children: "questions affecting education, the protection of young girls, child welfare, the milk supply, and temperance" fell into this category (August 28, 1920, 1073). This sort of social activism, aimed at the promotion of the common good, was a natural result of true religion, and its absence was an indication of a false faith (January 31, 1920, 14).

Between 1920 and 1930, Montgomery wrote no fewer than six pieces for *The Baptist* in support of national prohibition and one against gambling.[28] In her presidential address to the Northern Baptist Convention, she spoke in favor of Prohibition, world peace, and improved labor conditions for workers (June 17, 1922, 625–26, 641). In an open letter to the convention during her presidency, she advocated disarmament (September 24, 1921, 1081). In each of these cases she recommended political activism on the part of her fellow Baptists and especially the women.

Prayer and political activism, evangelism and social action, Bible study and the study of social problems—all of these went together in the mission theory of Helen Barrett Montgomery. She saw them all as essential if Christians were to enter into Christ's ministry, especially his ministry of emancipation on behalf of women everywhere in the world. In the opening paragraph of her address to the Baptist World Alliance, she echoed the great theme of her ministry: "Jesus Christ is the great Emancipator of woman. He alone among the founders of the great religions of the world looked upon men and women with level eyes, seeing not their differences, but their oneness, their humanity. He alone put no barriers before women in his religious teaching, but promulgated one law, equally binding upon men and women; opened one gate to which men and women were admitted upon equal terms" (August 25, 1923, 944).[29]

Identification of the Concerns of the Women's Missionary Movement with Baptist Ideals

Montgomery identified the emancipation of women with the core of Baptist identity and with radical New Testament Christianity. She was an experienced writer and speaker, so it is perhaps not surprising that she would make her feminist appeal to a Baptist audience in this way. Nevertheless her identity as a Baptist was very important to her personally. She felt Baptists were the vanguard of New Testament Christianity in the modern world: "It is but natural that so democratic a body as the Baptists should be among the first to further and to recognize the emancipation of women. For hierarchies, of every name, have an instinctive reaction consistently opposed both to democracy and its handmaiden, the emancipation of women. It has been the radical Christian groups who have seen most clearly and maintained most fearlessly the separation of church and state, and the full participation of women in all the activities of organized Christianity" (August 25, 1923, 944).

Montgomery credited the democratic spirit in Christianity with establishing the foundation for all of the liberties of Western civilization, even though at times they have been denied and obscured. Christianity, she asserted, is the root of "the growing power of democracy" and "the enlarging sphere of women." Christ is the one who stands behind "all the urge of democratic ideals as regards state and sex" (August 25, 1923, 944).

Montgomery tried to show, through the study of woman's missionary organizations, that the freedom and voluntary responsibility of women were crucial to the advancement of the cause of mission. She believed the mission movement ought to capitalize on what she felt were women's unique qualities, particularly "woman's genius for organization" (August 25, 1923, 945). Yet by 1927 it seemed as if the opposite was happening in the Northern Baptist Convention, at least as far as the women's mission societies were concerned. Montgomery was quite critical of the fact that the funds raised by the women's missionary societies had been merged with the general contributions under the unified budget plan of the New World Movement. Her conclusion: "The secret of the power of these women's organizations lies in fixing financial responsibility" (September 12, 1927, 1419).

The problem she found in the new arrangement was that women had been made passive and powerless. Because the mission gifts were not kept separate from other kinds of contributions, there was no reason for women to give separately from their husbands. The husband made the decision about what to give "with or without consulting his wife"; and though the wife shared in the gift, she was not "conscious of giving. She makes no contribution out of her allowance; she is conscious of little or no sacrifice" (September 12, 1927, 1419). In consequence, Montgomery made a rather startling statement for someone in her position as a denominational leader: "We all believed that we were working for the best when the women accepted the present plan, but I have come to think that perhaps we were mistaken; at least, it has not worked out well" (September 12, 1927, 1419, 1429). Certainly, it had not worked out well for the Northern Baptist women, who had less responsibility, less autonomy, and less authority; and their loss had meant the impoverishment of the entire denomination.

Finally, through her study and translation of the New Testament, she tried to show that the emancipation of women was essential to the true Gospel of Christ. Baptists regard themselves as a people of "the Book." If it could be clearly shown that the emancipation of women is taught clearly in the pages of the New Testament, no Baptist could argue with it in principle.

Montgomery used the story of Jesus' encounter with the woman at Jacob's well (John 4:3–30) to show that Jesus had a "caste-less, sexless attitude" towards people. It was an attitude so novel and radical that the apostle Paul was forced to circumscribe the Christian liberty of women in order to protect the public reputation of the early church.[30] Nevertheless Montgomery thought the biblical testimony to the freedom of women in the early church was clear. She cataloged these women: "the seven daughters of Philip who prophesied; Priscilla and her husband . . . Phoebe, servant of the church, . . . and that long list of women who find a place in the closing greetings of Paul's letters" (August 25, 1923, 944).[31]

Conclusion

The organizing principle of the ecumenical women's missionary movement was a gender-based theology of mission expressed in the slogan, "Woman's Work for Woman." In her writings for *The Baptist,* one can observe how Helen Barrett Montgomery promoted and defended that theology within her own denomination, and how she attempted to utilize its methods and resources to meet the challenges her denomination faced in the 1920s. For Montgomery and the women of the movement she represented, "Woman's Work for Woman" included personal involvement in local and national issues of civic reform, faithful service to the Kingdom of God through one's local church and denomination, ecumenical unity among Christian women, and solidarity with women around the world through foreign missions. Long before the phrase was coined, these women were thinking globally and acting locally. Should they be understood as partners in the social gospel movement? If so, the social gospel must be redefined to make room for a gender-based theology focused on the emancipation of women—not only in the United States, but also worldwide.

Notes

1. Rooted in Victorian gender roles and theories of domesticity, "Woman's Work for Woman" taught that Christian women had a unique calling from God to proclaim the gospel by ministering to the particular needs of women and children around the world. After World War I, the theology of "Woman's Work for Woman" gave way to a new theology of "World Friendship." See Dana L. Robert, *American Women in Mission: A Social History of Their Thought and Practice* (Macon, Ga.: Mercer University Press, 1997), 125–88, 272–302. While Montgomery advocated and affirmed many aspects of "World Friendship" in her last book, *From Jerusalem to Jerusalem* (1929), she was more directly responsible for articulating the theology of "Woman's Work for Woman."

2. These include *Christus Redemptor: An Outline Study of the Island World of the Pacific* (New York: Macmillan, 1906); *Western Women in Eastern Lands* (New York: Macmillan, 1910); *The King's Highway* (West Medford, Mass.: Central Committee for United Study of Foreign Missions, 1915); *The Bible and Missions* (West Medford, Mass.: Central Committee for United Study of Foreign Missions, 1920); *Prayer and Missions* (West Medford, Mass.: Central Committee for United Study of Foreign Missions, 1924); *From Jerusalem to Jerusalem* (West Medford, Mass.: Central Committee for United Study of Foreign Missions, 1929).

3. See Shirley S. Garrett, "Sisters All: Feminism and the American Women's Missionary Movement," in *Missionary Ideologies in the Imperialist Era: 1880–1920,* ed. Torben Christensen and William R. Hutchison (Cambridge, Mass.: Harvard Theological Review, 1982), 221–30. See also Sharyn Dowd, "Helen Barrett Montgomery's *Centenary Translation* of the New Testament: Characteristics and Influences," *Perspectives in Religious Studies* 19 (Summer 1992): 133–50; Roger A. Bullard, "Feminine and Feminist Touches in the Centenary New Testament," *Bible Translator* 38 (January 1987): 118–22.

4. Wilhermina C. Livingstone, "Helen Barrett Montgomery," pamphlet (New York: Woman's American Baptist Foreign Mission Society, n.d.), unpaged.

5. Robert, *American Women,* 271.

6. This is Montgomery's self-description. See Helen Barrett Montgomery, *Helen Barrett Montgomery: From Campus to World Citizenship,* with tributes by her friends (New York: Fleming H. Revell, 1940), 34.

7. For a more complete biographical sketch, see the booklet by Conda Delite Hitch Abbott, *Envoy of Grace: The Life of Helen Barrett Montgomery* (Valley Forge, Pa.: American Baptist Historical Society, 1997).

8. Robert, *American Women,* 256.

9. The $42 million includes one million dollars raised by the jubilee offerings. See Louise A. Cattan, *Lamps Are for Lighting: The Story of Helen Barrett Montgomery and Lucy Waterbury Peabody* (Grand Rapids: Eerdmans, 1972), 51, 60.

10. Robert, *American Women,* 305.

11. R. Pierce Beaver, *All Loves Excelling: American Protestant Women in World Mission* (Grand Rapids: Eerdmans, 1968), 154–55.

12. Ibid., 153; *The Story of the Jubilee: An Account of the Celebration of the Fiftieth Anniversary of the Beginning in the United States of Woman's Organized Work in Foreign Missions 1860–1910* (West Medford, Mass.: Central Committee on the United Study of Missions, 1911), 6.

13. William R. Hutchison, *Errand to the World: American Protestant Thought and Foreign Missions* (Chicago: University of Chicago Press, 1987), 101.

14. Robert, *American Women,* 293.

15. The following characterizations of the social gospel, by Gary J. Dorrien, Susan Hill Lindley, Janet Forsythe Fishburn, and Rosemary Skinner Keller, were presented at the second annual Social Gospel Conference, March 18–20, 1999, at Colgate Rochester Divinity School, Rochester, N.Y.

16. William H. Brackney, "Helen B. Montgomery, 1861–1934, Lucy W. Peabody, 1861–1949: Jesus

Christ, The Great Emancipator of Women," in *Mission Legacies: Biographical Studies of Leaders of the Modern Missionary Movement*, ed. Gerald H. Anderson et al. (Maryknoll, N.Y.: Orbis Press, 1994), 66.

17. Cattan, *Lamps*, 86.

18. Livingstone, "Helen Barrett Montgomery."

19. Brackney, "Helen B. Montgomery," 66.

20. "Hear the President's Message," *The Baptist* 2 (August 13, 1921), 874. All further quotes from *The Baptist* will be noted with parenthetical references in the text listing the date and page number of the item.

21. Montgomery, *Western Women*, 206.

22. See Robert, *American Women*, 308–9.

23. "Soul competency" is the belief that God makes each person responsible for his or her own soul; and since each person is individually responsible before God, every person ought to be free in matters of religion to follow the dictates of conscience without coercion from church or state.

24. For example, see Montgomery's *The King's Highway*, 17–34; *The Bible and Missions*, 167 95; and *Western Women*, 205–7.

25. Convinced of a Bolshevik plot to overthrow the U.S. government, Palmer and his assistant, J. Edgar Hoover, responded by targeting the immigrant community. They used the Espionage Act of 1917 and the Sedition Act of 1918 to censor the press, intimidate critics of the government, and round up, imprison and/or deport alleged radicals. Merely criticizing the government could be considered a criminal act, and Palmer's agents frequently violated the civil rights of the accused. See *The New Encyclopaedia Britannica*, 15th ed., s.v. "Palmer, A. Mitchell"; Kermit Hall et al., eds., *The Oxford Companion to the Supreme Court of the United States* (New York: Oxford University Press, 1992), s.v. "Abrams v. United States," "Sedition Acts," and "Schenk v. United States"; *Dictionary of American History*, rev. ed. (New York: Scribner's, 1976), s.v. "Sedition Acts"; Ian Purchase, "Normalcy, Prosperity, and Depression, 1919–1933," in *America's Century: Perspectives on U.S. History Since 1900*, ed. Iwan W. Morgan and Neil A. Wynn (New York: Holmes and Meier, 1993), 54–55; Steven J. Diner, *A Very Different Age: Americans of the Progressive Era* (New York: Hill and Wang, 1998), 241; Jack P. Green, ed., *Encyclopedia of American Political History: Studies of the Principle Movements and Ideas* (New York: Scribner's, 1984), s.v. "Nativism."

26. See also Montgomery, *Prayer and Missions*, 66–67.

27. Richard Carwardine calls this sort of evangelical piety "'Calvinist' involvement" in contrast to "'Pietist' withdrawal." It grew out of the Puritans' organic view of the community and was passed down to nineteenth-century evangelicals through those traditions most powerfully influenced by the Puritans' political views. See Richard J. Carwardine, *Evangelicals and Politics in Antebellum America* (New Haven: Yale University Press, 1993), 14–30. The Calvinism of the Particular Baptist tradition has exercised the dominant influence on the Baptist tradition in America. Nevertheless, the extent of the Pietist influence on Baptists is a topic of some debate. See H. Leon McBeth, *The Baptist Heritage: Four Centuries of Baptist Witness* (Nashville: Broadman Press, 1987), 32–40, 49–56.

28. See *The Baptist* for December 31, 1921, 1526; April 29, 1922, 396; October 11, 1922, 1178; July 23, 1923, 815; August 11, 1928, 990; November 3, 1928, 1330; September 21, 1929, 1148.

29. Compare this with similar statements in Montgomery, *Western Women*, 66–74; and Helen Barrett Montgomery, "Women and the New World Movement," *Watchman-Examiner*, April 15, 1920, 503.

30. See similar arguments in Montgomery's *Western Women*, 72–73, and *The Bible and Missions*, 86.

31. See Montgomery, *Western Women*, 69.

PART 5

Expanding the Conventional Boundaries of the Social Gospel Movement

CHAPTER 11

Gender and the
Social Gospel Novel

Susan Hill Lindley

The American social gospel and the role of women in American religion have emerged as significant concerns for religious historians in recent decades, after a period of relative neglect. In 1976 Ronald C. White Jr. and C. Howard Hopkins called for a fresh, more inclusive look at the social gospel, pointing to women as among the "neglected . . . reformers" in social gospel study.[1] Scholarship on women and religion has exploded in the last decade, focusing not only on important individuals and traditional religious images of women, but also on women's own ideas and activities. This essay is presented with the hope that it may add to the study of the history of women in American religion and also contribute to a new understanding of the social gospel movement.

There is considerable scholarly debate on the exact nature and duration of the social gospel movement. For the purpose of this essay, I have considered the social gospel movement to extend from the 1870s through World War I, although, of course, it had roots before and continuities after this period. The concern of the social gospelers was to relate the Christian message to the needs of their age, especially the problems associated with the emerging labor movement and structures of American economic and political systems. Theologically, the social gospel was allied closely to nineteenth-century liberalism. However, it did not exclude evangelical roots, evident in such an unquestioned leader as Walter Rauschenbusch, and its proponents spanned a theological spectrum from mild conservatism to Christian socialism.[2] Distinctive theological insights of the social gospel, such as the conviction that the social nature of sin and salvation is at least as important to understand as individual sin, reform, and salvation, are clearest in the most articulate and theologically trained leaders and perceived most easily in retrospect; yet they were implicit if not fully self-conscious operating principles of other participants as well.

The social gospel novel is particularly useful in exploring less "professional" theological aspects of the movement, for it constituted a significant form of popularization, one influential way in which the social gospel penetrated to people in the pews. The novels were intentionally didactic: their authors used them to urge readers toward a particular set of values and course of action, hoping to touch their affections as well as their intellect. Thus we find in the social gospel novel a sense of how authors and readers interpreted the social gospel message.

Studying the social gospel novel is also a way to understand the impact of gender on the movement. This form of fiction allowed, even impelled authors to comment more broadly on the roles and images of women as they attempted to portray "real life" situations. It was relatively easy for social gospel theologians to ignore women as women in their sermons and essays; it was more difficult (though by no means impossible) to construct a story with no female characters. Moreover, the novel was a form of literature more socially acceptable for women themselves to write at the time, thus providing a broader female as well as male view of women.

But what is a social gospel novel—beyond the widely familiar example, *In His Steps*?[3] There were many fictional treatments in the late nineteenth and early twentieth centuries of urbanization and industrialization in America, and rare was the novel at that time which did not touch on religion. As a working classification, I have adopted three criteria to identify the social gospel novel. First, it shows significant concern for the theme of urban, industrial, economic conditions in America during the period of the movement. Second, there is an important role proposed for the church or Christianity in responding to those critical conditions. Third, the novel is in sympathy with social gospel aims (thus excluding those works that were primarily religious defenses of the status quo) and reflects distinctive social gospel themes like the concern with structures and social salvation. Within these parameters, one still finds a wealth of works, which justly can be called social gospel novels.[4] Like the social gospel itself, they range from moderate to radical in their views and proposals. This essay will focus on three major questions: first, what images of women are found in the social gospel novel; second, what, if any, significant differences can one find between the novels written by men and by women; third, what else do the novels suggest about women and the social gospel?

The prominence, number, and roles of female characters in social gospel novels vary widely. In some cases, women are so peripheral as to be virtually invisible. Men alone do the significant talking and effective acting. More frequent are women characters as stereotypes, though one learns about the social gospel view of women from the frequency and shape of such types. But most interesting are the women who appear in some of the novels as fully developed actors.

Among the female types presented in social gospel novels is, as one would expect, the minister's wife, in the classic role of support for the direct religious and social work of the minister-hero. By and large, these women are admirable, devoted, devout, domestic, and extremely dull. Only occasionally is the minister's wife a more fully developed person who is given some credit and scope as a genuine partner in ministry, and few of the complex realities of the lives of nineteenth-century ministers' wives are reflected in the novels.[5] Other "good wives," whose main function is to support their husbands and families, appear in the novels. They are conventionally religious; sometimes they are involved in a kindly, neighborly charity. If their husbands' concerns take them into major social action, they follow dutifully, but they seldom initiate such movement. Their greatest worry, especially in Sheldon's novels, appears to be the drinking and dissipation of their sons.

A third type found with relative frequency but little character development is the wealthy, eccentric older woman who aids the cause, the hero, or the heroine—a financial deus ex machina. Less sympathetic but more prominent is the snobbish society matron. Usually she is shallow, hard, and unkind; at best, she is weak and unhappy. Madam Page, Mrs. Winslow, and Mrs. Sterling, familiar to readers of *In His Steps,* have their counterparts in numerous other novels. The predictable condemnation by social gospel writers of rich women who live for material and social show is extended to the characters' lack of success in their domestic roles: most lack genuine love from and for husband and children.

The society matron's counterpart is the society belle, beautiful but lacking in moral depth. Yet there are two sorts within the relatively undeveloped examples of the belle: first, the thoroughly unsympathetic, cold and heartless young woman; second, the belle who is basically shallow but kindhearted when pressed and when it does not interfere with her comfort. The latter may become involved briefly in "good works," but with no deep concern for social justice. More interesting and surprisingly frequent are the heroines of this type. Their primary quality is beauty; they may also have some redeeming strengths of character—flashes of kindness, intelligence, cheerfulness, integrity—but clearly they are *not* deeply committed to moral and religious issues in social gospel terms. Yet they are objects of love and devotion to the heroes—manly, saintly, deeply committed men who always seem willing to excuse the women's shallowness for the sake of their beauty.[6] A mild inconsistency appears: while the society matron without social concern is condemned or pitied as lacking in true religion and genuine family love, some of the younger society women, similarly lacking in social concern, are not judged so harshly. Their beauty and purity are sufficient to win admiration from other characters, the heroes, and the authors themselves. Yet there is some dissent, and it is telling, for it appears on the lips of female characters in novels by women. For example, in *A Listener in Babel,* Vida Scudder portrays a beautiful-but-shallow heroine, Dorothy Gerard Ferguson, who gives an impression of depth and sensitivity and is attractive to the socialist hero. But Scudder notes that "Dorothy's sorrowful questionings arose from indolence as much as from sincerity, and . . . the unutterable things hinted by her troubled brow and thoughtful, tremulous lips, could never be uttered, because they were not there."[7] Later in the novel, when even the most admirable male characters continue to find Dorothy's beauty and motherhood sufficient as social contributions, the women are clearly less impressed.[8]

Two slightly older semiheroines further illustrate the woman author's critique of conventionally admirable women. Isabel Lathrop in *A Listener in Babel* and Pauline Emery in Florence Converse's *The Children of Light* are ideal women, or are seen as such by many of the novels' characters: refined, sensitive, beautiful, and womanly, calling forth a protective instinct not only from men but also from their children, for neither has ever really grown up. Isabel refuses to accept, let alone share, the social passion of her husband and daughter; she lives in the past and makes antimaterialism an excuse for her own comfortable selfishness. Pauline is a self-described mystic and follower of Saint Francis who thinks of herself as sharing and inspiring the social passion of her sons, but whose idea of significant social concern is to spend an afternoon on a transatlantic steamer crossing reading *Idylls of the King* to the people in steerage.[9] If Scudder and Converse present these women with pity as well as condemnation, perhaps it is in recognition that they have fulfilled so completely the refined, womanly ideal their class and time set for them—they are victims sinned against as well as sinning.

The young, beautiful heroine without social conscience appears frequently enough to deserve comment, but more often the heroine is a beautiful young middle- or upper-class woman who is also socially and religiously sensitive. Rachel Winslow, Virginia Page, and Felicia Sterling of *In His Steps* are typical examples, but one could list two dozen similar women in other novels. With few exceptions, each marries the manly, religiously and socially concerned hero or another equally worthy male. Many are involved before marriage with some appropriate form of social service: Rachel's music, Virginia's philanthropy to a Christian newspaper and to the "fallen girls" of Raymond's Rectangle, Felicia's classes at the settlement on cooking and domestic economy. Work with poor children, especially in Sunday schools, is another favored activity for young social gospel heroines, as is friendship and philanthropy for factory girls. This typical social gospel heroine fulfills cultural expectations (and the author's romantic interest) by marrying, but her choice is always worthy, never made for financial considerations. Whether or not the pattern was related consciously to Bellamy's ideal in *Looking Backward* (one can assume the authors had read that popular work), it fits his prescription. Bellamy's Dr. Leete describes the situation in Boston in the year 2000: "Our women have risen to the full height of their responsibility as the wardens of the world to come, to whose keeping the keys of the future are confided. Their feeling of duty in this respect [marrying only the "best" men] amounts to a sense of religious consecration. It is a cult in which they educate their daughters from childhood."[10]

There is a deviation from the typical social gospel heroine in two of Sheldon's novels: a young woman who is middle-class but not financially secure and thus must join the working world directly. Faith Kirk in *Malcom Kirk* is a minister's daughter who goes to Chicago to earn her own way and help her genteelly impoverished family. At first she finds work as an artist in a photographer's studio, but she is laid off, can find no other work, and in desperation, takes a job as a domestic servant. Barbara Clark in *Born to Serve* has a college degree from Mount Holyoke but can find no appropriate job to support herself and her widowed mother, so she too enters domestic service, much to her class-conscious mother's horror. Neither stays in her position long (Barbara marries the local minister; Faith finds another artist's job and eventually marries), and of course neither is a typical hired girl. Indeed, when each is reestablished in her "proper" sphere, she continues to address the "hired girl problem" by setting up a training school for the girls and interceding with mistresses to convince them to be more humane. What is striking is that Sheldon deals at all with this form of female labor and its problems. Despite the reality of domestic service for many American laboring women of the time, reformers gave far less attention to it than they did to factory and sweatshop labor.[11] Sheldon's portraits are not very realistic, and his proposed solution is unconvincing; nevertheless, his description of his heroines' difficulties as hired girls fits well with late nineteenth-century analyses. Barbara nearly quits, not because of low wages, but because of her small, uncomfortable room over the kitchen, social stigma, the absence of any chance for improvement, and her lack of regular work hours and the consequent loss of freedom.[12]

Marriage as culmination is the dominant pattern for social gospel heroines, but one occasionally finds a young woman who fits the heroine's role in every other respect but who remains single by choice. In every case I have found where the woman is a significant and developed figure in the action, the novel was written by a woman.[13] Perley Kelso in *The Silent Partner* is the rich, pampered daughter of a mill owner. When her father dies, Perley determines to learn about "her" mills and refuses to be a silent partner conveniently married to the son of her father's partner. She proceeds to investigate life in the mills, make friends with the workers, and invest some of her share of the profits in improvements in their living conditions and cultural opportunities. Their response is gratifyingly positive, and she is happy and fulfilled by her new active life. Not surprisingly, she breaks her engagement to the insensitive junior partner, but she also refuses to marry Stephan Garrick, a new partner who has worked his way up from the mills and shares her concerns—a "worthy" suitor. As Perley explains her decision: "The fact is . . . that I have no time to think of love and marriage, Mr. Garrick. That is a business, a trade, by itself to women. I have too much else to do. As nearly as I can understand myself, that is the state of the case. I cannot spare the time for it. . . . I believe that I have been a silent partner long enough. If I married you, sir, I should invest in life, and you would conduct it. I suspect that I have a preference for a business of my own."[14]

Helen Baldwin in *The Children of Light* is another interesting, active, fully developed character who stays single by choice. Helen is aggressively self-sufficient and outwardly cynical, but her actions show her idealism and dedication. After a childhood in a Methodist utopian commune, Helen works her way through college; after graduation, she chooses a job in a settlement over a higher-paying position in a boarding school. At times she seems to scorn the theories and dreams of the socialists, but it is because her vocation lies in the relentlessly concrete world: political petitions, immediate aid for the settlement's immigrant neighbors, and labor organization.

Hilda Lathrop, the partly autobiographical heroine of Scudder's *A Listener in Babel,* loves the socialist Lawrence Ferguson, but when she loses him to Dorothy, she does not consider her life ended. She refuses a job teaching art at her alma mater in order to join a settlement as a "listener"; eventually she decides to go into the factories for ten years to find "the possible field for handicraft in modern industry."[15] A few other female characters in more minor roles, though young and apparently marriageable, also choose to remain single and are fulfilled vocationally; again, they are found mainly in novels by women. It appears that male authors simply could not imagine an eligible, admirable young woman who *chose* not to marry and yet had a full, fulfilling life; that option was conceivable only to women. (One could justly ask whether male authors could imagine a male, presumably eligible hero who chose to remain single. The answer is yes.)

Thus far I have dealt only with middle- and upper-class women in the novels; they are, overwhelmingly, the dominant female characters. Lower-class or working women as full, named characters are far less prominent. Most appear as nameless victims or very minor characters: factory workers, seamstresses, wives or mothers of drunken (and thus nonsupporting) men. Prostitutes also are portrayed generally as victims, naive or desperate girls driven to a life of shame by poverty or tricked by unscrupulous men. Several other working-class women who play some serious role in the action are also primarily innocent sufferers. But the ultimate victim is *The Silent Partner's* Catty Garth. Because her mother was required to work overtime in the mill's heavy season while she was pregnant, Catty is deaf, mute, and physically repulsive. Her own pitiful work in the mill finally costs her her eyesight, and she dies in a flood because she cannot be warned off a collapsing bridge. Catty is not an attractive victim—she is selfish and greedy as well as pathetic—yet the indictment of the system is at least as effective in her harsh portrait as in the more appealing plight of her romantic sister-victims. And that is the main point of the female lower-class victims in the novels. They are rarely active, developed persons themselves; rather, they represent the woman's underside of America's industrialization. The presumably middle-class reader is called not to identify with but to pity them and thus to be spurred to action.

Not all the lower-class women in social gospel novels are victims. One finds the young factory girl or domestic servant who is a bit flighty or vain but not bad, who delights in cheap finery and resists middle-class efforts to improve or convert her. The best such women can expect, the authors imply, is to find a good, hard-working, sober husband. A second lower-class type not primarily a victim is the good wife who is staunchly loyal to her husband, a devoted mother, deeply religious, and cheerful through adversity.

A few authors go beyond typical female roles, however, and portray working women of complexity and strength. Survival is a dominant characteristic of three women in *Metzerott, Shoemaker*. Sally Price is an older woman who goes through the bitter poverty and grinding labor of piecework without being crushed, as is her weaker sister Susan. When at last an opportunity arises to run an immigrants' social hall and cooperative, she seizes it and makes her own success. She is devoted to family and friends, kind but no-nonsense, uneducated but wise. She is religious—accepting even when she cannot understand fully the ways of God—yet she is tolerant of "infidels" whose Christ-like actions outweigh, for her, their lack of orthodoxy. Beside Sally, her niece Polly is a pale figure, yet she too begins in poverty and survives. Less sympathetic but equally strong is Anna Rolf. At the start of the novel, she is healthy and happy, a wife and mother who continues to earn her own money by dressmaking. As her impractical husband becomes more absorbed in his "invention" (ultimately useless), she grows harder, and her earning becomes the family's sole support after his suicide: "Anna Rolf arose from her bed with her beauty wasted, her youth gone. Instead of the brilliant, joyous girl, there remained the sharp-featured, sharp-tongued woman, whose sound health, clear head, and practical abilities were now, instead of a source of self-satisfaction, viewed by herself merely as a stock in trade, her only capital for the business of taking care of her children."[16] Take care of them she does; she survives at the price of bitterness, and her struggle evokes compassion and admiration in the reader. Survival has its costs.

Sip Garth in *The Silent Partner* is also a survivor. The daughter of generations of mill-workers, she is resigned to the only life she knows, despite dreams of becoming an actress. She is drawn to Perley Kelso; yet Sip knows that Perley can never truly understand life in the mills. Sip is commendably and completely devoted to Catty, her only surviving relative, and she responds with rapture to a "fine" picture Perley gives her—both examples of romantic middle-class expectations for lower-class heroines. But Sip is also realistic: for her the chances at education or a better job don't work, not because Sip is stupid or doesn't try, but because, as she says, it's too late. After Catty's death, she, like Perley, refuses to marry a worthy suitor, but not because her life is already full: "I'll never marry anybody, Dirk. I'll never bring a child into the world to work in the mills. . . . I'll never bring children into the world to be factory children, and to be factory boys and girls, and to be factory men and women, and to see the sights I've seen and to bear the things I've borne, and to run the risks I've run, and to grow up as I've grown up, and to stop where I've stopped—never."[17] Sip's fatalism takes a different twist at the end of the novel: after experiencing a religious conversion, she becomes an itinerant preacher to the mill people, preaching a Christ of the poor who brings comfort and resignation as the only solution—not changes in laws or conditions. Sip's conversion is less convincing than the rest of her portrait; nevertheless, she is an unusual character, not only as a survivor and a woman who remains single by choice, but because she, as a lower-class woman, is portrayed as a complex and perceptive being despite her lack of education.

Unions do not appear in Phelps's relatively early novel, but later novels present several women actively involved in the labor movement, including two major characters. Bertha Aarons (in *The Children of Light*) is an immigrant worker and radical. Passionately devoted to the union and the closed shop, she is also wry and clever; she tells the strikers, "And for pickets now: I want all the very little, weak girls; all the little girls that ought to be under sixteen, but of course they ain't."[18] Bertha becomes involved with the weak liberal, Tristram Lawrence, half from a reluctant attraction, half from hoping he can help the workers' cause. She knows he is using her, and "to be used that way don't flatter *me*. . . . But I stand it because I want to win."[19] Bertha ultimately leaves the shop to marry another radical, but with a firm intention to go on working with the Women's Trade Union League.

Jeanie MacDougal Casey in *The Burden of Christopher* is another strong union woman. She first appears when she asks Christopher Kenyon, the enlightened factory-owning hero, for her sick father's job and his wages—and gets them.[20] Later in the novel, after Jeanie has become a wife and mother, she goes back into the shops—not Christopher's, but those of his unenlightened capitalist rival, and not for money, but to organize the workers from within. The scenes of her organizing in the shops are unusual in a social gospel novel for their lively picture of factory work and of the women's hopes, fears, and jealousies. Jeanie is later discredited for lying to the forelady, a lie that tears apart Jeanie's own Calvinist soul, but is done for the sake of the workers and the union. The union fails, as does Christopher's experiment in enlightened management—this is no novel of success—but Jeanie emerges as a complex woman who freely chooses to sacrifice her own comfort and interests, not for a family but for a cause she believes in.

What, then, can one conclude of the images of women in social gospel novels? In most cases, middle- and upper-class women conform to dominant nineteenth-century values and patterns for women, but some further expectations are raised. First, admirable women show concern beyond their immediate families, although for most authors it takes appropriately feminine and supportive form and should not interfere with domestic duties; however, some moderate rebellion against parents or society—not husbands—for the sake of the social gospel is permissible and even worthy. Furthermore, women characters frequently demonstrate a more personal and intuitive sympathy for the working poor, especially women and children, than do their less sensitive male relatives. This activity and perception, along with the traditional role of "inspiration," are the major contributions most authors see women making to the social gospel. Second, and less frequently, a more radical statement is made through female characters, usually in the works of women authors. Marriage is by no means condemned, but neither is it seen as the only choice available to a woman. Women, too, may feel impelled to serious social commitment and action that become a life's work beyond philanthropic charity, part-time benevolence, or a vicarious, supportive ministry through a worthy husband. Such women have an identity, which is not simply, or primarily their familial one.

In social gospel novels, working-class women appear most often as victims, but a few are active, complex characters. Again, the differences between male and female authors are striking. Of thirty-five lower-class female figures who merit at least a name and minimal activity in the novels I have read, twenty are found in novels by women, and of these, nine appear in *Metzerott, Shoemaker,* one of the few works where fully half of the action occurs among and by working-class people.

The degree to which novels reflect social gospel expectations for women should be tested by other social gospel writings, but their evidence does suggest a fairly traditional view of women on the part of male social gospelers. This conclusion is strengthened if we look at two related issues in the light of the novels: the "feminization" of religion in nineteenth-century America; and marriage, motherhood, and the home. Several of the novels are concerned with "feminized" religion, and a few are quite explicit in suggesting ways to draw men into the churches.[21] Minister-heroes are always "manly" or exemplars of "true manhood" and frequently "prize athletes."[22] While social gospel authors never advocated irreligion for women, they were more worried about Christianity's poor image with men and tried to correct the problem in their comments and male role models. On the other hand, it is almost impossible to overstate the reverence for Christian marriage and the Christian home found in social gospel novels. Marriage is a high and holy institution; the home is the foundation of all that is good in society. Social gospel authors occasionally criticize men for their neglect of family duty, but more often, the well-being of family and home is tied to woman's purity and motherhood. As Sheldon writes in a typical passage, "Ah, mother-love! It is the most wonderful thing on earth, next to the love of God. It is even that, for it is the love of God expressing itself through the mother, who is the temple of the loving God."[23] Whatever other cultural or religious beliefs of the age the social gospel novelists may have questioned, marriage, home, and motherhood remained sacred. However, although female authors tend to concur with male ones on the importance of home and motherhood, they question its exclusivity for all women.

Another point at which women authors dissent from the typical male ideal for women is women's religious identity. In most of the novels, women are naturally religious; they do not truly struggle over their religious beliefs. Women who are irreligious are "bad" in other ways, socially or domestically. The closest a male author comes to showing religious conflict in a woman is Sheldon's Barbara Clark, who never doubts the substance of her Christianity, but only struggles to reconcile her class-consciousness and personal desires with her Christian understanding of service. Yet in some novels by women one finds women who struggle over religious belief, women for whom it is not automatic or natural. Indeed, it is the very religious struggle that contributes to the interest and complexity of these characters.

Alice Randolph in *Metzerott, Shoemaker* is a society girl who defies her family and gives up her inheritance to marry Dr. Frederick Richards, socially acceptable but a "free-thinker," an atheist *because* of his sensitivity to human suffering and his inability to reconcile evil with a good and powerful God. The marriage is happy, though Alice wishes Frederick shared her faith and her attempts to resign herself to God's will in the death of one of their children and the crippling of another. Yet she is also tormented: is God punishing her children for her own "sin" of marrying an infidel? In a crisis, the superficial faith of her childhood collapses, and in its place she adopts her husband's creed: "I believe that there are those whom I must live to help."[24] Eventually, helped by the suffering and faith of others, Alice's faith returns, but only as a resource for her, not as a standard for judgment of others on the basis of belief or unbelief. Like Sally Price in the same novel, Alice finds Christ-like actions more significant than professions of orthodoxy.

Agnes Gillespie in *The Burden of Christopher* is the precocious only child of a widowed college professor. She knows what she does not like—modern conditions and benevolent "charity" as a solution—but she is searching for a hero, someone or something to believe in. She finds both in Christopher Kenyon and his experiment with a cooperative factory, and she spurs him to more radical positions. Yet the young Agnes is a self-proclaimed agnostic, and when she comes at last, by way of her love for Christopher and their mutual ideals, to Christianity, it is for her a faith of both intellect and emotions. That faith sustains her when Christopher's experiment fails and when he himself fails to be the hero she believed in, misusing trust funds to sustain his factory—though it is for the workers' sake and not his own. Agnes is disillusioned, but she goes on after Christopher's suicide, both for the sake of her son and because one must. As she says at the end of the novel: "After a while I shall get dulled to [pain and disillusionment] and I shall set my whole mind and heart to the work; that does not fail me; I shall kindle to the work, thank God! But—the difference in life will never go away from me. It seems as if the earth had turned, and were going round another way. After a while I shall not be dizzy. After a very long while."[25]

Hilda Lathrop never fully resolves her struggle with Christianity. Her early faith is conventional and aesthetic, but it soon proves weaker than her growing passion to do *something* for suffering humanity and her distaste for the socially insensitive church of her day. In *A Listener in Babel*, Hilda tries to find ways to translate feelings of identity and sympathy for the poor into programs and actions, and no simple solution is given. Nor is there a simple Christian faith for her to embrace. When Hilda is particularly discouraged, a Roman Catholic friend takes her to a religious retreat of the "Friends of the Holy Way." There she finds Christians who share her social passion, but rooted in and blended with a deep spirituality. "Here was no group of indolent persons, spiritually luxurious, comfortably shifting the burden of the world's woe to the broad shoulders of the Almighty, but a band of soldiers who had merely paused for breath."[26] Hilda is renewed, but still denies being a Christian, even after a long theological discussion with Father Phillips, the retreat leader, whose faith she admires but cannot adopt. So he advises her to live in hope, and "if you do not believe in Christ, you can follow Him; that is more important."[27] The advice takes her through two more years at the settlement and into the next step in her life: "After years of speculation and years of experiment, she dared at last to take the great word Socialism with confidence upon her lips,—not as a dogma of the end to be achieved, but as a description of the process to be furthered. If toward the greater word, Christianity, she remained silent, through profound distrust of the Church in history and in the modern world, nevertheless the image of a Leader of men dwelt in the secret places of her soul."[28]

In *The Children of Light*, Clara Emery's religion is a blend of her childhood experience in a socially radical Methodist commune and her youth spent with her cousins Lucian and Cyrus, sharing their fascination with Saint Francis. She has no overt conflict with a Christianity deeply set by her early experiences, but she does try to mediate between the deep, almost monastic piety of Cyrus and the freethinking of adult Lucian as she struggles to define her own position as one who is both wealthy and radical. On one side, there is the concrete help of the settlement and of Cyrus's personal work with immigrants, which Clara appreciates, though she shares it only indirectly. On the other hand, there is the theoretical and political approach of socialism. Clara sympathizes with the socialists' critique of the ameliorative work of the settlement that fails to tackle unjust structures, and she shares their vision. Yet her Christianity makes her worry about their tactics. Her dilemma and probing of her own class bias despite her professed radicalism and work on the socialist paper continue through the novel's dramatic strike and election. Only Cyrus's martyr's death precipitates her decision to act despite the ambiguities of all action. For her, as a Christian, the symbol of action is to join the socialist party. "It isn't a choice between Socialism and Christianity that I make. It isn't leaving Christ's party to join the

Socialists'. Christianity is the road we travel to the kingdom of heaven, and for me, one of the sign-posts on the way is Socialism."[29]

The religious struggles of the four women are different, yet each is portrayed as genuine and each results in a faith that is implicitly or explicitly Christian and social. Since these struggles are presented by women authors who are themselves religiously and socially committed, it seems that the lack of religious struggle in male-created heroines says more about male misperceptions than it does about the reality of women's religious lives at that time. Surely there were women who were conventionally and superficially religious, just as there were men so; but religion was not natural or automatic to all women. (Again, in fairness, one should ask if male authors portray serious religious struggle in any male characters. They do.)

It is not within the scope of this study to attempt an exhaustive comparison of novels by male and female authors, beyond differences already mentioned on roles and images of women. Yet the works of Scudder and Converse in particular are suggestive for a deeper understanding of women in the social gospel than male authors provide. Theirs are the most radical social gospel novels I have read, in the sense of posing a serious challenge to political and especially economic structures of America in that period. (This radicalism is not surprising, for both women were associated in Boston with leaders of the "left-wing" of the social gospel like W. D. P. Bliss.)[30] An additional strength of their novels is their sensitivity to complexities. Scudder and Converse portray with sympathy a variety of honest responses to the social issues facing Americans at the time, demonstrating strengths and weaknesses of different alternatives. They propose no easy answers, no panacea to social problems.[31]

Let me suggest two specific examples. In *The Children of Light,* there is tension between settlement workers, who give immediate aid, and socialist party leaders, who focus their attack on the system, preferring to use propaganda and political action. The dilemma takes concrete form in a contested election. For political purity's sake, does one support the socialist candidate, who has no real chance to win, knowing that the socialist vote may throw the election to the "machine" candidate? Or does one support the liberal reform candidate, who promises aid to labor, but the depth of whose social commitment and even honesty one questions? Or, is it best to hope for a machine victory, on the theory that things must get even worse to ignite the revolution? No simple answer emerges.

A personalized illustration of complexity occurs in the friends and residents of the settlement in *A Listener in Babel.* Each person is presented both critically and sympathetically; no clear winner has the "right" answer. Of the men, O'Hagan is a labor leader, Mervyn a liberal, and Simpson a radical Russian socialist. Henrietta Morse teaches college economics and takes her radicalism to the classroom. She even tries, unsuccessfully, to bring principle to bear on the administration of the college. (In one scene where the college's acceptance of "tainted" money is debated, Henrietta makes several telling points, most of which are ignored until they are voiced by a man!) Mildred Ellis, a Roman Catholic mystic, leaves the settlement to "live" socialism in a cooperative setting of voluntary poverty. Jessie Bancroft marries a reformer to work with him, a solution especially commended by the male characters. Janet Frothingham, the most radical woman, leaves for Colorado to edit the *Anarchist Banner*. The daughter of an abolitionist, she perceives herself as a "crank" or "gadfly," an honest and valuable role for one who despairs of charity and piecemeal changes while structures remain unchanged:

> Every time that we teach a working woman to make her wages or her husband's go a little farther we set in motion a force of suction which tends to lower the universal wage. Every time we give one of these boys moral and industrial training, make him quick, competent, virtuous, we are teaching him to rise to success upon the necks of his fellows, pushed lower than they were. Could all women be trained to live on less, could all men be raised to a higher point of economic efficiency, the grudging sum which the world allows them for a livelihood would sink in proportion, and the process of demoralization be repeated. So much for sentimental philanthropy! The only consolation is that we shall never effect anything on a large enough scale to count. But that is cold comfort,—for it throws us back upon the old despair.[32]

While no one else chooses Janet's course, all respect her integrity and deep commitment. Hilda Lathrop decides to enter the labor force directly, not "simply to roam about in disguise for a few months and take notes for magazine articles,"[33] but to take ten years to study and learn. Miss Abbott, the director, stays at the settlement. Hilda's judgment speaks for them all and for the novel: find your own task and do it; keep the vision, even if you don't live to see it accomplished.

Both Scudder and Converse also cover directly "theological" issues. Like Rauschenbusch in *A Theology for the Social Gospel,* they try to adapt traditional Christian beliefs to a social environment. For example, Scudder, through a long discussion between Hilda and Father Phillips, admits that the doctrine of immortality has been "a terrible hindrance to social idealism. It engendered an intense sense of the moral responsibility of the individual, but socially speaking, its tendency was fatalistic. It fostered indifference to the destiny of man on earth, prevented the oppressed from struggling and the oppressor from remorse." Yet she insists that it *can* be a "great creed of social hope" for the activist deeply sensitive to social solidarity, the wasted lives of the poor and oppressed, and the slowness of change.[34] Converse stresses social identity and action rather than resignation as the core of Christian love and self-sacrifice in a speech by Cyrus Emery before an audience of striking workers:

> Christ said—"Ye have heard that it hath been said, an eye for an eye, and a tooth for a tooth: but I say unto you, that ye resist not evil: but whosoever shall

smite thee on thy right cheek, turn to him the other also.' . . . But I do not find him anywhere saying, If any one smite thy brother on his right cheek, do thou stand by and hold thy hand while thy brother is beaten to death. . . . No; He said—"This is my commandment, That ye love one another, as I have loved you. Greater love hath no man than this, that a man lay down his life for his friends." . . . to refuse to work for a wage on which your brother must starve; to refuse to work at all unless your brother be given wages and industrial conditions that shall keep his soul and body in health; to endure hunger, cold, nakedness, even unto death, that your brother may live—this, this it is to love your brother as yourself![35]

In sum, the novels of Scudder and Converse are important social gospel documents, deserving much fuller treatment than they can be given here. To the degree that "the" social gospel novel is identified with and confined to *In His Steps,* our understanding of the social gospel novel and the movement itself is the poorer.

This study of women and the social gospel novel suggests that for most authors, particularly men, any radicalism that the social gospel inspired did not extend to the home, the family, and traditional sex roles. For the most part, women are victims, inspirations to men, or responsibilities for men, not significant thinkers, actors, or initiators. One can cite two exceptions to this generalization. First, the most admirable women in the novels show concern for the plight of the urban poor, for a world beyond the immediate domestic circle. Women are not automatically excused by reason of their sex from awareness and even limited action on urban economic problems. Indeed, social gospel motives are seen as justifying a woman's moderate rebellion against social standards or parents (not husbands—but then, a woman should marry a worthy man against whom rebellion would be unnecessary). Second, the novels written by women challenge conventional roles and expectations for women in that period through portrayals of strong single women who choose a socially conscious career over marriage and of women's religious struggles.

It is also in novels by women that one finds admirable women who are not conventionally religious and judgments, like that of Sally Price in *Metzerott, Shoemaker,* that Christ-like actions are a truer gauge of Christian commitment than professions of orthodoxy. The voices of these female authors and characters support the importance of "doing theology"—of practice rooted in a social understanding of the gospel message—as at least as important as having a clear theological position in definitions of the social gospel movement. The distinctive social gospel note of concern for social structures and social identity in that practice distinguishes it (as does motivation) from "mere" social concern or charity.

Finally, the social gospel novels suggest indirectly an area for further study of women and the social gospel. In the novels, three concrete strategies for putting the social gospel into practice emerge with frequency. First, one can become a minister and, by preaching and example, inspire one's congregation to social consciousness and action. Second, one can put one's own factory or business on a cooperative basis, paying greater attention to the claims and well-being of the workers and regarding them as persons and not a commodity. Third, one can go into some form of settlement work. (None of the concrete solutions proposed in the novels is particularly appropriate to members of the working class, though some novels commend union organization indirectly. Social gospel novels were, by and large, written from the perspective of and to readers of the middle and upper classes.)

The settlement or cooperative social hall is found in many social gospel novels, and women are very active in them. Although there is broad agreement among the authors on the importance of the settlement, differences between male and female authors again are striking. For the men, it is men who do or should lead the settlements. The most blatant example is Sheldon's *The Reformer*. Grace Andrews has been director of the settlement for twelve years, and Sheldon describes at length what a wonderful Christian she is. But it is the young male hero, John Gordon, who really begins to get results when he joins the settlement. Grace has fought the local political boss for years with little result; in a matter of months, John and another man defeat him. Not only does Grace not resent John's taking over, she welcomes his protection and leadership.[36] In contrast, women in the settlements portrayed in *The Children of Light* and *A Listener in Babel* and in the immigrants' social hall in *Metzerott, Shoemaker* (not strictly a settlement but similar in function) work with men on an equal basis and are even leaders. Of course, in fact both men and women were active in the settlement movement. But as a movement, it was especially important for women. To return to the three concrete strategies: women could not be ministers, and even in the rare instances where they could have been ordained, there was still the problem of public acceptance; making one's own factory a cooperative was theoretically possible for women, but unfortunately it was limited to those who inherited a factory in the first place. Settlement work remained as the most viable, concrete, and significant option of the three for a woman seeking a "career" in the social gospel movement.[37]

The women and men who wrote the social gospel novel forcefully expressed the importance of "doing theology," of *practicing* a social understanding of the gospel message. Yet the significance of *proclaiming* this message in a form that was agreeable and accessible to the general public must not be underestimated. Given that women were generally barred from professional ministerial leadership and preaching, this literary genre was one powerful, socially acceptable means for women to exercise far-reaching didactic influence in the communication of the social gospel at the popular level. For this reason, it is an especially rich source for learning about women's, as well as men's ways of thinking about the social gospel, and comparing the differences between them.

Notes

This essay first appeared as "Women and the Social Gospel Novel," *Church History* 54, no. 1 (March 1985): 56–73, and is reprinted here, with minimal alterations, with permission from the American Society of Church History.

1. Ronald C. White Jr. and C. Howard Hopkins, *The Social Gospel: Religion and Reform in Changing America* (Philadelphia: Temple University Press, 1976), 119–26.

2. See Robert T. Handy, ed., *The Social Gospel in America, 1870–1920: Gladden, Ely, and Rauschenbusch* (New York: Oxford University Press, 1966), 5–7.

3. Charles M. Sheldon, *In His Steps* (Chicago: Advance Publishing Company, 1899). White and Hopkins cite *In His Steps* as the only social gospel novel to reach "mass market circulation that is impressive even in the twentieth century" (143); it is the social gospel novel most frequently cited in surveys of American religion and it is still in print.

4. C. Howard Hopkins, *The Rise of the Social Gospel in American Protestantism, 1865–1918* (New Haven: Yale University Press, 1940, 1967), 140–48, provided a valuable start in searching out social gospel novels. Also useful were Walter Fuller Taylor, *The Economic Novel in America* (Chapel Hill: University of North Carolina Press, 1942), and Fay M. Blake, *The Strike in the American Novel* (Metuchen, N.J.: Scarecrow Press, 1972). Thirty-seven novels were considered for this article, with publication dates from 1871 to 1921. Of these, ten were written by women and twenty-seven by men, including eleven by Charles Sheldon, unarguably the most prolific social gospel novelist.

5. See Dorothy in Charles M. Sheldon, *Malcom Kirk* (Chicago: Church Press, 1898).

6. See Irene Lawrence in Amanda M. Douglas, *Hope Mills* (Boston: Lee and Shepard, 1880); Pinkie Randolph in Katharine Pearson Woods, *Metzerott, Shoemaker* (New York: T. Y. Crowell, 1889); Lilian Kishu in Albion W. Tourgee, *Murvale Eastman, Christian Socialist* (New York: Fords, Howard, and Hulbert, 1891); Luella Marsh in Charles M. Sheldon, *The Reformer* (Chicago: Advance, 1902); and Dorothy Girard Ferguson in Vida D. Scudder, *A Listener in Babel* (Boston: Houghton Mifflin, 1903).

7. Scudder, *Listener in Babel*, 13.

8. Ibid., 265–93.

9. Florence Converse, *The Children of Light* (Boston: Houghton Mifflin, 1912), 218–19.

10. Edward Bellamy, *Looking Backward: 2000–1887* (Boston: Ticknor, 1888), 269. Bellamy's utopian vision sees radical changes for women, such as female service in the industrial army, socialized housework, and financial independence, but maternity is still central. Women leave the industrial army to bear and raise children, and "the higher positions in the feminine army of industry are intrusted only to women who have been both wives and mothers, as they alone fully represent their sex" (261). It is a fascinating male image of what would be ideal for women, trying to respond to contemporary criticisms but unable to discard a male perspective and a core of traditional roles for women, from separation and subordination of the female industrial army to the continued social practice of having ladies leave the table after dinner so men can indulge in serious talk.

11. Two important exceptions were women: Lucy Maynard Salmon, *Domestic Service* (New York: Macmillan, 1901); and Helen Campbell, *Prisoners of Poverty: Women Wage-Workers, Their Trades, and Their Lives* (Boston: Little Brown, 1887; reprint, Westport, Conn.: Greenwood, 1970). See also Daniel E. Sutherland, *Americans and Their Servants: Domestic Service in the United States from 1800 to 1920* (Baton Rouge: Louisiana State University Press, 1981).

12. Charles M. Sheldon, *Born to Serve* (Chicago: Advance, 1901), 34–42; see Campbell, *Prisoners of Poverty*, 223–32.

13. Two partial exceptions must be made to this statement. Virginia Page does not marry in *In His Steps*, but she does in Sheldon's sequel, *"Jesus Is Here!"* (New York: Hodder, Stoughton, George Doran, 1913, 1914). Grace Andrews in *The Reformer* is a kind of social gospel heroine and single,

but her advanced age (thirty-six) more than her own choice precludes her marriage to the hero, who is only thirty.

14. Elizabeth Stuart Phelps, *The Silent Partner* (Boston: Houghton Mifflin, 1871), 260, 262.

15. Scudder, *Listener in Babel*, 315.

16. Woods, *Metzerott*, 60.

17. Phelps, *Silent Partner*, 287.

18. Converse, *Children of Light*, 189.

19. Ibid., 209.

20. Florence Converse, *The Burden of Christopher* (Boston: Houghton Mifflin, 1900), 40–41.

21. See Washington Gladden, *The Christian League of Connecticut* (New York: Century, 1883); Charles M. Sheldon, *Richard Bruce* (Chicago: Advance, 1899); and Woods, *Metzerott*.

22. For social gospel concern for the manliness of religion, see Janet Forsythe Fishburn, *The Fatherhood of God and the Victorian Family: The Social Gospel in America* (Philadelphia: Fortress, 1981), 28–33. For the "feminization" of nineteenth-century American religion, see Ann Douglas, *The Feminization of American Culture* (New York: Knopf, 1977), and Barbara Welter, "The Feminization of American Religion," in *Dimity Convictions: The American Woman in the Nineteenth Century* (Athens, Ohio: Ohio University Press, 1976).

23. Charles M. Sheldon, *Robert Hardy's Seven Days* (Chicago: Advance, 1900), 73.

24. Woods, *Metzerott*, 123.

25. Converse, *Burden of Christopher*, 313–14.

26. Scudder, *Listener in Babel*, 247.

27. Ibid., 263.

28. Ibid., 296.

29. Converse, *Children of Light*, 291.

30. The two women were close friends, sharing a household with Scudder's mother. For biographical data, see Arthur Mann, *Yankee Reformers in the Urban Age* (Cambridge, Mass.: Belknap Press of Harvard University Press, 1954), 210–28; Peter J. Frederick, "Vida Dutton Scudder: The Professor as Social Activist," *New England Quarterly* 43 (1970): 407–33; and Theresa Corcoran, "Scudder, Vida" in *Notable American Women: The Modern Period*, ed. Barbara Sicherman and Carol Hurd Green et al. (Cambridge, Mass.: Belknap Press of Harvard University Press, 1980).

31. In a sense, the lack of a creative, definite program is also a weakness. Whether a neat solution was possible at the time is another question. Allen F. Davis, *Spearheads for Reform: The Social Settlements and the Progressive Movement, 1890–1914* (New York: Oxford University Press, 1967), suggests the dilemma in concrete terms: "Here was the settlement workers' problem in human terms, and it was also faced by the labor leaders—how hungry did the children have to become before one gave up fighting for principle, or even for a living wage, and chose conciliation?" (118–19).

32. Scudder, *Listener in Babel*, 135.

33. Ibid., 315.

34. Ibid., 258–61.

35. Converse, *Children of Light*, 276–77.

36. Sheldon, *Reformer*, 223–26, 255.

37. See Davis, chap. 2, on the religious component in the early settlements. Of course not all settlement workers were inspired directly by the social gospel; neither were all ministers.

CHAPTER 12

True to Our God: African American Women as Christian Activists in Rochester, New York

Ingrid Overacker

African American women played the central role in nurturing and sustaining the African American church during the first four decades of the twentieth century. How is it, then, that scholars of the social gospel movement have managed to miss most of the Christian activity of African American women (and men) in addressing the needs of their people in urban centers throughout America? How is it that most of the scholarship on African American religious development during this same period, with some recent stellar exceptions, has not attended to the Christian activity of African American women?[1] That the contributions of African American women remain hidden, or are considered to be supportive and secondary rather than central and primary, reflects the focus of the scholarship to date and its particular perspectives on race and gender.

African Americans practiced a Christian activism and social engagement that predated the social gospel movement when they resisted slavery, throughout the abolition movement, and during the development of the free church. Despite this, scholars who address the social gospel movement view it primarily as a movement conceived and led by whites in which some African Americans, notably male clergy, participated.[2] From this perspective, the presence of African Americans in the social gospel movement depended upon how much African Americans cooperated with white social gospel leaders, and how much their efforts resembled what white churches were doing. This perspective also limits the ability of scholars to discern the differing perspectives and beliefs that may have informed the participation of African Americans in the social gospel movement.

When examining the efforts of Christian churches to embrace the social gospel, for instance, scholars note the proliferation of institutional churches, recreation centers, employment bureaus, and other organizations as evidence of the movement. If one assumes a connection with white leadership and a mimicking of white structures, then the truly astonishing efforts on the part of African American urban congregations, which did not follow this model, remain invisible.

The separation of the history of the social gospel movement from the history of African American Christian activism also reflects differing perspectives on racism and its role in preventing the coming of the Kingdom. Scholars of the social gospel movement include racial injustice as one among many of the social evils that leaders believed interfered with bringing Christians closer to God's plan. For African American Christians, racism, while one of many evils, was *central* to their critique of American society. In their eyes true Christian fellowship, fundamental to the creation of the Kingdom, could not exist as long as some Christians considered themselves superior by virtue of race.[3] A focus on racism as basic to the plight of African Americans in urban centers separates African American Christian activists from most white social gospel adherents, whether or not they acknowledged the issue of race.

Scholars of the social gospel movement are not the only ones who neglect the contributions of African Americans to Christian activism during this time period or do not reveal the importance of African American women to that activity. The work on African American religious and church development, despite a growing challenge, still tends to support Gayraud Wilmore's scathing indictment of the African American church and its leaders during the early decades of the twentieth century.[4] Wilmore has asserted that during these years, African American clergy departed from their historical tradition of political and social protest. Wilmore's charge that African American clergy became obsequious, accommodationist, politically expedient, and cowardly has tinged much of the discussion of the church, particularly its leadership, during that period. Paradoxically, virtually all studies on the growth and development of African American communities in northern urban centers cite the importance, even centrality, of the mainstream Christian church.[5]

In order to address this paradox, and to offer a historical place to the efforts of African American women who worked to create a Christian society for their people, one must understand, first, the theological stance of African Americans who engaged in social and political action, whatever some male clergy might or might not have done.

For an elaboration of the theological underpinnings for African American Christian activism, one needs to examine the research of scholars who have explored the sociological and historical development of the African American mainstream Christian church.[6] This body of work reveals that during the first four decades of the twentieth century, African Americans had formulated a set of theological precepts that guided their lives in the church and society. These precepts rest on specific meanings attached to freedom, equality, justice, sin, and salvation, and they reveal a historical legacy that originated long before the decades during which the social gospel had force among white Christian Protestants. Not all African Americans adhered to these precepts. During the early twentieth century there was great diversity among African American Christians, and a growing number of African Americans chose alternatives to Christianity or eschewed religion altogether. Still most African Americans at the time belonged to mainstream churches (especially Baptist and Methodist). The following theological precepts were not the only theological view within the mainstream church, but they informed the behavior of many Christian activists.

First, God is immediately and personally present in the lives of human beings and is the informative force in history. Jesus offers the primary evidence of this, and following Jesus' living example, African Americans work for the liberation, salvation, and resurrection of the oppressed.

African Americans are God's children and are therefore responsible to answer God's call. They are all equally responsible to God and must therefore be free to respond to God immediately. Anything that interferes with the African American, and human, ability to respond to God's call is evil and must be confronted, actively and immediately, in order to establish African American, and human, equality and freedom.

Racism creates oppressive institutions and discriminatory practices that interfere with the African American response to God by limiting the ability of people to fulfill their human potential and therefore call. Racism is therefore sin, for some the primary sin that requires attention in our society. According to Peter Paris, African American Christians differentiate between the sin of personal transgression and the sin of a people's broken relationship with God. Paris explains that "the thought of black churches distinguishes the 'sins' of black people from the 'sin' of white racism, which is considered by far the most wretched. White racism . . . is considered the greater evil and possibly the source of all sin. . . . Consequently, all action that is aimed at correcting the social injustice of racism is viewed as moral action."[7]

Justice demands the redress of existential conditions that limit the ability of human beings to respond to God's call. Because the realities of the world can impinge on a person's opportunity to realize her or his gifts either in preventing a recognition of what these gifts are or in circumscribing their application, justice demands that reality bend in service to the realization of human potential.

It is therefore the responsibility of African American Christians to create communities in which African American women, men, and children can learn who they are as God's children and what they are capable of as individual human beings so that they can answer God's call. It is the responsibility of the church to provide a setting for that community. African American Christians can therefore acquire the sense of self and character that will enable them to address racist practices in our society.

Finally, fulfilling these responsibilities will involve suffering but will also lead to new life—that is resurrection, and the ultimate salvation of both African American and white society.

These precepts helped African Americans to recognize the barriers of poverty, ignorance, and personal weaknesses as corollaries of racism. God's purpose became obscured through the practices of discrimination and oppression. They believed therefore that their own church communities had to develop structures, programs, resources, classes, and services that would imbue the membership with the strength needed to confront racism. The Christian structures and practices that African Americans developed during the early decades of the twentieth century did not then necessarily look like the structures that white practitioners of the social gospel movement created. While African Americans created institutional churches, recreation centers, good government clubs, YWCAs and YMCAs, clubhouses, libraries, orphanages, and other institutions, most African American churches had neither the resource base nor the perspective toward those in need that leaders of the white movement had.

Coupled with the centrality of racism to their critique of American society, African American Christian activists differed significantly from traditional white social gospelers in the stance they took toward those in need of aid and succor in the city. For African Americans, the agents and subjects of service, or reform, or programmatic aid were the same. African Americans were working on behalf of themselves, of each other, of their own. In contrast to white Christians who often viewed the recipients of aid as the *other* (quite often foreign immigrants), African Americans viewed their Christian commitment in terms of saving their own people and thus furthering the salvation of American society.

This context meant that African Americans did not necessarily see the need to create structures external to the church in order to meet their Christian responsibility. They did not require institutional distance, since the needy were relatives and friends, or at least people who shared the bond of racial identification. Therefore, African American churches continued to practice Christian education and activism within their congregations on a face-to-face, informal level that proliferated in committees, clubs, and programs that addressed the delivery of services, education, economic development, and political engagement.

If the ultimate goal of Christian activism is the confrontation with racism on a daily basis as it affects the lives of ordinary African Americans, and if congregations and churches developed internal mechanisms to fulfill this goal, then the study of African American Christian activism requires a close examination of local churches and communities and their internal efforts. The primary setting for Christian activism was the local church community. Shifting the focus of analysis from national organizations and nationally known leaders has the immediate effect of illuminating the role and activity of women. African American women were the backbone of local church communities. The women in the church community of Rochester, New York, offer one example of this.

From 1900 to 1940, there were four churches in Rochester that formed the center of the African American community. The members of Memorial AME Zion, Mount Olivet Baptist, Trinity Presbyterian, and Saint Simon's Episcopal churches provide a rich tapestry of evidence for the beliefs and activities of women committed to the future of their people.

African American women in Rochester adhered to the gender norms of their times, which for African Americans included a fluidity concerning women's economic and political contributions. While African American women might, for example, appreciate the opportunity to stay home and nurture children while men provided the economic support for the home, both history and present circumstances encouraged African American women to cross gender lines. The criterion for acceptance of women's active economic and/or political roles was that all such activity be in support of the health of the community. Most African American women in Rochester worked outside the home in order to maintain economic viability and make sure their children were fed and clothed. In accordance with their primarily role as nurturers and caretakers, the women in the church took responsibility for making sure basic needs were met; they visited the sick, fed the hungry, clothed the naked, and, especially, raised the children. In securing a safe setting for African American people, women organized the congregations, raised the funds to support the church, and made certain that the children attended. In promoting educational and economic development, women were full partners with men and promoted such achievement on the part of both girls and boys. In political leadership, most women viewed themselves in a supportive role, and unlike some other women nationally, did not directly challenge men's control of the pulpit or the political structure of the church. African American women in Rochester worked actively to make sure that they were visible in the community as people of character and responsibility who challenged racist notions of African American women's moral fiber and abilities.

The evidence from the lives of the African American women in Rochester best illustrates their Christian activism. Two women's stories in particular offer alternate approaches. One was a woman who forged her own path in confronting racism; the other was a woman who molded the character of her children to do the same. Their stories together offer examples of the ways women nurtured the personal growth and development necessary for African Americans to battle racism.

Elsie Scott

Elsie Scott was born in 1907 and came with her parents and five siblings to Rochester in 1909.[8] The Scott family lived with Charlotte Herndon, Elsie's grandmother. Elsie's mother, Lucinda Herndon Scott, primarily stayed home to raise the six children in the family, but when she went out to do day work to supplement her husband's income, Charlotte Herndon took care of Elsie.

Charlotte Herndon was a staunch member of Mount Olivet Baptist Church from its inception in 1910. She, her daughter Lucinda Scott, and all six of her grandchildren went to church every Sunday. They attended every service or event during the week, and the children were active in Sunday School and the Baptist Young People's Union (BYPU) from a very early age. Elsie Scott recalled that "every time the door was open, we went in." Elsie sang in the junior choir and attended BYPU every week. BYPU combined Bible study with lessons on appropriate behavior and academic habits. The students would memorize passages from the Bible, such as the Ten Commandments or the Twenty-third Psalm, and would be expected to interpret Jesus' purpose and teachings. Mount Olivet had a close relationship with Colgate Rochester Theological Seminary and students there would come to present programs. Elsie Scott remembers these times as opportunities for the youth to talk with seminary students, and as a time for the students from Colgate to get to know them.

Having her children participate in this kind of youth development was important to Lucinda Scott and to other parents, who "didn't want the children to get misled and go out in the world and do things that they shouldn't do so if they gave them things to do within the church then they would know where they were and who they were with." School was of primary importance to Elsie's mother. She had only a third-grade education herself, but she wanted all of her children to graduate with at least a high-school education so that they would have better opportunities than she and her husband had. (He had graduated from high school but had not been able to get professional work.) Both of Elsie Scott's parents believed that if you got an education, "you could do things that *you* wanted to do," which meant going beyond high school.

When she was seventeen years old Elsie Scott decided she wanted to be a nurse. She learned what she would have to do to reach her goal and took preparatory courses during her remaining two years in high school. Graduating from East High in 1926, Elsie applied to all the hospitals in Rochester for nurse's training. None of them would take her. "They *suggested* to me that I go to a hospital where I could get in, so then I called Harlem in New York City and they said yes so then they sent me applications."

Elsie Scott was severely disappointed. She wanted to stay in Rochester, and she had never encountered such racial hostility before. Her experience as an African American child in the Rochester public school system had not prepared her for it. Before the 1950s in Rochester, African American children met with very little overt prejudice, and African Americans in general in Rochester encountered racial hostility only when they tried to break what were clearly inflexible racial lines. African American women could not be nurses in Rochester, despite the quality and progressive nature of its medical school, nursing school, and hospitals.

"When they said no, I said, well, I'm still gonna be a nurse." When one looks at the church foundations and role modeling she received, such a response is not surprising. From a very early age, she had been exposed to the concept that education was the key to a future that involved freedom of choice. She had met, learned from, and received respect from college students, some of whom were African American. The pastor of her church, Reverend James Rose, was himself a graduate of Colgate Rochester Theological Seminary and was actively pursuing graduate studies while he pastored her. When asked what she remembered about Reverend Rose, the first thing Elsie Scott said was that he was a graduate of Colgate.

Elsie Scott went to New York and entered the nursing program at Harlem Hospital. She thrived on the work and felt a wonderful sense of uplift from helping people, "because they need it. It fulfills a need." And, she was "very proud of that white uniform." In her struggles she drew upon the foundations of her youth and actively sought solace and guidance from the church. She knew that she would need the church to make it through nursing school. "That's why," she said, "when I got to New York to become a student nurse I got affiliated with the Abyssinian Baptist Church." During her ten years in New York as a student nurse and while she sought work, Elsie Scott leaned heavily on the spiritual inspiration she found at the Abyssinian Church. Adam Clayton Powell Sr. was pastor there, and his reputation for active social engagement is well documented. His sermons provided Elsie Scott with the messages she needed to deal with discrimination and to continue seeing herself as a nurse even when she couldn't find work. "It meant a lot to me to go. I enjoyed the spiritual uplift that I got from going. The message . . . would help me in my everyday life so that things weren't so difficult, it'd be easier for me. . . . It gives you a lift and helps you carry on because some people are so evil and I had to deal with that, so when you go to church and have that foundation there it gives you help, it helps you, so I appreciated the help that I got."

Even with her education, however, it was almost impossible for Elsie to practice as a nurse. When she graduated from Harlem, in the middle of the Great Depression, the only places hiring black nurses were the tuberculosis centers. All fifteen of the black nurses hired faced horrible working conditions. Though Elsie does not draw this direct connection, in part it may have been the influence of Reverend Powell and the Abyssinian Church that encouraged her to request an investigation from the city into these working conditions, after which the supervising nurse was dismissed and conditions improved. However, the TB centers soon closed.

Elsie Scott does credit Reverend Powell and the worship services at Abyssinian with reinvigorating her faith, and this faith helped keep her identity intact. Beginning in the late thirties, and for more than ten years, Elsie Scott could not find work as a nurse and instead worked as a domestic. She returned to Rochester in 1938, hoping to find conditions improved there, but she could not get a nursing job. If she had to work as a domestic, she thought, she might as well do that in New York. She went back to New York City and earned thirty-five cents an hour doing housework throughout World War II. Her faith "took me over." For all of those years, she said, "I believed it would only be temporary. Look at Job, he went down to skin and bones. So that kind of carries you over, beliefs like that. [You may be] down today, but not tomorrow. . . . The foundation is there, see," she says, "and if you're built on a Christian foundation, you're not going to swaver [*sic*] too much. Might swaver a little, but you always get back to that."

Elsie Scott returned to Rochester after the war. In 1949, she decided to apply for a nursing job at Highland Hospital. They hired her on the spot. "It was the quickest hiring I ever got. I went up there one day and she told me to come to work the next." She worked at Highland as a nurse from 1949 to 1969. During that time she put her son through college. He received his doctorate in education from the University of Rochester.

This account of one woman's development in faith and understanding of Christian commitment illustrates the foundations of African American women's Christian activism. Elsie's mother and grandmother adhered to gender norms appropriate for that community to nurture children and work to sustain economic viability. The goal was to imbue Elsie with the strength to know herself and her relationship to God, and with an ability to discern God's call. Elsie Scott became a nurse. She did this in the face of severe racial proscription, which she never allowed to convince her that she was wrong in her commitment or in her assessment of herself. Local congregations, both in Rochester and New York, sustained her in her path, through leadership that constantly challenged racist images of African Americans and provided a daily and weekly environment for the exercise of talent, mutual respect, and Christian duty. The biblical mandates to suffer and persevere, like Job, informed her adult life, as it had informed the lives of her parents and her grandmother. Her role models were not only James Rose and Adam Clayton Powell, but also Lucinda Scott and Charlotte Herndon.

From an African American social gospel perspective, Elsie Scott personifies the themes already outlined. She believed in herself, her Christian responsibility, and the future of her people. She saw the evil of racism and was undeterred by it. Her achievement furthered God's purpose through a personal response to call and a challenge to socially constructed barriers.

Pearl Garnett

Pearl Garnett is a woman who fulfilled her primary role as mother, but a mother very much in the world. She was a strong individual who confronted racism so that her people could prosper.[9] She migrated to Rochester from North Carolina in 1908. She had been recruited into private service and worked for a pastor's family. Her employers wanted her to have a church and helped her find Memorial AME Zion, which she attended regularly. She met her husband on its steps and raised three children in the church. When she married, her husband's wages allowed her to leave domestic service and stay at home.

Pearl made the church the focus of everything she and her children did outside the home. They spent all day Sunday in church, going to services and attending Sunday school. When the children were old enough, they attended Christian Endeavor with the other youth of the church. During the week, Pearl took her children to the Gospel Tabernacle so that they would be steeped in biblical knowledge. Her son, Daniel Garnett Jr., remembers that he and other children from Memorial who got this double dose of religion during the week excelled in their knowledge of the Bible.

Pearl Garnett also participated actively at Memorial. In addition to Sunday school, she was a member of the Women's Missionary Society. What Daniel remembers most, however, are the things his mother did for people informally, like rounding up the neighborhood children for church events during the week, when their parents had to work and couldn't take them. It was important to Pearl Garnett that no children be left out of what the church could offer and she always made and brought plenty of food for everybody. Why was it so important to her that her own and other African American children be so tied to the church? Daniel Garnett explained: "Church was quite important . . . to keep the kids in the right path, more or less. To keep them spiritually motivated 'cause knowing what you had to tangle with during the week, it would make you much stronger in the week." Pearl Garnett immersed all of her children in the church for that very purpose and her son Daniel found this to be of critical importance to him as he entered the working world as an adult.

When Daniel Garnett began his career at ITECH, the white workers spat on him.[10] They threw things at him and created hazardous working conditions. They called him "nigger" and "SOB" and "all this other stuff." Because he had a firm faith, Daniel says, "I could take all those insults, all that spitting on me, spitting at me, calling me all those names, telling the boss that I don't want that nigger working with me, I don't want this and that. . . . [Religious training and constant involvement in the church] made me better 'cause I knew when I left there that I went home, I had a happy family, I was taking care of the head of the family—father, mother, sister, and brother. I was the breadwinner. I went home with a happy feeling and the services and things fortified me spiritually to know that somewhere in the future there was a better thing for us and so I was able to endure that."

Let there be no mistake. Daniel Garnett is speaking about a future in this world for himself and his family and other African Americans. "You don't have to wait till you die, you could be getting your rewards on earth, it doesn't mean that you have to die to wait somewhere in eternity to get your reward. You can get it." Still, until he began his job, he did not know what he would have to do, or how much it would cost.

Daniel Garnett remembers that at ITECH other blacks came and went. He watched them break under the pressure or refuse to put up with the insult to their humanity. He remembers one incident vividly that occurred just after he started working there. Another skilled African American from the South started at about the same time. Daniel recalls, "They were ripping him apart. Told him he wasn't wanted, he wasn't doing good work, nobody wanted him there. And then the foreman handed him a broom and told him to sweep the floors." This man lasted two weeks, took his paycheck and left, saying he had lived in the South, he didn't want to bring the South with him. Now Daniel was the only black man left in the department. The foreman came up to him and gave him the broom. "Between my God and five other people I said, look, where do you want me to start?" He swept the floors better than those who were paid to do it. What did it matter to him? He thought, "I still got paid the same. I drew my twenty-four dollars. And when I got home I had my family, my God and all. And then, that check fed my family." Daniel Garnett was not only feeding his family. He was feeding his community, and the future. Daniel remembers the additional strength and self-respect he gained from seeing the pride his father took in him. His father would boast to friends and neighbors, "My son works at ITECH. He makes a difference." Daniel still feels the pride and satisfaction of being able to see others coming up through the ranks, even passing him and achieving more. During the years he worked for ITECH, Daniel Garnett saw other African Americans come into the business and occupy executive positions. He knows that wouldn't have been possible had he not had the faith to endure. He says that he and others like him "scrubbed floors and took the beating," and he takes personal satisfaction in having done so. These are his rewards.

When he almost gave up, in the face of open hostility, physical threats, and workplace sabotage, he talked it over with his mother, saying he could not take this beating any longer. Some of his coworkers had told him they knew where he could get a job where he wouldn't have to put up with it. His mother asked him, "Where do these people who are giving you this advice live? Do they own their own home? Why would they want you to leave? Son, what do you mean, quitting?" He stayed for forty years.

Both of Daniel Garnett's parents were instrumental in supporting him in this extremely painful and important stand against racial hostility in Rochester. Pearl Garnett occupies what many would see as a background role to this story. Yet her presence is vital and it is instructive of what African American women, through their church communities, were attempting in Rochester. It was Pearl Garnett who raised Daniel in the church, made sure he got there, encouraged his participation in Bible study, and was most explicit about the spiritual foundation Christian faith and fellowship would provide for him and other African American children, as they attempted to better themselves in a world that placed severe racial restrictions on African Americans. As Daniel Garnett explained, "You've got to pay the price in those early years. But you've got to have a foundation . . . to come in here Monday to go to work. Got to. See, 'cause if you don't have nothing to grab onto, you're lost, see. You've got to have something. Even the ones that worship idols and things, there's something other that they've got to grab onto. We might call them atheists or pagans. . . . We say our God is the true God. Our God is the living God . . . but they've got to have something to bring them together. And so that's what held me together. . . . You don't realize you take things for granted until these sort of things happen and you have no way else to turn." God held Daniel Garnett together, but his mother made sure that he made God's acquaintance, that he took God into his heart, and that he never gave up.

Were these African American churchwomen in Rochester practicing the social gospel? If we define the social gospel as a movement designed to hasten the realm of God through a combination of personal conversion and active challenge to those barriers in society that prevent human beings from living in fellowship with each other under God's law, then, yes, certainly, they were. Yet the circumstances and challenges facing African Americans defined their efforts, and their particular beliefs shaped their response.

African American Women and Their Strategies for Christian Activism

Elsie Scott and Pearl Garnett belonged to different congregations and developed individual responses to the African American Christian mandate to work for the future of their people in a society that reflected God's purpose.[11] They moved within a wider African American community whose women purposefully built a Christian base that would support such work. How did they do this in Rochester?

The strategies and practices these African American women employed were multilayered, complex, and roughly generationally implemented; yet they followed a course that can be mapped. The first step was to establish a strong, personal relationship with God. From this, they could nurture and sustain relationships with their families and community members. The relationships among family and church members were based on moral behavior and attention to each other's needs, and they were practiced on a daily basis and from a very early age. The work that people did within the church trained them for what they would encounter in the wider world and provided both a buffer and a setting for the exhibition of talents and skills. Armed with the love and appreciation of their community, the members of that community could break down the barriers to individual or community achievement. Despite certain failures, they never abandoned the cause.

First of all, women made sure that the people attended church. Sunday was the day you went to church. You went every Sunday, sometimes twice on Sunday, and a couple of times during the week. Overwhelmingly it was the women—

grandmothers, mothers, sisters, or aunts—who made sure of this. Women strictly enforced church attendance for a number of interrelated reasons, spiritual rejuvenation and "learning about the Lord" being paramount. Praying, listening to the word, and meditating on God's purpose personally fortified people.

Learning about the Lord entailed more than participating in the spiritual exercises of worship and prayer that connected individuals to God and to the examples of Jesus' life. Regular church attendance drummed into people the lessons of Christian behavior and character. It inculcated positive mores and allowed the monitoring and encouragement of particular behavior. For example, everyone learned to respect one's elders, the family unit, and the church community. Children communicated respect for elders and elders communicated respect for the family and church community most clearly in the reciprocal child-caring and child-disciplining roles the adults of a particular community assumed. If an adult caught a child doing something he or she wasn't supposed to (running around, swearing, talking back, lying), the adult would either take custody of the child and return her to her parents or administer punishment on the spot. "And you didn't struggle," remembered one such child. If you struggled or complained to your parents, things invariably got worse. Parents talked to each other about their children's behavior, reinforcing effective mores and extending parental influence from the home to the church and into the community. It was women who most often took care of, watched over, and disciplined children.

Women's insistence that their children and families attend church regularly, every week, provided the grounding for the formation of positive community relationships and interpersonal connections. Through regular attendance and active participation in worship as well as church events and activities, children learned and adults practiced Christian behavior. This behavior had clear social and political implications, but its intrinsic value came from its connection to the will of God. Father Brown, the first priest at Saint Simon's Episcopal Church in Rochester, taught the young people there that "whatever you do and wherever you go, it's all right as long as you can take God with you."

Regular church attendance established one as a member of the community, someone who could call upon others in need and who could in turn answer calls for help when asked. The infrastructure of the church, again organized primarily by women, reinforced the spiritual foundations established on Sundays.

Furthermore, the focus of women's activity was to sustain the church itself so that it could function as haven and support for its members. The organizational structures that carried out the work of the church consisted of formal governing bodies, like trustees, elders, and deacons, and less formal groups called "clubs." Women were present and cooperated with men by forming deaconess, stewardess, and usher boards, but they were perhaps more fundamental to the sustenance of the church through their club activity. The most obvious purpose of clubs was to raise money for the church. The involvement of women in church organizations and clubs has led historians to conclude that women raised most of the funds on the local level for church work. This was clearly true in Rochester. With few exceptions, all church clubs had women presidents, and most were explicitly women's organizations. Thus women were the primary force behind maintaining church solvency.

For the women in Rochester, fund-raising served as an organizing force and the primary purpose for club work. Financial support of the church was both a goal in itself and an expression of the Christian character that these groups promoted. The organizational activity within the churches created interpersonal relationships of mutual support. It fostered the act of giving in many practical and material ways and culminated in financial sacrifice for the common good. Whatever their articulated purpose—to teach, socialize, study the Bible, or assist the pastor—these various organizations focused on Christian practice in their day-to-day operations. The activities of a Sunday school class illustrate this point. Among the duties of Sunday school class leaders and members were to visit members who missed class; to take collections, one for the poor and another for the support of the pastor; to care for both sick and poor members; to apply to the steward for relief of needy members; and to collect for the needs of the wider denomination. More women than men taught Sunday school, just as more women than men organized and ran clubs. Often, as in the case of Memorial AME Zion, all the members of a congregation, adults and children, belonged to intergenerational Sunday school classes.

The informal connections arising from common club and organizational work provided the primary avenue through which church members brought each other's needs to light and worked to meet them. This established a solid foundation of caretaking upon which wider efforts could rest.

African American women also supported the creation of programs, networks, and agencies with the express purpose of bettering the condition of African Americans in Rochester. Women's missionary and deaconess societies organized and supported efforts to "redeem" women from the red-light district of Rochester, to provide domestic science and academic training for young women to enhance their employment opportunities, and to establish a YWCA and then a YMCA, church libraries, orphanages, day care, and recreation centers. When formal structures could not be sustained, women (and men) incorporated these services within their clubs, Sunday school classes, and boards. The most obvious example of this was the fosterage of children during the Great Depression. The women of the African American church community in Rochester fostered hundreds of children, relatives and strangers alike, usually on an informal basis.

As the examples of Elsie Scott, Pearl Garnett, and others attest, women focused their efforts on acquiring higher education and professional training in order to increase the economic and social resources of the community. All of their club and organizational activities served to identify talented youth and foster their talents and abilities, first within the church and then in the wider world.

Armed with the strength of their faith, the support of their community, and knowledge of their own abilities, individual African Americans could challenge racial discrimination, and did so. The women in the churches in Rochester carried out a generational assault on racial barriers. Children would gain an education and become economically prepared, then they could articulate a challenge to racial discrimination based on equality of talent, training, and ability. The grandmothers, mothers, and aunts provided means for the community to accomplish these goals. Both the men and women of the community never passed up an opportunity for political protest. While we have concentrated here on the efforts that took place during 1900–1940, each succeeding generation yielded a larger cadre of educated, professionally trained, and politically active leaders who addressed the conditions of African Americans in Rochester.

It would be surprising if the church community in Rochester were unique in the strength and determination of its women to foster such Christian activism. A great deal more work needs to be done to examine the internal life of local congregations. The African American community has much to teach us about mutual and reciprocal relationships, between those in need and those who answer another's need one day but may call upon their neighbor the next. The true meaning of fellowship rests upon the understanding that those who serve and those in need are the same. Additionally, the African American church community has a great deal to tell all of us about the connections and disjunctions between personal transgression and the transgression of an entire people who practice racism or other forms of exploitation and oppression.

The African American women and men in the church community in Rochester stood upon a foundation of faith that called them to act in the world as Christians. Their faith led them to engage in the world through individual efforts to better themselves and through active challenges to what they saw as obstacles to God's plan. Yet African American Christians in Rochester appear to have had few connections with white social gospel practitioners, of which there were many in the city, most notably Walter Rauschenbusch. Their Christian understanding and their active commitment were rooted in a much older religious tradition that had operated among African Americans since they embraced Christianity under slavery. While there are similarities in theological stance, social critique, and active involvement in social issues, African Americans in Rochester were practicing a social gospel inherited from African American Christian and communal tradition rather than from white Christian perspectives and influences.

Notes

1. The exceptions include Frances Joseph Gaudet, *He Leadeth Me* (New York: G. K. Hall, 1996); Evelyn Brooks Higginbotham, *Righteous Discontent: The Women's Movement in the Black Baptist Church 1880–1920* (Cambridge, Mass.: Harvard University Press, 1993); and Judith Weisenfeld and Richard Newman, eds., *This Far by Faith: Readings in African American Women's Religious Biography* (New York: Routledge, 1996).

2. For treatments of race and racial cooperation see Ralph Luker, *The Social Gospel in Black and White: American Racial Reform, 1885–1912* (Chapel Hill: University of North Carolina Press, 1998) and Ronald C. White Jr., *Liberty and Justice for All: Racial Reform and the Social Gospel (1877–1925)* (San Francisco: Harper and Row, 1990).

3. While both Gayraud Wilmore and Peter Paris make this point, the best expression I have found is a statement by James Rose, pastor of Mount Olivet Baptist Church in Rochester, New York: "The Caucasian race which embraces Christianity in its organized form cannot practice real brotherhood with the colored races of the earth as long as it feels itself superior to them. You cannot have brotherhood when one brother is admitted to certain places and the other is excluded, but organized Christianity sanctions it." "Jesus Our Way to Brotherhood," article from unidentified periodical, dated 1932, in Mount Olivet archives, Rochester.

4. Gayraud Wilmore, "Deradicalization of the Black Church," in *Black Religion and Black Radicalism* (New York: Doubleday, 1972).

5. Some of the more well known, with appropriate quotes, are Gilbert Osofsky, *Harlem: The Making of a Ghetto: Negro New York 1890–1930* (New York: Harper and Row, 1966), in which he states, "After the collapse of the Afro-American Realty Company, Negro churches played a more important role in the development of Harlem than all other institutions in the Negro Community" (113); James R. Grossman, *Land of Hope: Chicago, Black Southerners, and the Great Migration* (Chicago: University of Chicago Press, 1989), who observed, "The most important institutions founded by the migrants were their churches" (156); and Joe William Trotter, *Black Milwaukee: The Making of an Industrial Proletariat, 1915–45* (Urbana: University of Illinois Press, 1985), who wrote, "Similar to the pattern in other black urban communities, the church was the oldest and most stable black institution in pre–World War I Milwaukee" (31). For a concerted effort to include the church in northern African American community development, see Milton Sernett, *Bound for the Promised Land: African American Religion and the Great Migration* (Durham: Duke University Press, 1997).

6. The classics are Carter Woodson, *The History of the Negro Church* (Washington: Associated Publishers, 1972); W. E. B. Du Bois, *The Negro Church* (Atlanta, Ga.: Atlanta University Press, 1903); Benjamin Elijah Mays and Joseph William Nicholson, *The Negro's Church* (New York: Negro Universities Press, 1969); E. Franklin Frazier, *The Negro Church in America* (New York: Schocken, 1974); C. Eric Lincoln and Lawrence H. Mamiya, *The Black Church in the African American Experience* (Durham: Duke University Press, 1990); Peter Paris, *The Social Teaching of the Black Churches* (Philadelphia: Fortress, 1985); Albert J. Raboteau, *Slave Religion: The Invisible Institution in the Antebellum South* (New York: Oxford University Press, 1978); Monroe Fordham, *Major Themes in Northern Black Religious Thought, 1800–1860* (Hicksville, N.Y.: Exposition Press, 1975); and Sernett, *Bound for the Promised Land.*

7. Paris, *Social Teaching,* 16.

8. The account of Elsie Scott's experience is taken from Ingrid Overacker, *The African American Church Community in Rochester, New York, 1900–1940* (Rochester: University of Rochester Press, 1998), 115–19; all quotations are from these pages.

9. The account of Pearl Garnett's experience is taken from Overacker, *African American Church Community,* 143–48; quotations are from these pages. Garnett is a pseudonym assigned to members of this family at the request of those interviewed.

10. ITECH is a fictitious acronym that could connote any of the technological imaging or optic companies in Rochester.

11. The rest of this article is based on the analysis presented in Overacker, *African American Church Community.*

CHAPTER 13

In the Legacy of Martin Luther King Jr.: The Social Gospel of Faye Wattleton and Marian Wright Edelman

Michael Dwayne Blackwell

The social thought and action of Martin Luther King Jr. was paradigmatic of what the social gospel really is, or ought to be, in the contemporary world. King credited his early reading of the social gospel theologian Walter Rauschenbusch, along with Mahatma Gandhi's ethic of nonviolence, as a strong influence in the development of his social views. In recent decades, King's legacy has been embodied and expanded in the lives and work of Faye Wattleton and Marian Wright Edelman, whose careers have focused upon the rights and well-being of women and children. Before examining these personalities, however, it is important to redefine and re-vision what the social gospel is.

The Social Gospel Redefined

The social gospel is an affirmation that individual salvation is not enough; social institutions must also be redeemed in order to approach the realization of the commonwealth of God. This perspective recognizes the complementarity of theology and ethics, the interconnectedness of individual and community life, the dynamic interplay of theory and practice, and the coherence of means and ends. Rooted in evangelical liberalism, the social gospel is the identification of the principles of Jesus and the application thereof to society at large. Not only is the Christian ethic of love to be correlated with social facts and issues, but the critical warnings of the Hebrew prophets are to be marshaled against perceived social evil.

The social gospel is a disposition to be seriously and urgently concerned with the multiple and cumulative causes of the physical, intellectual, psychological, and spiritual abuses that affect the lives of countless Americans. The social gospel is the recognition of the fact that the integrity of a nation is not characterized by individual successes, rather by how the dispossessed and disaffected are treated, handled, or addressed.

The social gospel is a discernment that one is never solitary; one is always a person-in-community. As such, the person who embraces the social gospel does not merely have an inclination towards others in an arbitrary, inconsequential, and self-congratulatory way; instead, that person is impelled by conviction to do the hard work of applying theory to practice—not only to address the problems daily confronting the lives of the disadvantaged and the negligence infecting the lives of the better off, but also to redress these matters in progressively efficacious ways. The social gospel is a marshaling of all the tools at one's disposal to seek to identify and eliminate the inequities that frustrate the lives of many and disallow their full participation in the dynamics of citizenship.

Finally, the social gospel is a conviction that there is no genuine security until everybody has life's existential needs: food, water, shelter, clothing, income, sense of belonging, spiritual wholeness, a sense of meaning and purpose, and ability to communicate. It is an ongoing process that leads to a comprehension of the causes of systemic social problems faced by oppressed peoples, which in turn leads to the movement from a disposition of caring to constructive engagement, informed advocacy, and radical action.[1]

The Legacy of Martin Luther King Jr.

The classic period of the civil rights movement is framed by the public career of Martin Luther King Jr.: from December 5, 1955, to April 4, 1968. During this period, King was the undisputed, symbolic, and actual leader of the nonviolent direct-action campaigns primarily targeting Jim Crow segregation in the South. There are several aspects of his leadership that are the major constitutive elements of his enduring legacy.

First, there is the principle of dissent. One of the essential tenets of any democratic republic where freedom and responsibility are tandem features is the right to dissent. The first day of the Montgomery bus boycott, King asserted his belief not only in the "teachings of Jesus" but also in the "weapon of protest."[2] In January 1956, King reiterated his support of dissent by declaring American democracy's "right to protest for right."[3] On April 3, 1968, the day before he was assassinated, King affirmed the greatness of America, in part, as "the right to protest for right."[4] In his famous "Letter from Birmingham Jail," King states: "I submit that an individual who breaks a law that conscience tells him is unjust, and who willingly accepts the penalty of imprisonment in order to arouse the conscience of the community over its injustice, is in reality expressing the highest respect for law."[5]

Second, based on this respect for law, King believed in following one's convictions despite the consequences or ramifications of one's actions. He was disposed to say, if a person has not found something to die for, that person is not fit to live, a remark made in the wake of the murder of the civil rights leader Medgar Evers.[6] In essence, physical death under such circumstances of conscience is "redemptive."[7] When he broke his silence over the Vietnam War in 1967, King stressed the importance of listening to and acting upon one's moral conscience.[8]

Third, King articulated hopefulness found in the belief that the universe is on the side of justice. Nevertheless, he was not simply an eternal optimist.

King's utilization of the Hegelian dialectical process to reach a fuller understanding of choices and the creation of the best possible society, therefore, constitutes a fourth component of his legacy. For example, his choice of a socialistic perspective was the result of canceling out the extreme positions of capitalism and communism. Another instance is his belief that community and justice are mutually necessary: that we must avoid the extreme of having community without justice (i.e., "colonialism"), which is hollow, on the one hand, and the extreme of having justice without community (i.e., "paternalism"), which is blind, on the other hand.[9] Strongly attracted to this progression from thesis and antithesis to synthesis, King was compelled to reject extremism in favor of "mediation and conciliation" as well as "education and legislation."[10]

Fifth, King broadened his horizons, that is, he evolved. King's emphasis on the obligation to love during the early stages of the Montgomery bus boycott grew into the application of Gandhian philosophy and nonviolent method to segregation in the South. After the passage of the Civil Rights Act in 1964 and the Voting Rights Act in 1965 and his being awarded the 1964 Nobel Peace Prize, King enlarged his focus from concerns such as integration in public accommodations to more intricately systemic issues such as the elimination of ghettoized communities, economic injustice, increased military spending, U.S. participation in the Vietnam War, and white privilege.

Sixth, King had a strong affinity to the biblical witness. Prophets such as Amos, Micah, and Isaiah stressed the importance of doing right, effecting justice in the land, and redressing the concerns of the poor and the oppressed. King also found in the words of Jesus confirmation for relieving the burdens of "the least of these" (Matthew 25:31–46) as well as reconciliation with one's enemies.[11]

Seventh, King had a pride in his cultural heritage. Many of King's speeches were peppered with references to diverse heroes and heroines, such as Frederick Douglass, Ida B. Wells-Barnett, Willie Mays, Rosa Parks, Langston Hughes, Roland Hayes, Paul Robeson, Marian Anderson, and Mary McLeod Bethune. He was very much concerned with the oppression of apartheid in South Africa and imperialist plundering by Western countries on that continent.[12] As he became more involved in addressing economic conditions and U.S. foreign policy, King broadened his concern to all in the African diaspora as well as people of color around the world and eventually, to the empowerment of all of humanity.[13]

Finally, King believed in nonviolence not simply as a method of protest, but also as a way of life. Nonviolent direct action could serve to deal with the tensions in the body politic in creative ways, and it could also help to address tensions in one's personal life with a strong inclination towards peace and reconciliation. Nonviolence was the way in which King devoted himself to the hoped-for realization of the beloved community.

The Social Gospel of Faye Wattleton

Faye Wattleton, president of the Planned Parenthood Federation of America (PPFA) during 1978–92 and founding president of the Center for Gender Equality, helps and challenges us to extend King's human rights initiatives in the areas of reproductive rights, gender equity, and, in the final analysis, the preservation of America's fundamental liberties.

In 1959, at the age of sixteen, Wattleton entered Ohio State University Nursing school, and she became the first person in her family to receive a college degree, in 1964. Wattleton met an obstetrics professor in undergraduate school who encouraged her to pursue midwifery. In her training as a nurse, however, Wattleton felt the hand of her mother, who insisted that whatever she did must be in the service of God. Balking at the idea of becoming a missionary nurse, however, Wattleton commenced working as a maternity nursing instructor for the Miami Valley Hospital School of Nursing in Dayton.

Subsequently, she decided to take her professor's advice and enrolled at Columbia University's studies in midwifery on a government stipend. During her tenure in New York City, she interned at Harlem Hospital, where the importance of access to safe abortion and the necessity of informed decision-making with regard to fertility issues became clear to her. She saw numerous women, over six thousand in a single year, who came into the hospital with complications from incomplete abortions. Abortion was illegal at the time, and the health of many women was jeopardized because of the criminalizing of acting on unwanted pregnancy.

Earning a master of science degree in maternal and infant health care from Columbia in 1967, with certification as a nurse-midwife, Wattleton elected to return to Dayton to work as a consultant and assistant director of Public Health Nursing Services in the City of Dayton Public Health Department. It was there that she joined the local PPFA board. Wattleton's involvement in Planned Parenthood would continue to develop. In 1970, she began service as executive director of the local agency's board. Under her leadership, the number of clients tripled and the budget increased from less than four hundred thousand to almost one million dollars.

In 1975, she became chairwoman of the national executive director's council of PPFA. The Supreme Court had legalized abortion in 1973 with Roe v. Wade, but the emotional conflict over reproductive rights did not subside. In 1977, Planned Parenthood of Miami Valley came under attack from a local Baptist group and Right-to-Life chapter. Furthermore, it came under federal scrutiny into its use of government financing. During that same year, PPFA clinics in Minnesota, Virginia, Nebraska, Vermont, and Ohio were burned or bombed.

Despite these attacks, Wattleton continued on with the courage of her convictions after the manner of King. She tried to promote the other programs of the PPFA clinics, such as prevention of unwanted pregnancies, educational programs, reproductive health services, cancer screening, and treatment of venereal disease. Her equanimity and articulateness in discussing these difficult and emotionally charged issues were impressive. These communication and social skills, coupled with her compassion, professionalism, and organizational competence, helped her to gain appointment to the presidency of PPFA. She was the first black person, the first woman, and the youngest individual to head the national organization.

Paralleling King's view of the ultimate friendliness of the universe, Wattleton believes that in the darkest hour, there is still hope, because Jesus, though vilified and crucified, was resurrected. She holds that the resort to malefaction or bitterness is self-destructive, for it gives power to others and drains oneself of the spiritual nurture needed to persist in a cause one thinks is just. Thus, despite death threats, racial and sexual slurs, picketing, boycotting, and the like, she has been able, like King, to find succor in her personal faith. She prayed that God would keep her alive to raise her daughter, Felicia, into independent adulthood, without capitulating to anger, violence, and fear. Out of her relationship with her daughter, Wattleton felt drawn to discuss in public her views on sexuality. In 1986, Doubleday published *How to Talk with Your Child about Sexuality,* which she coauthored with Elisabeth Keiffer.

In keeping with King's interest in the beloved community, Wattleton has consistently been concerned for the quality of life for children. She reminds critical listeners that as a midwife she has helped numerous women to give birth. She is not pro-abortion but rather pro-choice, and she is interested in assisting women to make reasonable and healthy decisions about contraception, birth control, planning families, and effective parenthood.

In 1995, she founded a "think tank," the Center for Gender Equality, which was incorporated in New York City on August 25. It was formed with an endowment of one million dollars and designed with the notion that scholars would come together there to address issues of gender that women would face in the twenty-first century. After leaving PPFA, she continued lecturing, debating, and engaging in dialogue with others. Wattleton also wrote her memoirs, which were published by Ballantine Books as *Life on the Line* in 1996. In the same year, Wattleton won the Margaret Sanger Woman of Valor Award and appeared on National Public Radio's *Talk of the Nation.*

Like social gospel leaders almost a century before her, Wattleton was appalled over the lack of adequate health care services accorded to the poor, particularly blacks, in Dayton and in Harlem. Recalling her mother's admonition to make work be in the service of God, and having been raised on the virtues of neighborliness and compassion, Wattleton could not do otherwise than to find ways to reach out to despairing women and girls who found themselves in the throes of controversy because of their desire to determine the fate of their own bodies.

It was the disposition of reconciliation her mother taught her that prompted Wattleton to face her antagonists not with fear or trepidation, but, instead, with the greatest aplomb and an inclination towards realistic compromise. In line with King's personalism, she learned to fight against or for people's perspectives rather than their personhood. Wattleton states: "My care and compassion was not conditional. Each deserved respect and to be treated with human dignity."[14]

One of Wattleton's enduring messages, which bodes well for the future of women, is that the responsibilities of citizenship are multifaceted and participation in the political process is mandatory. Wattleton believes that women are not holding politicians accountable for addressing their needs, and that the fault for this sin of omission lies with those who constitute a little over 51 percent of the population. Realizing the overwhelming character of the governmental process and the fear it induces, Wattleton points to the idea that progress comes incrementally with hard work, and that failure is almost always part of the pathway to success.[15]

It is clear how Wattleton's concern for human rights, particularly the rights of women, her public persona, her compassion for the poor, and her emphasis on participatory democracy square with the definition of the social gospel outlined above and harmonize with distinctive elements of King's legacy identified earlier. However, there is an understandable ambiguity about how Wattleton's support for the removal of an evolving "life" within a woman's womb coincides with King's legacy of nonviolence. How can such an action fit within the legacy of nonviolence?

An answer lies in how Wattleton's perspective is understood. Wattleton's role has been primarily to inform females about their reproductive choices. In the process, she has listened to what her clients express as wants or needs, and she has responded in a counseling and consultative way. Even though many under her purview have gone on to receive abortions, Wattleton has not been as much a promulgator of abortion as she has been an advocate for a woman's right to choose. Furthermore, as a midwife, she has encouraged many women regarding prenatal and infant care, and she has given birth herself to a daughter she has subsequently raised with a zest for life, a concern for others, and a pride in her cultural heritage.

Wattleton has promoted better education, career opportunities, health care, and welfare, and she has insisted on the need for the continuance of affirmative action policies—issues clearly consonant with King's vision. Moreover, she has argued that her concern has been to defeat this white, patriarchal, and sexist society by empowering women to take control of their own lives and to make their positions known and supported.[16]

At the end of the prologue of her book, *Life on the Line,* Wattleton gives a message to her daughter in the form of a letter, much like the work of Rauschenbusch for social awakening and King's correspondence from a jail cell in Birmingham. She encourages Felicia to find her way and to be unconventional and nonconformist like Sojourner Truth and her own grandmother. They had confidence in themselves and believed in themselves, Wattleton asserts. She continues: "Your grandmother crisscrossed the country with a message of salvation from eternal damnation. I have traveled many of the same roads, and more, with a message of respect, tolerance, and compassion—salvation from the injustices of this world."[17] Wattleton's eloquence indisputably matches the substance and fluidity of Rauschenbusch and King as she elaborates on the principles taught and practiced by her mother by which she, in turn, now lives and teaches to Felicia: "honesty, loyalty, integrity, respect and compassion for others, diligence, perseverance, and faith in God, . . . [knowing] right from wrong. I have tried to convey the same principles to you, although with less absolutism."[18]

Toward the end of that letter, Wattleton encourages her daughter to fight with all the tools available to her against forces poised to weaken "the sustaining promise of your liberty, embodied in the promise of our Constitution."[19] Wrapped into this statement is the interplay of theory and practice, the use of the social sciences, and the appeal to the nation's documents of freedom. Named "one of the best speakers in the United States" by *New Woman* magazine in 1994, Wattleton is a celebrated lecturer who urges: "It's time to define what women will be. We need a different vision for the next millennium. If we're not vigilant enough and if we don't say enough or do enough, we will have only ourselves to blame."[20]

The Social Gospel of Marian Wright Edelman

Marian Wright Edelman was one of several students who joined Martin Luther King Jr. in the protest against Rich's department store in Atlanta in March 1960. Later, having worked in Mississippi with the poor, Edelman implanted the seed in King's mind to address the perniciousness of poverty out of which the Poor People's Campaign eventually sprouted.[21]

Marian Wright, named after Marian Anderson, whom she heard sing as a child, was born the youngest of five children on June 6, 1939, the daughter of Arthur Jerome Wright and Maggie Leola (Bowen) Wright, in Bennettsville, South Carolina. Her father was pastor of Shiloh Baptist Church and encouraged his children to pursue higher education and to serve the local community. Practicing what he preached, Arthur Wright established the Wright Home for the Aged in the segregated town of Bennettsville, and Maggie Wright ran it.

In 1956, Marian Wright graduated from Marlboro Training High School and entered Spelman College in Atlanta, Georgia. Prior to graduating valedictorian of her class, she participated in one of the largest sit-ins in Atlanta's city hall. Fourteen students were arrested, including Wright. While a senior in undergraduate school, and because of her desire "to serve the community," Wright set her sights on law school. She applied to Yale University Law School, was admitted, and entered as a John Hay Whitney Fellow in the fall of 1960.

During spring break of her last year in law school, Wright chose to travel to the Mississippi Delta to get involved in the voter registration drive that was gaining momentum under the guidance of her friend Robert Moses and others. Moses was field secretary for the Student Nonviolent Coordinating Committee. A year after graduating from Yale, Wright returned to Jackson, Mississippi, where she worked as one of the first two interns for the NAACP Legal Defense and Education Fund. In addition to heading the fund from 1964 to 1968 in Mississippi, she passed the bar examination in 1965 and opened a law office primarily for the purpose of getting student workers out of jail.

In 1968, Wright received a Field Foundation grant to study how to make laws work for the poor, and she moved to Washington, D.C., to inaugurate the Washington Research Project. By this time, Peter Edelman, a Harvard law graduate who had worked for Senator Robert Kennedy, had already entered Wright's life. They were married in July of that year.

In 1971, the Edelmans left Washington for Boston, where Peter became vice president of the University of Massachusetts, and Marian became director of the Harvard University Center for Law and Education. Marian Edelman was unwilling to relinquish her Washington Project, however, and made weekly trips to Washington to oversee the activities of her organization. By this time, they had already had two sons, Joshua and Jonah, and *Time* magazine had named Marian one of America's two hundred young leaders.

Concerned about providing systematic and long-range assistance to children and about lobbying for improvements in public policy regarding children's needs, Marian Wright Edelman founded the Children's Defense Fund (CDF), a nonprofit child advocacy organization based in Washington, D.C., in 1973. With the long commute beginning to take a toll on family life, and the birth of another son, Ezra, in 1974, the Edelmans chose to return to Washington, where Peter obtained a teaching position at Georgetown University Law Center in 1979.

The 1980s witnessed a rise in teen pregnancy, particularly in the African American community. Just as Faye Wattleton was involved with the PPFA's concern over unwanted pregnancies, Edelman and the CDF began a long-term national campaign to get out the message of pregnancy prevention and to show young women the way to positive choices and alternatives. Taking her responsibility in this cause seriously, Edelman launched a multimedia campaign. In addition, she promoted the establishment of local, volunteer child-watch coalitions in more than seventy communities in 60 percent of the nation's states. As a result of her dedication to improving the lives of children, especially the disadvantaged, poor, and members of racial and ethnic minorities, in innovative ways, Edelman received the prestigious MacArthur Foundation Prize Fellowship.

Having won such acclaim for her efforts to improve the quality of life for children, Edelman was invited to give the W. E. B. Du Bois Lectures at Harvard in 1986. The lectures were published by the university's press as *Families in Peril: An Agenda for Social Change* the following year. In the preface of that text, she gives the motto for the CDF as "the best way to help poor black children is to show that white children are similarly affected."[22]

Edelman and the CDF staff research and interpret data related to the plight of the nation's children. They have been recognized for generating statistics and other valuable resources about children. In 1987, they were largely responsible for Senator Alan Cranston's Act for Better Child Care. *Time* magazine noted her again in an article, which held that Edelman was "one of Washington's most unusual lobbyists" whose "effectiveness depends as much on her adroit use of statistics as on moral suasion."[23]

Following the passage of the welfare reform bill in 1996, Edelman became more active at the state level. She organized a march called Stand for Children in D.C. that was attended by 200,000 people. The purpose of the demonstration was to highlight the needs of the nation's youth. For her bold, indefatigable, and unwavering support of children, the National Black Caucus of State Legislators granted Edelman the Nation Builders Award.

Edelman's concern for and advocacy in behalf of children is beautifully expressed in her book *Guide My Feet: Prayers and Meditations on Loving and Working for Children*. The book is a collection of prayers and reflections, many from Edelman's own pen, that seek guidance from God to grant strength and wisdom to men and women as they commit themselves to providing care for children.[24] In her preface, Edelman emphasizes the contributions of many black leaders. She laments that black children of today are not afforded the opportunity to learn—or even choose not to learn—about their cultural heritage. Many of the persons she celebrates in her book remind one of the heroes and heroines that King cited in his various addresses.[25] In a passage on service, Edelman underscores her principled upbringing in the Baptist faith and the Christian tutelage of her parents. Moreover, the prayer manifests an understanding of the social gospel and the coherence of means and ends: "O God, help us to work together for our children—to use the rich variety of our leaders, organizations, talents, disciplines, and experiences to serve and save our children. Remind us daily that we and our institutions are the means to serve rather than the ends to be served."[26]

The prayers and meditations of Marian Wright Edelman hark back to her childhood days of piety and service with her father, a pastor, and her mother, a church organist and choir director. They are reminiscent of the prayers of Rauschenbusch and King. The lessons they teach repeat the lessons she learned in childhood: the "enduring God-given and life-giving values of faith, integrity, and service." As she gets older and wearier, she finds herself praying to God more and more, and on numberless occasions she waxes prophetic: "As we face a new century and a new millennium, the overarching challenge for America is to rebuild a sense of community and hope and civility and caring and safety for all our children. I hope God will guide our feet as parents—and guide America's feet—to reclaim our nation's soul, and to give back to all of our children their sense of security and their ability to dream about and work toward a future that is attainable and hopeful."[27]

Edelman learned from an early age that "service is the rent we pay for living. It is the very purpose of life and not something you do in your spare time."[28] Even as her father lay dying when she was fourteen, he taught her "that race and gender are shadows; and that character, self-discipline, determination, attitude, and service are the substance of life."[29] Arguably, one of the strongest messages Edelman sends to all children is the importance of humanity. She exhorts them to "never defer to another on the basis of his or her race, religion, gender, class, fame, wealth, or position."[30]

In her book *The Measure of Our Success,* Edelman expresses concern for the future of America and charges each American to "commit personally and as voters to a national crusade of conscience and action that will ensure that no child is left behind." She continues: "Only we—individually and collectively—can transform our nation's priorities and assure its future as we face a new century and begin a new millennium."[31]

On the one hand, Edelman urges U.S. children to be gadflies to the status quo: "Be a flea for justice wherever you are and in whatever career you choose in life and help transform America by biting political and business leaders until they respond."[32] On the other hand, she acknowledges that one can be "a quiet servant-leader and example in [one's] home, school, workplace, and community."[33] Like Wattleton, Edelman holds up the abolitionist and women's rights activist Sojourner Truth as a role model,[34] and like King, she urges America to "finish what we started in the Declaration of Independence and Constitution" and to make sure liberty and justice belong to the children of today and tomorrow.[35]

At the CDF, Edelman has worked to build networks and coalitions with other social institutions, including churches, to support the causes of children in the United States, especially the poor and the oppressed. She has established a variety of institutes for child advocacy in the hope of creating a "moral witness for children."[36] One way that the lines of communication and information are kept open is through a worldwide Web site that is constantly updated. In addition, there are list-serves and other electronic vehicles to enhance coordination of resource and lobbying efforts.

Edelman's commitment to the causes of and services to children is a self-sacrificial one. The whole of her adult life has been a response to the call of her father and mother to serve the community. That is why, in the beginning of *Families in Peril,* she pays homage to her parents through Du Bois's prayer about having the courage of one's convictions.[37]

Conclusion: A Vision for the Social Gospel in the Twenty-first Century

In many ways the concerns of today and tomorrow are very similar to those at the turn of the nineteenth century during the development of the social gospel movement. Urban areas are still wastelands of poverty, unemployment, disease, powerlessness, and crime, and those who live in small rural areas are finding it increasingly difficult to make a living off the soil or livestock. Overcrowded communities are not a thing of the past as the birth rate is rising and material resources are thinning both domestically and globally. The chasm between the rich and the poor, the haves and the have-nots, is growing, and in an age of heightening technological know-how, the building of genuine community from the local level to the international arena is truncated.

Nevertheless, we should be encouraged because we have seen the focus of the social gospel expand from the concerns of a marginal wing of Protestant denominations that catered to white workmen, to include the civil rights movement, woman's right to choose, and child advocacy. The social gospel gives us a legacy for the future: it tells us that, regardless of the present and unforeseen social issues that might face us, we must have the disposition and the will to identify what is best in our society and to discover ways to effect change in such a manner that we draw closer and closer to just, sustainable, and holistic community.

Faye Wattleton and Marian Wright Edelman introduce us to the possibilities of a greater, more enriching life for those born in the new century. Their unique voices, their concern for women and children of all races and ethnic backgrounds, their continuing courage in facing adversaries, and their deep and abiding faith in God both honor and enlarge the social gospel tradition—correcting the mistakes of myopia in the past, challenging the complacency of the present, and anticipating the further realization of the beloved community in the future. King's question Where do we go from here? lingers in our consciousness and we are haunted by the silence of ignorance. Are we going to find ourselves in chaos, ignoring the words of conscience; or will we find some way to live more appreciatively of one another through the thoughtful and deliberate work of saving the world of the human, our planet, both individually and collectively?

Notes

1. Laura Meagher, *Teaching Children about Global Awareness* (New York: Crossroad, 1991), 24, 40.

2. Martin Luther King Jr., *The Papers of Martin Luther King, Jr., Vol. 3: Birth of a New Age, December 1955–December 1956,* ed. Clayborne Carson (Berkeley: University of California Press, 1997), 72–73.

3. *Legacy of a Dream: Martin Luther King, Jr.,* film narrated by James Earl Jones (1990 MPI Home Video, orig. prod. by Martin Luther King Jr. Center for Nonviolent Social Change, 1974).

4. Martin Luther King Jr., "I See the Promised Land," in *A Testament of Hope: The Essential Writings of Martin Luther King, Jr,* ed. James Melvin Washington (San Francisco: Harper and Row, 1986), 282.

5. Martin Luther King Jr., *Why We Can't Wait* (New York: Mentor, 1963, 1964), 83–84.

6. Martin Luther King Jr., untitled speech given at Cobo Hall, Detroit, Michigan, June 23, 1963, Southern Christian Leadership Conference, audio cassette in collection of the author.

7. Martin Luther King Jr., June 5, 1964, in *The Wisdom of Martin Luther King: In His Own Words,* ed. staff of Bill Adler Books, Inc. (New York: Lancer Books, 1968), 144.

8. Martin Luther King Jr., *The Autobiography of Martin Luther King, Jr.,* ed. Clayborne Carson (New York: Warner Books, 1998), 342.

9. John H. Cartwright, "Foundations of the Beloved Community," *Debate and Understanding* (Fall 1977): 175.

10. Ira G. Zepp, *The Social Vision of Martin Luther King, Jr.* (Brooklyn: Carlson Publishing, 1989), 202–6.

11. See Martin Luther King Jr., *Strength to Love* (Cleveland: Collins-World, 1963).

12. See Lewis V. Baldwin, *To Make the Wounded Whole: The Cultural Legacy of Martin Luther King, Jr.* (Minneapolis: Fortress, 1992); idem, *Toward the Beloved Community: Martin Luther King, Jr., and South Africa* (Cleveland: Pilgrim Press, 1995).

13. Martin Luther King Jr., *Where Do We Go from Here: Chaos or Community?* introduction by Coretta Scott King (New York: Bantam, 1967, 1968), 27–77.

14. Faye Wattleton, "Women and Leadership," speech delivered for the Mary Lyon Lecture Series, Mount Holyoke College, September 30, 1997, <http://www.mtholyoke.edu/offices/comm/misc/faye/faye.shtml>; accessed February 22, 1999.

15. Kerrita McClaughlyn, *Northeastern News,* April 9, 1997, 10. Speech delivered by Faye Wattleton to the Ford Hall Forum at Northeastern's Egan Research Center.

16. Wattleton, "Women and Leadership." See also "Faye Wattleton Calls Women to Action as Leaders," *College Street Journal,* Mount Holyoke College, <http://www.mtholyoke.edu/offices/comm/csj/971010/watttleton.html>; accessed February 22, 1999.

17. Faye Wattleton, *Life on the Line* (New York: Ballantine Books, 1996), xvii.

18. Ibid.

19. Ibid., xx.

20. Wattleton quoted in Christina Schoen, "Wattleton Asks, 'What about Women?'" *Mount Holyoke News,* October 2, 1997, 1.

21. Coretta Scott King, *My Life with Martin Luther King, Jr.,* rev. ed., introduction by Bernice, Dexter, Martin, and Yolanda King (1969; New York: Henry Holt, 1993), 276–77.

22. Marian Wright Edelman, *Families in Peril: An Agenda for Social Change* (Cambridge, Mass.: Harvard University Press, 1987), ix.

23. Nancy Traver, "'They Cannot Fend for Themselves': That Is Why Marian Edelman Became a Top Lobbyist for Children," *Time,* March 23, 1987, 27.

24. Marian Wright Edelman, *Guide My Feet: Prayers and Meditations on Loving and Working with Children* (New York: Harper Collins, 1995), 37.

25. See also Marian Wright Edelman, *Lanterns: A Memoir of Mentors* (Boston: Beacon Press, 1999).

26. Edelman, *Guide My Feet,* 149.

27. Ibid., xxviii.

28. Marian Wright Edelman, *The Measure of Our Success: A Letter to My Children and Yours* (Boston: Beacon Press, 1992), 6.

29. Ibid., 7.

30. Ibid., 26.

31. Ibid., 20.

32. Ibid., 60.

33. Ibid., 68.

34. Ibid., 59–60.

35. Ibid., 74–75.

36. Children's Defense Fund slogan; see, for example, <http://www.childrensdefense.org/msmainrelaff.php>; accessed February 25, 1999.

37. Edelman, *Families in Peril,* vii.

Contributors

Elizabeth N. Agnew is assistant professor in the Department of Philosophy and Religious Studies at Ball State University in Muncie, Indiana. She is currently writing a biography of Mary Richmond.

Michael Dwayne Blackwell is director of multicultural education and adjunct professor of philosophy and religion at the University of Northern Iowa, Cedar Falls, Iowa. He has also taught at Gordon-Conwell Theological Seminary, Southwest Missouri State University, and Curry College.

R. A. R. Edwards is assistant professor of history at Rochester Institute of Technology, Rochester, New York.

Wendy J. Deichmann Edwards is associate director and associate professor of history and theology, United Theological Seminary at Buffalo, New York. She has published numerous articles about the social gospel movement and Protestant missions, including "Forging an Ideology for American Missions: Josiah Strong and Manifest Destiny," in *North American Foreign Missions, 1810–1914: Theology, Theory and Policy,* edited by Wilbert R. Shenk (forthcoming). She is currently writing a biography of the internationally known social gospel leader Josiah Strong.

Christopher H. Evans is associate professor of church history at Colgate Rochester Crozer Divinity School in Rochester, New York. He is the editor of *Perspectives on the Social Gospel* (1999) and *The Social Gospel Today* (2001) and author of *Social Gospel Liberalism and the Ministry of Ernest Fremont Tittle: A Theology for the Middle Class* (1996). He is currently writing a biography of Walter Rauschenbusch.

Janet Forsythe Fishburn is professor emerita, the Theological School and the Graduate School of Drew University in Madison, New Jersey. She is the author of numerous articles and several books, including *Confronting the Idolatry of the Family: A New Vision for the Household of God* (1991) and *The Fatherhood of God and the Victorian Family: The Social Gospel in America* (1982).

Carolyn De Swarte Gifford is a research associate in the gender studies program at Northwestern University, Evanston, Illinois. She is the editor of *Writing Out My Heart: Selections from the Journal of Frances E. Willard, 1855–1896* (1995) and has written numerous articles on American women's religious experience and reform activity.

Paul William Harris is professor of history at Minnesota State University Moorhead and author of *Nothing but Christ: Rufus Anderson and the Ideology of Foreign Missions* (1999).

Susan Hill Lindley is professor of religion at Saint Olaf College, Northfield, Minnesota. She is the author of *You Have Stept Out of Your Place: A History of Women and Religion in America* (1996) and "'Neglected Voices' and *Praxis* in the Social Gospel," *Journal of Religious Ethics* (Spring 1990). She is currently editing the *Westminster Dictionary of Women in American Religious History.*

Kendal P. Mobley is a Th.D. candidate at the Boston University School of Theology in Boston, Massachusetts. He is the author of "Adoniram Judson (1788–1850), Baptist Missionary," in *The Biographical Dictionary of Evangelicals*, edited by Timothy Larsen (2002). He is writing a dissertation on the Baptist social reformer Helen Barrett Montgomery.

Ingrid Overacker is assistant professor of history at Jefferson Community College in Watertown, New York. She has written *The African American Church Community in Rochester, New York, 1900–1940* (1998) and "School Reform in Rochester, N.Y., 1965–1980: The Challenge of Desegregation and Integration," *Alliance* (Summer 1994).

Dale E. Soden is professor of history at Whitworth College in Spokane, Washington, and author of *The Reverend Mark Matthews: An Activist in the Progressive Era* (2001).

Eleanor J. Stebner is associate professor in the theology department at the University of Winnipeg, Manitoba, and has also taught at Chicago Theological Seminary. She is the author of *Gem: The Life of Sister Mac* (2001), a biography of Sister Geraldine MacNamara, founder of a social settlement house in the inner city of Winnipeg, and *The Women of Hull House: A Study in Spirituality, Vocation, and Friendship* (1997).

Robert Trawick is assistant professor of philosophy and religious studies at Saint Thomas Aquinas College in Sparkill, New York. His publications include "Called to a New Ethic: Walter Rauschenbusch and the Resuscitation of Vocation," in *Perspectives on the Social Gospel* (1999), edited by Christopher Evans.

Index